AF512180

Dedicated to

Prof. K. Venkata Reddy

Aspects of Contemporary World Literature

Edited by

P. Bayapa Reddy

ATLANTIC

PUBLISHERS & DISTRIBUTORS (P) LTD

Published by

ATLANTIC

PUBLISHERS & DISTRIBUTORS (P) LTD

7/22, Ansari Road, Darya Ganj, New Delhi-110002
Phones : +91-11-40775252, 23273880, 23275880, 23280451
Fax : +91-11-23285873
Web : www.atlanticbooks.com
E-mail : orders@atlanticbooks.com
Branch Office
5, Nallathambi Street, Wallajah Road, Chennai-600002
Phones : +91-44-64611085
E-mail : chennai@atlanticbooks.com

Copyright © Atlantic Publishers and Distributors (P) Ltd., 2008, 2018

All rights reserved. No part of this publication may be reproduced, stored in a retrieval system, transmitted or utilized in any form or by any means, electronic, mechanical, photocopying, recording or otherwise, without the prior permission of the copyright owner. Application for such permission should be addressed to the publisher.

Disclaimer

The author and the publisher have taken every effort to the maximum of their skill, expertise and knowledge to provide correct material in the book. Even then if some mistakes persist in the content of the book, the publisher does not take responsibility for the same. The publisher shall have no liability to any person or entity with respect to any loss or damage caused, or alleged to have been caused directly or indirectly, by the information contained in this book. Hence, the book should be taken as a general guide only.

The publisher has fully tried to follow the copyright law. However, if any work is found to be similar, it is unintentional and the same should not be used as defamatory or to file legal suit against the author/publisher.

If the readers find any mistakes, we shall be grateful to them for pointing out those to us so that these can be corrected in the next edition.

All disputes are subject to the jurisdiction of Delhi courts only.

Printed in India at Nice Printing Press, A-33/3A, Site-IV, Industrial Area, Sahibabad, Ghaziabad, U.P.

Acknowledgements

1. Wail S. Hassan's "World Literature in the Age of Globalization," *College English*, Vol. 63, No. 1, September 2000, pp. 38-47.
2. Ronald Knowles' *Pinter and Twentieth Century Drama: The Cambridge Companion to Harold Pinter*, 2001, pp. 73-86.
3. Neilten Kortenaar, "Only Connect," *Research in African Literatures*, Fall 93, pp. 59-72.

Thanks are extended to the editors and publishers of these titles for permission to reprint.

Acknowledgements

1. Wail S. Hassan's "World Literature in the Age of Globalization," *College English*, Vol. 63, No. 1, September 2000, pp. 38-47.
2. Ronald Knowles' *Pinter and Twentieth Century Drama: The Cambridge Companion to Harold Pinter*, 2001, pp. 73-86.
3. Neilten Kortenaar, "Only Connect," *Research in African Literatures*, Fall 93, pp. 59-72.

Thanks are extended to the editors and publishers of these titles for permission to reprint.

Preface

K. Venkata Reddy belongs to a very rare breed of scholars, critics and teachers who are deeply involved in the serious and profound type of literary activity. With his passion for teaching for about four decades, his solid contribution to scholarly journals like *World Literature Written in English* and *Journal of South Asian Literature*, his publication of numerous books and papers on different literatures as well as higher education, and with his academic visits to countries like USA, UK, Japan, Singapore, and Malaysia, he is well-known in the world of letters both in India and abroad. He is not only a sound academic but also a committed social activist. He has been actively involved throughout his career in nation-building activities like eradication of social evils, removal of illiteracy and spread of scientific temper. He relentlessly yearns for and at the same time works diligently for a casteless and classless society. The festschrift for Venkata Reddy is quite in the fitness of things. Hope the festschrift, *Aspects of Contemporary World Literature*, competently represents Reddy's encyclopaedic range and variety of interests in the areas of literary and critical studies.

This book offers a balanced selection of the most representative global celebrities of contemporary times leaving the reader to explore and uncover for himself the canon's unrepresented and the less represented upwellings of creativity. It comprises five parts and each part is linked with the other parts with its overt emphasis on the strand of contemporaneity.

Rooted as it is in the concept of World Literature, Part—A studies interestingly, contemporary British literary artists. Part—B examines, not surprisingly but unabashedly, the modern American artistic sensibilities. While Part—C analyses meaningfully and conveniently, the most representative literary endeavours from the Third World excluding the great Indian subcontinent, Part—D scans most authoritatively, the selections from contemporary Indian writers in English. Part—E heralds tacitly and also articulates compellingly, a seamless global network of mass media including the affiliations with lexicography and critical theory.

I would like to conclude that this is admittedly a daunting task of exhibiting a tiny fraction of the infinite, irreducible diversity of contemporary world literature. I am deeply indebted to all the contributors for their well researched articles. I sincerely hope that this book will be a prized possession for any library—personal or institutional.

P. Bayapa Reddy

Contents

PART - C

PART - D

PART - E

PART - A

1

World Literature in the Age of Globalization: Reflections on an Anthology

Wail S. Hassan

Since the early 19th century, *Weltliteratur* (World Literature) has been one of the great Western humanistic ideas. Like many such ideas, it has both reproduced and reinforced a specially Western worldview. For a long time, "world literature" was synonymous with European literature, but with the vigorous interrogation from a number of perspectives of the primacy of the Western canon, the rise to global celebrity of scores non-Western writers (including several Nobel laureates and other equally canonized by the Western literary-critical establishment), and the increasing availability of English translations, the teacher of a world literature course today faces an unprecedented abundance of texts from which to choose. Yet this situation is fraught with difficulties of its own, for even as the "globalization of literary studies" emerges as the topic of the hour, the selective inclusion of non-Western texts in critical and pedagogical cadres often reveals new configurations of power and domination. I shall be arguing in this essay that the pedagogical application of the concept of "world literature" in the United States since WW II has developed in step with the political economic, and strategic remapping of global relations, sometimes in subtle ways that tend to mask its affiliations with power.

The globalization of literary studies is articulated in several interrelated domains—critical, curricular, pedagogical—all of which I cannot adequately address within the scope of this essay. I would like, however, to limit my discussion to one aspect of pedagogy, namely the evolution of the single most authoritative and widely used textbook in world literature courses in the United States, *The Norton Anthology of World Masterpieces.* I shall begin by revising the notion of "world literature" itself by way of setting up the following question: Has the *Norton Anthology* provided those of us who are committed to the teaching of world literature from non-Eurocentric perspectives with a useful tool, or does the anthology more subtly than ever reproduce the canon's ideological underpinnings? My attempt to answer this question, in turn, leads to a consideration of the extent to which the new notion of the "globalization of literary studies" departs from older concepts of "world literature" and whether multiculturalism has contributed something to this globalization that the Eurocentric assumptions of the traditional canon precluded. These issues, I believe, are central to any consideration of the teaching of world literature.

When Goethe coined the term *Weltliteratur* in 1827, he was envisioning a future state rather than naming a contemporary canon. As Rene Wellek writes, for Goethe "the term *world literature*...suggests a historical scheme of the evolution of national literatures in which they will fuse and ultimately melt into a great synthesis" (221). For Goethe, that ideal future was to be marked by open dialogue between "nations"—in Herder's sense of a nation as a collective cultural and linguistic community with a distinctive spiritual essence, or a *Volksgeist*. In this dialogue, each nation would be represented by its major writers, whose works would continue to reflect each nation's *Volksgeist* while achieving, as a result of the increased cross-cultural understanding fostered by reading foreign literatures, such breadth of vision as to express the universality of the human experience. In that sense, world literature was for Goethe an opportunity, not for the imposition of cultural hegemony by one nation over others, but rather for greater understanding of one's neighbors and of oneself that would foster harmony and lead to reducing conflict (Lawall, "Introduction" 13). Goethe's optimism about the future of humanity may not have permitted him to articulate the notion of world literature in the context of contemporary historical forces shaping Europe's imperialist expansion throughout the globe. His idealistic notion of *Weltliteratur* was a far cry from the cultural imperialism of Macaulay's grimly pragmatic program (advocated a few years later in the infamous "Indian Education: Minute of the 2nd of February, 1835") for the re-education of Indian youth in English literature on the grounds of its "intrinsic superiority" to the literatures of the "Orient" (722).

Rooted as it is in Enlightenment universalism, the concept of *Weltliteratur* was also in a sense Goethe's response to the greatly increased volume of trade and communication occasioned by the Industrial Revolution (Aldridge 9). Goethe's notion of world literature, therefore, is linked in an important way to the internationalization of culture that resulted from the emergence of capitalism as the dominant mode of production in modern Europe. Similarly, our contemporary notion of the globalization of literary studies is affiliated with the globalization of capital, or late capitalism in the post-Cold War era. This new paradigm for literary studies is articulated along the various trajectories of postmodernism, the poststructuralist critique of universalism and foundational philosophy, and the multiculturalist interrogation of the traditional Eurocentric canon from Third World, feminist, minority, and class perspectives. This kind of globalization encompasses a wide range of neoliberal and emphasize that they are far from being uniform either in their histories or in their content and that, in fact, considerable ambivalence and contradiction exist between them and the parallel—sometimes enabling—movement of corporate globalization. For example, the multiple and distinct histories of national liberation worldwide, women's movements, and Civil Rights struggles may have converged with poststructuralism in their interrogation of the Eurocentric bias of enlightenment universalism, but at the same time their projects may conflict in profound ways with postmodernism when it is understood, in Fredric Jameson's compelling argument, as "the cultural logic of late capitalism."

What I do want to identify on this wide spectrum of positions is the tendency, in the sphere of culture in general and literary pedagogy in particular, of some strands of globalization to reproduce uncritically the logic of global capitalism as the latest form of imperialism while at the same time posing as counter-hegemonic projects, This tendency often results in idealized notions of multiculturalism that superficially celebrate difference and diversity while commodifying cultural production. There are, however, other non-hegemonic conceptions of difference that self-consciously historicize their understanding of world cultures and literatures while maintaining "critical vigilance" (to use Gayatry Chakrovorty Spivak's term) toward their own affiliations with power. Such conceptions should, in my view, inform our efforts to construct a framework for the interpretation of culture and for teaching world literature that resists cultural imperialism, whether of Macaulay's or of the more subtle, late capitalist variety.

The Norton Anthology of World Masterpieces such a framework. A brief history of the anthology's eight editions will show how its Eurocentric definition of "world literature" itself has come to embody some of the most problematic aspects of multiculturalism. W.W. Norton's dozen or so anthologies are the most widely used textbooks in introductory and survey literature courses in American universities. Those anthologies are expertly edited by teams of highly distinguished scholars whose decisions are often informed by questionnaires sent out to hundred of professors regarding what they teach and how they do so. The often excellent introductions, helpful footnotes, and useful "Instructors's Guides" all contribute to making Norton's anthologies by far the most convenient textbooks available, and, therefore, the most concrete embodiment of the canon.

The *World Masterpieces* anthology, under the general editorship of Maynard Mack, first appeared in two volumes in 1956, then in successive editions in 1965, 1973, 1979, 1985, 1992, 1995 (the "Expanded Edition" of the sixth), and most recently 1999 (with Sarah Lawall succeeding Mack as general editor). On the title page of all seven regular editions (but not the "Expanded Edition"), the subtitle "Literature of *Western* Culture" (Emphasis added) tellingly sports the Eurocentric bias of the collection: Not only is "world literature" fully coterminous with "Western" literature, but the unabashed proclamation in the subtitle, reiterated in the preface of each edition, demonstrates just how normalized that Eurocentricism has been. Not surprisingly, those seven editions have followed the standard periodization of Western literature—classical, medieval, Renaissance, and on—and contained, in the first four editions, other than extracts from the Old Testament, no non-Western works. Curiously, however, the third (1973), fourth (1979), and fifth (1985) editions announced inside the front cover that a "companion volume" entitled *Masterpieces of the Orient* was available as a supplement to the main anthology. This appendage to the 4,000-page anthology was advertised as conveniently available in the abridged version of 379 pages and an enlarged version of 834 pages. Even more than the subtitle of the anthology itself, this strange, optional supplement at an additional cost uneasily, and grudgingly, acknowledged the Eurocentrism of the anthology. At the same time, this supplement revealed the uneven division of world literature into mainly Western, housed in the main anthology, and Oriental, available upon request in two "convenient" sizes. Shopper suit thyself.

Nor was that all. The fifth edition of 1985 listed the Indian R.K. Narayan, the Japanese Mishima Yukio, and the Nigerian Wole Soyinka—

not in the "Companion Volume," as one would expect, but in the main anthology under the heading "Contemporary Explorations." It is not clear why these three writers were placed in the main anthology and not in the companion volume, nor is it clear why these three particular writers, and no others, were thus Westernized by association. Even more interestingly, and with no explanation, the sixth edition of 1992 dropped all three, adding in their place the Nigerian Chinua Achebe and the Egyptian Naguib Mahfouz. The sixth edition also included the epic of *Gilgamesh* in the "Ancient World" section and a selection from the Qur'an in the "Middle Ages" section (note here the problematic posting of a transcultural medievialism: the period from the sixth to the fourteenth centuries C.E., which witnessed the emergence of Arab civilization, is subsumed in the *Norton Anthology* under the rubric of what became known in Europe as the Dark Ages). The most recent, seventh edition (1999) has maintained the non-Western selections of the sixth, adding three short Arabic "medieval" lyrics and a selection from *The Thousand and One Nights.* (Meanwhile, the seventh edition has grown to include Qur'an, *The Thousand and One Nights*, Achebe's *Things Fall Apart*, and Mahfouz's "Zabalaawi" simply *become* Western texts.)

Obviously, this confusion would not have occurred had Norton avoided the universalist pretensions of the title "World Masterpieces," and named its anthology for what it is: a library of Western literature. Yet the editors explain in the preface to the sixth edition that "for a very long time we have been experimenting with ways to expand this anthology into a collection of 'world' masterpieces *in the fullest contemporary sense*" (1992, xviii; emphasis added). One cannot help but wonder at the increasing elasticity of Norton's notion of "world." Short of a Copernican revolution in literary studies, which is yet to come, that logic justifies the need for periodical revision of the definition of " 'world' literature," or for including or excluding this or that foreign text, other than that of market trends? Consequently, the experience of reading becomes truly a "contemporary exploration" for the reader-tourist-consumer with a short attention span and thirst for exotic commodities. Reading and teaching world literature become a leisurely stroll in a global literary mall that is structured at once to satisfy and to reinforce Western modes of consumption and interpretation: Western periodization. Western thematics, and Western postmodern sensibilities.

Nevertheless, to market its anthology successfully, Norton must walk the fine line between pleasing both the "advocates of 'canonicity' and 'multiculturalism.'" This means assuring the former that the sixth and subsequent editions "will continue as in the past to evolve and grow, responding to the needs and preferences of those who wish to stress in the limited time at their disposal the Judaic-Greek-Roman-European-American traditions of thought and feeling" (1992, xiii), a promise that the seventh edition of 1999 has honored. As for the multiculturalists, the editors announced a new "expanded edition," which was published in 1995 and contained the entire sixth edition plus 2,000 pages of non-Western works. Here, finally, is globalization at work: no fundamental structural changes reflecting anew vision of global reality, but simply "expansion" (the term unambiguously implying territorial "colonization" or "annexation") by adding more and more foreign "masterpieces" to a consolidated Western canon. Yet this increase is emphatically, even his or her own preferred version of the world.

In this "expanded edition," the editors removed the categories of European literary history from the major section headings within the anthology and used instead a temporal scheme with which literary movements are clearly marked as culture-specific (e.g., "India's Heroic Age" or "China's Middle Period"). Nevertheless, it will be noticed that the temporal scheme itself (Vol. 1: Beginning to A.D. 100, 100 to 1500, 1500 to 1650; Vol. 2: 1650, 1800, 1800 to 1900, and the twentieth century) coincides with the standard periodization used in structuring literature curricula in most western literature departments in the United States: classical, medieval, Renaissance, enlightenment, the nineteenth century, and the twentieth century. Not surprisingly, the editors felt that some justification was necessary when this temporal framework failed, for example, to showcase more than handful of non-Western works, totaling 390 pages, in the sections covering 1500-1900 C.E., which consist of 1400 pages of Western literature. This is, of course, the period when the world was rapidly being subjugated by the colonial powers of Europe not only dominated about 85 per cent of the earth's surface, but also imposed its languages and curricula in ways that permanently changed countless non-Western cultures. Yet this unpleasant fact is not mentioned by the editors, who simply state that "selections from non-Western literature diminish (in those sections) because in any culture the upwellings of creativity that produce works of great stature obey no time schedule" (1995). Whose time schedule, one might ask, and whose criteria determine whether, which, and when such "works of great stature" ("timeless masterpieces") are produced? Without questioning the sincere efforts of the editors, who seem to be trying their best to amend an old and embarrassing notion of the canon, update their anthology in the light of new knowledge, and also sell their product, I cannot help detecting in that statement the implicit logic of the argument that colonialism affected peoples who were not simply weaker militarily than the European colonizers, but who were culturally bankrupt.

Obviously, no single course can ever hope to incorporate all of the contents of the anthology, or even a single volume of it, but the point is that the anthology authoritatively manufacturers and imposes a fundamentally slanted vision of world literature that has always obeyed the logic of imperialism. As Kristin Ross argues, " [w]hen we speak about breaking out of a Western bourgeois model in our teaching, we cannot speak merely of adding on or integrating culture...into a better, more representative totality, a fuller globe. For we will then merely reproduce what is essentially a Western bourgeois sociology of culture: Western civilization as world civilization" (670). This is precisely the paradigm of "expansion" that Norton used in the 1995 expanded edition. Furthermore, the evolutionary trajectory of the anthology in its successive editions, with its reverential treatment of the Western canon and random inclusion and exclusion of non-Western writers, parallels the historical trajectory of Western European and North American enunciations of global relations. Thus the "world" of "world literature," as represented in the early editions of the anthology, was coterminous with the "West," while the so-called "Orient" and its cultural production occupied an ancillary status, only slightly more ambivalent than Macaulay allowed. Then the category of "Third World Literature" emerged in the 1960s as a sort of alternative canon (Ahmad 78-86), the mere existence of which begins, two decades later, to be tacitly conceded by the *Norton Anthology*. At the height of decolonization movements and the Cold War, the Three Worlds Theory—at least insofar as it opposed First World to Third World—could be seen retrospectively as the new model for this institutionalized split between Western and non-Western literatures in the curriculum. With the end of the Cold War and the advent of what George Bush celebrated as a "New World Order," heralded by the dramatic affirmation of U.S. military supremacy in the Gulf War, the horizon of late-capitalist global market economy expands freely, aided by a hegemonic form of multiculturalism that has informed the anthology's development in the 1990s.

What does this symptomatic development tell us, then, about multiculturalism, the controversial movement cited by the Norton editors as the spur for "expanding" the anthology? Leftist analyses the critiques of multiculturalism (Zizek, San Juan, Juan, Lazarus, Dirlik)—notwithstanding the sometimes radically distinct specificity of their personalities—distinguish themselves from neoliberalism by stressing the continuities between the hegemonic tendency of global capitalism and its cultural cognates, postmodernism and multiculturalism. The argument goes like this: "if imperialism is the latest stage of capitalism, globalism is the latest stage of imperialism" (Sivanandan 5). Postmodernism, then, is described as the "cultural logic of late capitalism" (Jameson), and multiculturalism as the "positive guise" of the "cultural fragmentation" precipitated by global capitalism (Dirlik 30). The most radical form of this critique describes multiculturalism as a new kind of racism. In an essay with strong Jamesonian echoes entitled "Multiculturalism, or the cultural Logic of Multination Capitalism," Zizek's argues that

> the ideal form of ideology of this global capitalism multiculturalism...[which] is a disavowed, inverted self-referential form of racism, a "racism with a distance"—it "respects" the Other's identity conceiving the Other as a self-enclosed "authentic" community towards which he, the multiculturalist, maintains a distance rendered possible by his privileged universal position. Multiculturalism is a racism which empties its own position of all positive content (the multiculturalism is not a direct racist, he doesn't oppose to the Other the *particular* values of his own culture), but nonetheless retains this position as the privileged *empty point of universality* from which one is able to appreciate (and depreciate) properly other particular cultures—the multiculturalist respect for the Other's specificity is the very form of asserting one's own superiority.

The multiculturalist, In other words, is one who has "transcended" or "moved beyond" racial prejudice and into a privileged realm of late capitalist development that no longer depends on older forms of exploitation based on race; the multiculturalist has "left behind" those (mostly in parts of the world which have not attained complete capitalist development) who are still mired in ethnic, racial, and religious strife. The implicit reference here is to the history of capitalism, which depended in an earlier phase on colonial expansion, which in turn spurred the development of post-Enlightenment racial theory, Orientalism, and Similar discourses on Europe's Others. Now, in a late phase of capitalism that depends on globalization rather than colonial expansion, racism accordingly assumes a more subtle form.

Taken together with its professed model, Jameson's reading of postmodernism as "the cultural logic of late capitalism," Zizek's critique places multiculturalism squarely within the imperialist project of multinational capitalism; paradoxically, multiculturalism's professed anti-racism and acknowledgement of the validity of other cultural values and norms itself becomes an efficient vehicle for undermining the integrity of other cultures and a new form of racism. What enables this sleight of hand is capitalism's drive toward maximizing profit by any means necessary, so that the new racism, is not so much directed by one ethnic group against another, but by global capitalism (as an "empty point of universality") against its victims. In a slightly different but related argument, Dirlik writes that "the apparent end of Eurocentrism is an illusion, because capitalist culture as it has taken shape has Eurocentrism built into the very structure of its narrative, which may explain why even as Europe and the United States lose their domination of the capitalist world economy, culturally European and American values retain their domination" (30). Thus, if not strictly racist in the conventional sense, multiculturalism as the cultural logic of the globalization of capital is fundamentally Eurocentric and exploitative, despite its claims to the contrary.

To illustrate, take the billboard multiculturalism of "The United Colors of Benetton" and MCI's claim to have built a "seamless global network" of business communication. Benetton manufactures a kind of multiculturalism chic (translated into images of groups of stylist multiracial youngsters) designed to appeal to liberal-minded youth who can afford Benetton's expensive garments. Multiculturalism here mobilizes notions of racial equality that exist only in the eye of the beholder (and consumer), masking not only the social and global realities of inequality but also the very mechanism by which capitalist culture depends on exploitation and inequality.[1] The MCI example articulates a utopian vision of global capitalism in a series of television advertisements featuring Sam Neill as a corporate mogul standing in a grayish, metallic, high-walled enclosure that appears to be an abstract rendition of a corporate boardroom. He peeps stealthily through a small aperture in the wall—not a keyhole, he assures us in one of the commercials—but apparently some sort of cyper-panopticon from which he spies at one time on robotic, expressionless corporate employees dancing in a (vicious?) circle. "They seem rather happy," says Neill with confident authority. Both the claustrophobic abstract setting and the dehumanized state of the otherwise privileged employees ironically underscore the viciousness of this vision of homogenized global culture (in another advertisement, dozens of men uniformly clad in spotless white suites and hats, who ostensibly represent "local carriers and international carriers," exchange briefcases as they march mechanically in circles). In such a world of streamlined communications and global capitalist access, there is simply no place for the "unhappy": the poor, the women and children shamefully exploited in Third World sweatshops, and the underprivileged masses who constitute the functional waste of the "seamless global network." Within this New World Order, "four-fifths of the global population...are simply marginalized" (Dirlik 32).

Such representations by MCI and Benetton reveal the depoliticizing homogenizing, and idealizing dynamics of global capitalism. In much the same way, Norton has been idealizing and depoliticizing the globalized canon, in which the unpleasant realities of colonial history and exploitation are sanitized within an ever-expanding pantheon of "timeless masterpieces."

This is not the place to restate the argument for multiculturalism. From Rush Limbaugh to Dinesh D'Souza and their like, the Right has been busy demonizing and stereotyping multiculturalism, which it sees, with reason, as a menace to its parochialism. The project of multiculturalism is unquestionably valid, important, and ethical insofar as it challenges both the realities and the philosophical justifications (from Platonic monism to enlightenment universalism) of cultural, racial, religious, sexual, class and other forms of hegemony. The pressing question that, to my mind, Zizek's compelling argument forces us to confront, is this: How and when does multiculturalism turn into a superficial celebration of diversity that sanitizes difference and effectively co-opts it into the "seamless global network" ideal for corporate expansion? To tackle the issue from this angle, I think, is to begin to clear a space for an alternative model for the globalization of literary studies that carries within it the recognition that the world is a closely knit, although extremely diverse, human community that superficial forms of multiculturalism tend to homogenize and that the dynamics of global capitalism attempt to transform into a seamless global supermarket built on Eurocentric assumptions, norms, and attitudes.

As Aijaz Ahmad observes, "Internationalism...has been one of the constitute traditions of the Left, but in this age of late capitalism it is best to recognize that certain kinds of internationalism also arise more or less spontaneously out of circuits of imperialist capital itself, and the lines between the internationalism of the Left and the globalism of capitalist circuits must always by demarcated as rigorously as possible" (45). This distinction, also implicit in Zizek's critique of multiculturalism, is more critically important today than ever before and will become, I suspect, more so in the future.

I would like to conclude by offering a few suggestions to those who, like myself, find themselves forced to use the *Norton Anthology* in their world literature courses for lack of a viable alternative, since it is the only anthology available that attempts, however unsatisfactory, the admittedly daunting task of bridging Western and non-Western literatures. (I am emphatically not saying that one should ignore Western literature.) Other anthologies either focus exclusively on the West (Wilkie and Hurt) or on Asia, Africa, and Latin America combined (Barnstone and Barnstone).[2] The challenge one faces, therefore, involves not only balancing the content of the course, but also correcting the Eurocentric image of the world which the *Norton Anthology* suggests to the students who so much as read its table of contents.

One obvious solution to the shortcomings of this, or any, anthology is to supplement it with other texts and to devise creative ways of structuring a course. More important, I think, is that we engage our students in discussing the history of the anthology, its affiliation with imperialist discourses on the non-Western world, and the cultural and political implications today of reproducing their logic. Further, let us make explicit to our students our philosophies of teaching something as formidably vast as world literature. Let us also explain to them that, since we could not possibly, in the space of one or two semesters, introduce them to a tiny fraction of four millennia of world literature, we are offering them a particular selection that, while it cannot hope to represent, at least it could begin to suggest the infinite, irreducible diversity of the world in which we all live.[3]

NOTES

1. For an extended treatment of the politics of Benetton's brand of multiculturalism, see Giroux.
2. Prentice Hall's new anthology, *The World of Literature*, edited by Louise Westling et al., was published in 1999, after this article was completed. This anthology offers a more balanced selection of Asian African, European, and North and South American texts than the *Norton* while avoiding the latter's Eurocentric periodization, thus promising to be a valuable textbook. I have also learned that at least two other anthologies are in preparation at Macmillan and Beford.
3. I am indebted to many people who have generously offered encouragement or valuable comments on earlier drafts of this article: Stephanie Hilger, Jonathan Hunt, James Hurt, Thomas Joswick, R.S. Krishnan, Michael Palencia-Roth, Zohreh Sullivan, Ronald

Walker, and the anonymous reviewers at *College English*. An earlier version of this essay was presented at the 2nd Annual Red River Conference on World Literature held at North Dakota State University in April 1999 and appeared in its proceedings.

WORKS CITED

Ahmad, Aijaz. *In Theory; Classes, Nations, Literature*. London: Verso, 1992.

Albridge, A. Owne. *The Reemergence of World Literature*. Newark: U of Delaware P, 1986.

Anderson, G.L., ed. *Masterpieces of the Orient*. New York: Norton, 1961.

— *Masterpieces of the Orient*, Enlarged Edition. New York: Norton 1977.

Barnstone, Willis, and Tony Barnstone, eds. *Literatures of Asia, Africa, and Latin America*. Upper Saddle River, NJ: Prentice Hall, 1999.

Dirlik, Arif. "The Global in the Local." *Global/Local: Cultural Production and the Transnational Imaginary*. Ed. Rob Wilson and Wimal Dissanayake. Durham: Duke UP: 1996.

Gates, Henry Louis Jr. "Beyond the Culture Wars: Identities in Dialogue." *Profession*, 93 (1993): 6-11.

Girous, Henry A. "Consuming Social Change: The 'United Colors of Benetton.'" *Cultural Critique* 26 (1993-94): 5-32.

Jameson, Fredrick, *Postmodernism*, or, *The Cultural Logic of Late Capitalism*. Durham: Duke UP, 1991.

Lawall, Sarah. "Introduction: Reading World Literature." *Reading World Literature: Theory, History, Practice*. Ed. Sarah Lawall. Austin: U of Texas P, 1994, 1-64.

Lawall, Sarah, *et al.*, eds. *The Norton Anthology of World Masterpieces*. 2 vols. 7th ed. New York, Norton: 1999.

Lazarus, Neil. "Charting Globalization." *Race and Class* 40.2-3 (1998-1999): 91-109.

Macaulay: Thomas Babington. "Indian Education: Minute of the 2nd of February, 1835." *Macaulay Prose and Poetry*. Ed. G.M. Young. London Rupert Hart-Davis, 1952, 719-39.

Mack, Maynard, *et al. The Norton Anthology of World Masterpieces*. 2 Vols. New York: Norton: 1956.

— *The Norton Anthology of World Masterpieces*. 2 Vols. 4th ed. New York, Norton: 1979.

— *The Norton Anthology of World Masterpieces.* 2 Vols. 6th ed. New York, Norton: 1992.

— *The Norton Anthology of World Masterpieces* (Expanded Edition). New York: Norton, 1995.

Ross, Kristin. "The World Literature and Cultural Studies Program." *Critical Inquiry*, 19 (1993): 666-76.

San Juan, E. "Globalization, Dialogic Nation, Diaspora" *Beyond Postcolonial Theory*. New York: St. Martin's P., 1998, 195-226.

San Juan, E. "The Multicultural Imaginary: Problematizing Identity and the Ideology of Racism." *Beyond Postcolonial Theory.* New York: St. Martin's P., 1998, 113-54.

Sivanandan, A. "Globalism and the Left." *Race and Class*, 40.2-3 (1998-1999). 5-19.

Wellek, Rene. *A History of Modern Criticism: 1750-1950.* Vol. I: *The Later Eighteenth Century*. London: Jonathan Cape, 1955.

Westling, Louise, *et al.*, eds. *The World of Literature*. Upper Saddle River, NJ: Prentice Hall, 1999.

Wilkie, Brian, and James Hurt, eds. *Literature of the Western World.* 2 Vols. Upper Saddle River, NJ: Prentice Hall, 1997.

Zizek, Stavoj. "Multiculturalism, or the Cultural Logic of Multinational Capitalism," *New Left Review*, 225 (1997): 28-51.

2

The Matter of Somerset Maugham: A World with Properties

Howard R. Wolf

If it isn't accurate to say that the work of Somerset Maugham ever had central, even marginal, status in the American literary canon and academy, it is fair to suggest that literary critics and teachers on both sides of the Atlantic during the 1920-1960 period would not have shied away from making reference to his writing. Indeed, such references were, for students of my generation of literary students in America (the last such generation, I think), marks of worldliness and internationalism in a New Critical culture that seemed too preoccupied with the autonomy of the text.

This was particularly true for students of the emergent middle class, often children of immigrants who had the opportunity, as the result of G1 Bill and post-WW II economic boom to go on to higher education in the best colleges and universities. Even as these students sought to climb the Halls of Ivy, they knew that there was a larger and harder world beyond the quads and compuses; they knew that money, class, snobbery, and prejudice were part of the real furniture of the world.

Empson and Brower, Wellek and Austin Warren, Brooks and Robert Penn Warren, the critical worthies, provided ways of stepping back from history, and many of us too the invitation for a while; but we knew secretly that the evasions of history were risky and costly, even dangerous. We knew about the Holocaust, after all. Maugham, despite his limitations, perhaps because of them, was there, with some other middle range writers (James Hilton, John P. Marquand, O'Hara), to remind us that life and literature were grounded in history—social, material, political, geographical. Few of our instructors talked in these terms (I had one at

Amherst College, C.L. Barber), but we knew that we could have to work out our lives in real cities. "Imaginary toads" were fun to think about, a testing ground for sensibility, but we knew that social boundaries, no garden fences, circumscribed our lives.

I want to suggest that all writing is historical: a product of, and response to, the "circumstances" of its historical moment. Writers may wish to rise above historical circumstances, and critics may wish to theorize away a certain kind of materialism; but I believe it is still possible and necessary for some writers to deal in a significant way with a world of intrinsic properties, with a world of Newtonian properties, with some version of realism—if our culture is to survive with some coherence.

Charles Townsend, the Assistant Colonial Secretary of Hong Kong, says something like this, to the chagrin of Kitty Fane (the wife of Walter Fane, medical bacteriologist) in Maugham's *The Painted Veil*:

> But, my dear, I love you. Only we're not living in a desert island and we've got to make the best we can out of the circumstances that are forced upon us. You really must be reasonable. (72)

From the time of Defoe to Maugham, the English novel and, somewhat later in its different way, the American novel took for granted a certain solidity of specification. As Defoe virtually weighs Moll's life in terms of coins and possessions in *Moll Flanders* (the weightiest novel in the old metallic canon), so Maugham takes the measure of things in all his writing.

It is perhaps not coincidental that in 1722 Defoe writes about the plague in *A Journal of the Plague Year*, the first great non-fiction book and the precursor of the New Journalism, while Maugham writes about a cholera epidemic in *The Painted Veil.* Both writers were drawn to the same sensible world that incited Dr. Johnson to kick a stone in refutation of Bishop Berkeley. One looks at the world with journalistic eyes, the other with medical objectivity. Or we might say that the interest in objectivity led one to journalism and the other, for a while, to medicine. Defoe and Maugham frame the beginning and end, for some critics, of the post 17th century empirical revolution.

If criticism loses respect for facts and circumstances, or if it will acknowledge only one set of facts (in, say, Marxist or Psychoanalytic criticism), then a certain kind of fiction will fall between the cracks. In no time at all, yesterday's sturdy wall will become tomorrow's archeological ruin. Something like this happened to Maugham. A strong current of intellectual history— what we associate with Modernism-called another kind of social history into question. Put on a scale of values with Woolf, Joyce, and Kafka, and other avant-gardists, allegedly realist naturalist writers such as Maugham, Marquand, Sinclair Lewis, John O' Hara fared badly in the weigh off. I say alleged because even a realist like Maugham acknowledges the role of construction in our knowledge of the world:

> Beyond certain fundamental data which they call the given, and the existence of other minds, which they infer, men can be sure of nothing. All the rest of their knowledge is fiction, the construction of their minds. (*The Summing Up* 171)

But "fundamental data" and "other minds" are no small matters.

To the extent that criticism turned towards the sort of Modernist values—solipsistic and subjectivist values that were pushed towards arbitrary ones in post Modernism—it was inevitable that the writing of Somerset Maugham would get undervalued, if not devalued.

Virginia Woolf advances this view of consciousness (a world of inner "atoms") in her influential 1919 essay, "Modern Fiction":

> Life is not a series of gig lamps symmetrically arranged; but a luminous halo, a semi-transparent envelope surrounding us from the beginning of consciousness to the end. Is it not the task of the novelist to convey this varying, this unknown and uncircumscribed spirit, whatever aberration or complexity it may display, with as little mixture of the alien and external as possible? (*The Common Reader* 154)

What could be more alien to Maugham that a world "with as little mixture of the...external as possible"? Indeed, it is hard to imagine the world of Somerset Maugham without hotels, such as the Oriental in Bangkok, from the verandahs of which he made so many of his observations, to say nothing of the District officers' bungalows in *The Gentlemen in the Parlour* and other travel writings.

Edmund Wilson's summary dismissal of Maugham, in his essay "The Apotheosis of Somerset Maugham," can best be understood as a consequence of the former's commitments to "advanced" Modernism, the sort of commitments he was defending in *Axel's Castle*:

> It has happened to me from time to time to run into some person of taste who tells me that I ought to take Somerset Maugham seriously, yet I have never been able to convince myself that he was anything but second rate. (*Classics and Commercials* 319)

Wilson's judgement is consistent with his understanding of the new Modern temper, especially what he calls in the same essay "relativistic theory," thinking of Joyce and Proust and Maugham's dismissal of Joyce (325). Maugham just isn't, for Wilson, "relativistic" enough. Maugham still inhabits a Newtonian universe where solid objects affect each other; he doesn't pay sufficient attention to new concepts of time and space. For Wilson, there is too much furniture in Maugham's world, and it lends to stay put.

Maugham stands for a set of certainties—individual, social, even cosmological—that Wilson would dismiss in the light of new notions about the nature of time, space, and matter in relation to consciousness. Instead of using Joyce to extend the representational possibilities of fiction, Wilson urged an erasure of previous Maughamian possibilities. Instead of adding Einstein to Newton, using each other where appropriate, Wilson urged, as it were, a total Einsteinian description of the world. In the world of Maugham, however, junks, freighters, and social hypocrisy do not travel near the speed of light. We need to be mindful of, and tolerant towards different ways of seeing, interpreting, and describing the world.

In this spirit, I hope to show that what is a deficit for Wilson possibly may be refashioned by us at the this time as a positive value serving to guide us towards a post-Modernist sensibility as we enter a new century. An X-ray or MRI of Maugham's world can outline a still anatomy for writers who believe in "human nature," a stubborn and obdurate social environment, and a cosmos based on traditional religion.

Joseph Epstein states the main point in his article "Is it all right to read Somerset Maugham?" He tries to shore up Maugham's reputation by naming some impressive "supporters," including Orwell (who praised Kipling, we may recall), and by pointing to Maugham's firm grasp of "human nature," without which concept the world of Maugham (and, in our time, Updike and Mailer) collapses.

> The point Maugham stuck to throughout his long career was the investigation of that magnificent, comic, admirable, outrageous, depressing, impressive, grim, gracious, grudging, great, and elusive thing called human nature. (*The New Criterion* 13)

The problem here for Maugham and some of us is that the intellectual history of recent decades (let us call it Deconstructive for purposes of intellectual economy) has not favored an essentialist view of Human Nature—which I here capitalize as it might have been written in the 18th century, the century of Common Sense that shaped Defoe and paved the way (with cobble and stone) for Orwell and Maugham.

In order for Maugham to be reconsidered, there needs to be a change in critical perspective that accepts once again "the gentleman in the parlour," the person in a furnished world; and one may be available to us that wasn't quite accessible even a decade ago—the decanonization or, I would prefer, the recanonization of literature.

This may be the right moment to consider dimensions of pragmatic realism just as it may be an equally opportune moment to welcome a panoply and chorus of non-establishment voices. Radical criticism may end up at the same table with older voices. In effect, the work of Maugham lets us see what literary elements have been more or less excluded from academic criticism in recent decades, elements which need to be given weight again. I list these elements here:

(1) Confidence in his ability to observe a real world. This is clearly central to any re-evaleation of Maugham and writers like him, and it accounts for much of his appeal to adolescent readers. As Poe pierces the unconscious of the young reader and stays there for a lifetime, so Maugham's worldliness becomes an ocean liner or sampan for a young, restless mind and spirit eager to go beyond the confines of city caverns, village two paths, or suburban malls.

No one can carry the day when it comes to questions of ultimate reality, but physics keeps reminding us that matter does matter and that, in the end, it was matter, no anti matter that prevailed in the cosmos. To deny some kind of realism is to negate matter.

(2) Maugham's plain style with his well-known priorities of "lucidity, simplicity, and euphony" is the equivalent of a worldview. Maugham's sturdy, deceptively lyrical, and painterly style (he practiced as well as acquired Impressionism) serves him well as a travel writer and a writer who travels (closer to what he does). He enables us to "see" with him. Often he claims no more than the ability to see surfaces: "He looks like one of those sages that the Chinese artists painted in a rocky landscape or under Kang-hsi modelled in porcelain" (*On a Chinese Screen* 234). Maugham gives form to what most travellers bring back from voyages: visual impressions. He serves as a camera for us, and his photo album tend to be better than ours.

(3) Maugham sees the world through an autobiographical presence whom the reader is meant to regard as a real person. After Ashenden, it became "Mr. Maugham" for Maugham. Without making a case for any deep psychological sense of Self, Maugham's first person narratives in, say, *On a Chinese Screen*, refuse to dissolve into mere narrativity as they do in the work of John Barth.

Barth says, now famously, in "Life-Story,"

> He being by vocation an author of novels and stories it was perhaps inevitable that one afternoon the possibility would occur to the writer of these lines that his own life might be a fiction, in which he was the leading or an accessory character. (*Lost in the Funhouse* 116)

Barth's aesthetic self-reflexiveness played a creative and liberating role at a moment in the 1960's when American fiction was trying to remake itself by going beyond certain middle class preoccupations (Willy Loman's illusions and delusions) and by opening itself to European thinking (Levi-Strauss, Barthes, Robbe-Griller, Derrida).

By 1975, however, by the end of a Vietnam war, American fiction had rue out of "new" tricks, and it was disheartening to see lesser talents that Barth carry the same old spears in all too familiar parades. In a contest between ways of not making meaning and older ways of making sense, many writers and readers began to become sceptical about scepticism. Hence, the return to forms of realism in recent fiction.

(4) At the center of Maugham's world, more often that not, lies the conflict between the narrator's fairly comfortable role as British traveller-aesthete-observer and the misery of abject humanity which he observes. Maugham is often poised between the role of armchair traveller-writer and compassionate observer. He is very much a writer of the middle ground (as well as for the middle class). Maugham creates a comfortable "middle" zone in which he is, so to speak, safe away from home. There is often burning "charcoal" and a "hurricane lamp" in the berth where he is perilously "dropping down the river." He manages to make a "parlour" wherever he is (*Screen* 95).

Philosophically and aesthetically, all travel is for Maugham a recreation and reaching back to the epiphanic moment in the Heidelberg of his youth when the world opened up to him as a "plain"—the sense of prospect and vista are central to Maugham's aesthetic and serve perhaps as the ethical equivalent of freedom—and where he doubtless saw the possibility of escape from a moralistic England that might have punished him for same sex preferences. He sees a great deal, but he keeps his distance.

> The only symbol for happiness I know is a wide prospect all golden in the setting sun, with a shining stream of silver running through it, like the path of life or like the ideal that guides you through it, and far away the grey towers of an ancient town. (185)

Maugham's middle zone of upper middle class gypsy/artist is where many of us would like to live. To condemn him without scrutiny is to dismiss our own day dreams, to find ourselves second rate.

(5) This middle ground is established in "stories" in which each person has a character, an identity (often hidden to himself and the world), which, in relation to fixed circumstances, say the conventions of colonial Hong Kong or old China, shapes a destiny, usually a poignant unhappiness, or a failure that begets a quest. These stories often present a straggle with suppressed sexuality in which characters express themselves through adultery (Maugham's cover all for forbidden sexuality) and other illicit relationships (liaisons with "fallen" women).

Although their differences are greater than their similarities, it may not be unreasonable to link Maugham with D.H. Lawrence as a maker of modern sexuality. Maugham's "Rain," like Lawrence's *Lady Chatterley's Lover*, captured frankly the volcanic eruptions of sexuality from beneath the crust of convention. The perception of "civilized" life in the British Colonies (Malaya, Singapore, Borneo) was never to be the same after Maugham.

(6) A conflict between haute bourgeois privilege and democratic values defines many of Maugham's "civilized" journeys. Maugham can be both "fashionably" anti-Semitic (as he can be philo Semitic) and compassionate towards the overworked "coolie." He is capable of saying about "An American Jew called Elfenbein" that "He was the kind of Jew who made you understand the pogrom (*The Gentleman in the Parlour* 171-75)," but Maugham is also capable of moving through an aesthetic response to a Chinese laborer's "blue rags" to a heartfelt compassion in "The Beast of Burden" (*Screen* 77-79). Maugham gives us, among other things, a documentary guide to pre-WW II snobbery and class malice. It's part of the equation found also in Eliot and Fitzgerald, and it serves the purposes of literary and intellectual history to include such evidence in our studies.

(7) Maugham casts a cold eye on himself as observer and his character. He is fundamentally anti Romantic and makes himself and his experience representative. Closer to Defoe than Wordsworth, he controls the role of the self-observer, lest it become over indulgent.

As Eric Blair reinvented himself as "Orwell," Maugham makes himself the civil and cordial interlocutor he failed often enough to be in life. In writing, he overcame his stammer and his dark passions. He forced himself to speak for, and to observe common humanity. We see his social intelligence, not his idiosyncratic desires. This is at once an asset and liability, particularly in Maugham's travel writing. Maugham specializes, in his vignettes in *On a Chinese Screen*, on finding "types," albeit types subject to specific pressures. He is not interested in uniqueness of character. He wants to show that what is most deeply human in us will surface under certain conditions. He puts super ego where Freud locates the id. For Kitty, it is generous love, not passion, that is hidden. Her speech to her father in *The Painted Veil* is worthy of Austen and Dickens with its earned and controlled sentiment (6) Aphoristic and cunning on the surface, Maugham is most deeply an idealist, not a moral relativist at depth.

(8) Maugham has some faith in faith—what Kitty calls, in reference to the nuns, "a different world from ours" (148), what Waddington calls "Tao" (the way) in the form of God, opium, whisky, and lover (168). His mystical and cosmological yearnings for oneness are attached to traditional Buddhistic and Hindu ideas. Maugham's religious aspirants turn towards orthodox structures for revelation. His questers are not alienated loners. They have social affiliations even when they leave the world and are cloistered.

Maugham's depiction of East West antinomies tend, therefore, to be predictable: "Here was the East, immemorial, dark, and inscrutable. The beliefs and the ideals of the West seemed crude beside ideals and beliefs of which in this exquisite creature she seemed to catch a fugitive glimpse" (166-67). At the same time, this dichotomy has proven to be true for many world travellers who could not so succinctly express their beliefs.

I don't think it possible that these Maughamian values, as they often are expressed and realized by Maugham, can be made central to contemporary literary culture. Maugham's realism is too often the limited possession of a privileged observer who belongs to the world of Empire.

At the same time, I think it is imperative for criticism to pay attention to the foundations of Maugham like fiction and for the literary academy to include some examples of them in the curriculum, including Maugham's own work. If nothing else, and it is a good deal, we owe it to our students to show them and to share with them some of the literary pleasures that pleased so many people for so long. It is sometimes true that the judgement of common humanity makes sense.

At the end of the day, we owe it to our students to make as much of a case for sense, what Flannery O'Connor calls "experienced meaning" as Virginia Woolf makes for "disconnected and incoherent" pattern in "Modern Fiction" (155). The study of Maugham, along some of the lines I have suggested, gives us a chance to take the measure of some of the important literary issues of the century, to decide just what matters matter.

As we approach the end of the 20th century, we owe it to the next generation of students to consider the whole experience of an era. We don't want to give them the impression that everything was a matter of "discourse," as the Newer Critics are fond of saying, for us. In making reference to Maugham and Orwell (a higher, but still neglected, level of achievement), we shall remind the students of the next American century that tramps and tramp steamers were part of our world.

In banishing "sexual objects," virtuous critics too often throw out the objects of the world. In savaging Empire, the standard bearers of Political Correctness, whose ethical standards are often correct, often neglect to make concrete the actual suffering of people under colonial conditions of political and economic subjugation. Theory displaces experiences, and we are once again returned to the safe precincts of criticism (the "cave," as one colleague of mine calls it).

Maugham may not side with the disposed and despised, the maligned and persecuted, though he sometimes does, but he dramatizes their lives for us to contemplate. Like F. Scott Fitzgerald, a writer who bears some resemblance to Maugham, he reflects and refracts a world of all too real circumstances. Maugham can serve as a kind of Johnson's stone for critics who wish to say to the radical subjectivists, "I refute it thus."

WORKS CITED

Barth, John. *Lost in the Funhouse.* New York: Doubleday & Co., Inc., 1968.

Epstein, Joseph. "Is it all right to read Somerset Maugham?" *The New Criterion*, November 1995. 1-13.

Maugham, Somerset, *The Gentleman in the Parlour: A Record of a Journey from Rangoon to Haiphong.* 1930. London: Pan Books, 1986.

— *On a Chinese Screen.* 1922. New York: Paragon House, 1990.

— *The Painted Veil.* 1925. New York: Penguin Books, 1952.

— *The Summing Up.* 1938. New York: Penguin Books, 1963.

O'Connor, Flannery. "Writing Short Stories." *The Story and Its Writer: An Introduction to Short Fiction.* Ed. Ann Charters. Boston: Bedford Books St. Martin's Press, 1955, 1544-49.

Wilson, Edmund. *Classics and Commercials: A. Literary Chronicle of the 1940s. 1950.* New York: The Noonday Press, 1967.

Woolf, Virginia. *The Common Reader.* New York: Harcourt, Brace, and World, 1953.

3

Vedic Themes in Eliot's *The Waste Land* and *Four Quartets*

Ramesh Chandra Tungaria

To remember T.S. Eliot is to recapitulate the complete ethos of twentieth century because in writing himself he wrote his time more than any other man of letters. English literary historians have acknowledged him to be the greatest modern American-British poet. Therefore, there is no exaggeration in saying that to understand modernism is to understand Eliot. The present paper endeavours to show that T.S. Eliot is one of those representative poets like W.B. Yeats, Ezra Pound, and Henry James of the Modern Period of English Literature (1910-1936) who not only brought English Literature of Europe in the full stream of the European literary movement, but also participated as much as possible in the process of assimilation of art and religion of the East, particularly the Hindu doctrines (which are Vedic in origin and Upanishadic in content) of *The Bhagvadgita* and Patanjali's *Yoga Darshan* which had already made a considerable headway.

Eliot declared in 1927 that he was "...classicist in literature royalist in politics, and Anglo-Catholic in religion."[1] It tends to point out Eliot's religious position that he was an Anglo-Catholic; but it too can be demonstrated in the tone of plainest evidences from his poetry that some more religious trends have made indelible impressions on the art and mind of Eliot than mere Christianity. Of these trends mention may be made of Hinduism, or Brahmanism, Buddhism, and even Hebraism. The assimilation and operation and Hinduism—more particularly the doctrines of *Upanishads* and *Srimadbhagvadgita* in *The Waste Land* and

Four Quartets, both representative poems of Eliot, are to be examined and understood in this paper.

Like W.B. Yeats, Eliot was highly influenced by the Indian spirit and tenets of *Srimadbhagvadgita*, *Upanishads*, Patanjali's *Yoga Darshan*, and the teachings of Buddha.[2] There are copious evidences to show that Eliot had studied Sanskrit and Pali, "at Harvard for two years under the able guidance of Charles Lamman...." There, at the self-same Harvard University, he was almost overpowered "by Buddhism and the philosophy of *Bhagvadgita* and *Upanishads* through the lectures of Irving Babbitt and Paul Elmore More—the two great savants of oriental wisdom."[3] At the same time he learnt Patanjali's *Yoga Sutra* intensively for one year under the able guidance of James H. Wood. In his *After Strange Gods* Eliot says:

> Two years spent in the study of Sanskrit under Charles Lamman, and a year in the mazes of Patanjali's metaphysics under the guidance of James Wood, left me in a state of enlightened mystification. (Eliot)[4]

And also he admitted:

> My own poetry shows the influence of Indian thought and sensibility (Sen Gupta)[5]

To find and examine explicit references to and examples from Vedic scriptures like *Upanishads* and *Bhagvadgita* one may turn to Eliot's poetry—*The Waste Land (1922), Four Quarters (1935-42), and The Indian Who Died in Africa (1943).*

Looking to the insufficiency of space and certain other limitation of the nature and form of a paper like this which has been devised in the contextual perspective of this academic meet for attracting the attention of the scholars of Vedic literature towards the assimilation and operation of Vedic themes in the poetry of T.S. Eliot without expounding the contents of the poems in detail, the present writer endeavours to focus on the explicit allusions, examples and glimpses from the *Upanishads* and *Bhagvadgita* which have been incorporated in the poems under study with a view to fulfilling the dire necessity of peace and salvation in the mechanical, substantial, and lifeless survival of the modern men in alienation from God and spirituality.

The Waste Land runs into five movements. In the first movement the modern world is pictured as modern wasteland, as 'stony rubbish,' universe of death where spiritual fertility has shrunken hard and dry. It projects the chaotic urbanity of the modern world where humanity in surviving in isolation from God, and therefore, has succumbed by vacuity, boredom, draught, sterility, and dread. In such a waste land there is very little hope for peace and salvation of mankind, and scant possibility of regeneration and rebirth.

In the second movement the poet proceeds to unravel the main facets of this spiritual dreadfulness. In this regard it is worthwhile to remember that the foundation of healthy spiritual life of an individual as well as of the society depends on a healthy sexual relationship—a relationship governed by moral discipline and self-control. When sex becomes devoid of self-control and moral discipline, it—by causing perversions and abnormalities—breeds frustration, neurosis, and failure of conjugal amity.

In the third movement, which is captioned after Buddha's "fire sermon," the image of fire in Eliot's mind is associated with that of Lord Buddha and St. Augustine. In Buddha's teachings one can look for the possibility of the way out of waste land only by overcoming the lust of 'the study pleasure of sex' and passions, and thereby becoming free from attachment and by practicing happy detachment.

In the fourth movement the focus of attention shifts from the element of fire—consuming fire—to the element of water which was once an embodiment of God's blessings, love, spiritual purification, and rebirth.

In the fifth and final movement the element is 'air,' just as in the first and second it is 'earth' in the third 'fire' and in the fourth 'water.' In this movement the protagonist, the blind seer Tiresias, is said to have travelled through the "frosty silence in the garden" and the "agony in stony places," and now he hears the thunder of spring over distant mountains" which refers to possible rain, that the possibility of life or the water of life that the protagonist has been seeking all through the 'arid plains' and 'rocky mountains' of the waste land, but he fails to find the water of life—love as we read in the poem:

> Here is no water but only rock
> Rock and no water and the sandy road
> The road winding above among the mountains
> Which are mountains of rock without water
> If there were water we should stop and drink
> Amongst the rock one cannot stop or think
> Sweat is dry and feet are in the sand
> If there were only water amongst the rock

Dead mountain mouth of carious teeth that cannot spit
Here one can neither stand nor lie nor sit
There is not even silence in the mountains
But dry sterile thunder without rain
There is not even solitude in the mountains
But red sullen faces sneer and snarl
From doors of mudcracked houses
If there were water
And no rock
If there were rock
And also water
And water
A spring
A pool among the rock
If there were the sound of water only
Not the cicada
And dry grass singing
But sound of water over a rock
Where the hermit—thrust sings in the pine trees
Drip drop drip drop drop drop drop
But there is not water

"What the Thunder Said," *The Waste Land*

In the end of this movement Eliot recapitulates the waste land which is devoid of real love, fertility, virtue, and life. Eliot also establishes an analogy between this rocky, dry, and barren life in the waste land of the western world and the barren country and libidinous life of the mythical Fisher King. But he does not choose to be surrounded by the murk of disappointment ever encircling the thoughts with frustration; rather he looks forward for the sunshine of life and kindles hope that the modern society can be liberated from the curse of waste land only by seeking shelter in the shrine of oriental philosophy of *Upanishads.* In that Eliot has intensively exerted to survey the world literature to a great extent for seeking the hope for peace and salvation of the modern society; but in the last resort he had no choice except fishing in the deep waters of *Vedas* to set the 'waste land' in order. The poet tries to consult several cultural resources going back to the earliest origin in the Sanskrit *Upanishads.* And he draws the formula of three keys for the triple peace of mankind in the eternal truth of *Brihadaranyakopanishad 5, 2, 1-3.*

Datta, Dayadhvam, Damyata
Shantih, Shantih, Shantih.

"Give," "Sympathise," and "Self-Control" are the three keys with which triple peace and salvation—the birth of higher self—is possible. These closing lines are the core of the poem. This three-fold message, Da, Da, Da, which signifies give, sympathise and self-control—is given through thunder by Prajapati to his disciples—men, gods, and demons. Man himself is the microcosm of the three peculiar properties, human, angelic, and demonic. This formula should be taken together to form the three-fold path of deliverance of humanity from the darkness and sterility of spirit. Also this formula can be a path for social salvation which will make the blessings of Heaven descend on the tormented humanity like the refreshing gentle rain—Shantih Shantih Shantih—and lead to a state of peace which is beyond the finite, ken of human understanding.

Again to examine and understand how much Eliot was influenced by Indian philosophy one may turn to *Four Quartets* which takes recourse to the Upanishadic knowledge presented by *Bhagvadgita.* A reading of the second movement of "The Dry Salvages" in *Four Quartets* reveals that "Time" the destroyer is Time the preserver which verily recounts to the Vedic concept of Time in relation to eternity—timelessness. It explicitly alludes to Mahesh and Vishnu of the Hindu Trinity. Further, in the third movement of "The Dry Salvages" we come to the exhortation of Lord Krishna to Arjuna regarding *Karma Yoga* when he is in the grip of faint heartedness and attachment for his kinsmen. The Lord says:

> And do not think of the fruit of action
> Fare forward (*cf. Bhagvadgita: 2:47*)
> O voyagers, O seamen,
> You who come to part, and you whose bodies
> Will suffer the trial and judgement of the sea
> Or whatever even, this is your real destination.
> So Krishna, as when he admonished Arjuna
> On the field of battle.
> Not fare well
> But fare forward voyagers.

From these examples it emerges that Eliot attaches greater significance to the philosophy of *Karma Yoga* than any other type of yoga. Sunil Kumar Sarker rightly observes that[6]—

> Eliot also needed some spiritual influence.
> He wanted some sort of spiritual emancipation
> from the drabness of the dry civilization and he
> found a glimpse of spiritual emancipation
> particularly in the philosophy of *Bhagvadgita.* (24)

Bhagvadgita was so dear to Eliot that he called it "...the next greatest philosophical poem to the *Divine Comedy* within my experience." There are recurring references of *Bhagvadgita* in the poems under study and more particularly in the "Dry Salvages". Hence Eliot's philosophy was not different from the Indian philosophy of *Karma Yoga*. Lord Krishna's demonstration to Arjuna is almost a carbon copy of the philosophy of *Karma Yoga of Bhagvadgita*. Incorporation of allusion and examples from Sanskrit and other foreign literatures in the poems like *Waste Land and Four Quartets* is not a mere pointless assemblage of other poets and writers, rather it demonstrates Eliot's point about English people's loss of tradition. Though he was predominantly a Christian he acknowledges his indebtedness to Buddhism and Brahmanism, in his notes to the *Waste Land*, to secure peace and salvation for the rebirth of a civilization.

NOTES

1. Eliot, T.S. *For Lancelot Andrews*. London: Faber and Gwyer, 1928, IX.
2. T.S. Eliot's contemporary poet, W.B. Yeats was also influenced by the spirit of the same Indian scriptures through his two Indian friends and mentors: Mohini Chatterjee and Purohit Swami (Sarker 5).
3. Quoted by Sunil Kumar Sarker, in his *T.S. Eliot: Poetry Plays and Prose*, New Delhi: Atlantic Publishers and Distributors (P) Ltd. 1995, p. 5.
4. T.S. Eliot, *After Strange Gods*, Faber and Faber, 1934, p. 40.
5. Sengupta, Satya Prasad, T.S. Eliot (in Bengali). Calcutta: Employees' Comparative Industrial Society Ltd.
6. Quoted by Sunil Kumar Sarkar, p. 24.

WORKS CITED

Dwivedi, A.N. "Religious Trends in Eliot's Poetry," *New Responses to T.S. Eliot: A Birth Century Tribute*, ed. Narsingh Srivastava (Varanasi: Vishwavidyalaya Prakashan, 1989), 8-14.

Eliot, T.S. *Lancelot Andrews*. London: Faber and Faber, 1928, rpt., 1970.

Eliot, T.S. *After Strange Gods*. London: Faber and Faber, 1934.

Sarker, Sunil Kumar. *T.S. Eliot: Poetry, Plays and Prose*, New Delhi: Atlantic Publishers and Distributors, 1995.

Sengupta, Satya Prasad. *T.S. Eliot* (in Bengali). Calcutta: Employees' Comparative Industrial Society Ltd.

4

J.G. Farrell—The Man and Writer

V.R. Badiger

James Gordon Farrell, one of the modern British novelists, may be considered as an anti-modernist in the tradition of Joseph Conrad, George Orwell, Joyce Cary and Doris Lessing, who, in their metonymic and metaphoric fiction, dealt with the colonial experience in South Africa, India and the Far East. His best work consists of "powerfully imagined historical novels." (Waynes 1989:219). By his strong sense of irony, self-mockery and wry humour, Farrell may be clearly distinguished from other liberal-minded novelists like, E.M. Forster, M.M. Kaye and Paul Scott. In this paper a modest attempt has been made to introduce the writer and his novels, hinting at the biographical approach to the study of the man and the writer which are sometimes mutually inclusive as far as the creative process is concerned.

Farrell was born on 23rd January in 1935 in a nursing home at 150, Moscoe Drive at Liverpool in England, William Francis Farrell, his father, was a clerk-cum-accountant. His mother was Josephine, the precocious daughter of an English timber merchant. The Farrells moved to Chittagong as his father got an appointment as a manager of Pure Cane Molasses Company. The novelist had two younger brothers—Richard and Robert. As a boy he had "keen observation" (Binns 1986:18) and could comment even on Walter Scott's famous historical romance *Ivanhoe* as a 'novel of long tedious descriptions'.

As the World War II broke out in 1938-39, the Farrells returned to 'Bascobel,' a huge ancestral house in Ireland. There, they lived peacefully for some time till 1941 in which the building was damaged by a bomb during the air raids. So they were forced to shift their residence to another house in Saval Park Road, Dailkey in Ireland. This exodus from Ireland to England, caused by the war, had a deep impression on the boy James who had just begun to write some short stories of 'sentimental' love under the pseudonym of a girl "Dora Saval Park." At the age of twelve he joined Rosall School as a boarder in Lancashire coast. In the school, he was introduced to Perre Loti's *Pecheurd Islande* (1886) which considerably enthralled him. As a young man, he developed greater interest in French writings of Stendhal and Collette. At the same time he was exposed to himself to the great European masters' viz. Tolstoy, Conrad and Camus. In 1928, he sought an appointment of a teacher in a Prep School in Dublin. Later he migrated to Canada with the sole intention of becoming a writer but, there he, being forced by the circumstances, worked as a labourer, a fireman and finally as a clerk in the army. After a short tour in America he, with a renewed nostalgia of 'home,' returned to Ireland.

In 1956, Farrell got admission to Brasnose College, Oxford to study Law but he was unfortunately attacked by partial paralysis at the end of the first term. Overnight, he was transformed into an 'invalid.' The dreadful disease shocked him to the core of his heart and effected his creative work. Despite medical treatment, he could not completely recover from it. His zest for education was so strong that he once again started attending the classes in college, with an option for Modern Languages instead of studies in Law. As a paralytic, he, once forever, determined to grow into a writer, at least, for the sake of his livelihood. Circumstantially he was forced to compose his first novel, *Lung* (1963). After joining a school as a language teacher in Paris, he successfully completed the next novel, *A Man from Elsewhere* (1965). In 1966 he went to America on the Harkener's scholarship and worked out his third novel, *A Girl in the Head* (1967), which, against his hopes, received bad reviews. Then, he turned his attention to a larger and more crucial theme of the troubles in Ireland, his country. The *Troubles* (1970), the fourth novel, not only brought him Faber Memorial Award but also recognized his lost position as a novelist by his earlier novels. The immense success and resources brought by *Troubles* enabled him to buy a flat in posh suburb at 16, Eagerton Gardens in London. With a greater zeal and ambition, he embarked upon making of 'a trilogy' on the empire. For writing the first volume of it, he visited India and did a lot of research on Indian Mutiny. As a result, he published *The Siege of Krishnapur* (1973) which won him the Booker Prize, England's highest Literary Award and promoted a tour to Singapore and the Far East. During his tour he visited the bombed city of Saigon and personally experienced the horror of the war. On his return to England, he conceived and completed the fifth novel, *The Singapore Grip* (1979) which become a topical success. Immediately he started the next novel, *The Hill Station* but before its completion, he drowned in the seashore nearby his house and died in 1979.

The Lung (1963), 'a black comedy,' is based on his personal experience as a victim of the dreadful disease. Sands, the comic hero, who leads the life of a thoughtless 'bohemian,' is attacked by polio. Overnight he is transformed into a 'demi-skeleton.' To escape from the misery of his harsh reality, he imagines himself to be a man who lives inside an iron lung, trying to recover his health in the jovial company of an attractive nurse and patients. Much of Sands' sad story is admixtured with his vain attempts to gratify his main urges—sex and alcoholism. Bernard Shares, a reviewer says thus: "This is a humane and entertaining novel, and confirms, Mr. Farrell as a man with something to say and skillful way of saying it" (Binns 1986: 25).

A Man from Elsewhere (1965), written during his short stay in Paris, is about a dying novelist Regan who is yet to win the Catholic Prize for his best-selling novel on contemporary political problems—the violence in Algeria and France, a threat of nuclear annihilation and the Burling Crisis. The novelist,—a diehard communist, changes into a staunch individualist, by turning to the art of writing novels. Gerhardt, one of Regan's ex-comrade, sends Sayers, a journalist—spy, to dig up unpleasant things of the novelist's past with an intention to demoralize him. In course of narrative a variety of incidents prevent Sayers from fulfilling his journalistic mission to be carried out in the larger interest of the international communism. John Holloway, the critic, comments: "Farrell's most distinguished debut inspite of the novel's inherent faults." His skillful handling of the pseudo-political ideas in fiction is widely appreciated.

The more interesting one, *A Girl in the Head* (1967) is about a cripple called Count Boris Stattery whose personal misadventures are hilariously farcical, providing much fun and humour. He lives with Inez, a beautiful young girl, in a dull provincial seaside resort of Maidenhair Bay. The literary excellence lies in the novelist's self-conscious, innovative experiments with the narrative from with topographical trickery and deliberate effort for foreground the 'fictionality' of fiction by directly addressing his readers. In this funny novel, he seems to recognize a psychological link between the hero's inner disease and the external reality of his surroundings.

Troubles (1970) is the tragi-comic novel about Major Archer's stay in a decrepit hotel, named Majestic. The novel begins with an elaborate description of the old, huge and dilapidated hotel, which stands as a metaphor for the decaying state of the British Empire. The hotel does not merely stand for the empire but it is the empire itself by his skillful way of employing disease symbolism, focusing light on the corrupting impact of the imperialism. The central image is that of an abscess ('a cankerous tumour') which threatens to bring down the whole building. Seeing "the wooden giant abscess" quite mentally disturbs Major Archer, the tenant (*Troubles* 55). Being terrified by the imminent danger the Major and his wife, Sarah, go round looking for its suspicious bulges. This act of going round the hotel, at last, turns into a marvellous game of dark significance. Edward Spencer, the owner, on the contrary, declares "economy drive" when the furniture becomes broken and mirrors discoloured, and the quality of food declines. The disease aggravates with the troubles in Ireland. The timid occupants move from one room to another seeking safer, if not a better place. Even the electric generator "Do more" stops functioning. So are the gas mantles. Farrell, at this juncture, inserts a news-cutout for indicating the Britain's debts, its self-glorification of victory in war and a plea for financial assistance from her colonies. At the end the significance of the abscess becomes quite explicit when Edward kills an innocent Irish servant boy—an act of imperialistic jingoism. The Major condemns his act as "inhuman" and "intolerable." Edward himself feels better after the murder. Major, being the mouthpiece of the author, knows that the disease of the hotel beyond and diagnosis, treatment and cure. The defusing of Edward's insanity goes along with the further disintegration of the hotel. Another implication is that Edward, the owner is the symbolic emperor of the empire. The author reminds us of his philosophical tone "...nothing is invulnerable to growth, change and decay, not even one's most fiercely guarded memories" (*Ibid.* 259). The murder of the boy is, no doubt, the symptomatic of the strategical defect of the British in World War II.

The Siege of Krishnapur (1973) is a long satirical attack on the decadence of the empire in India. The historical theme is Indian Mutiny of 1857 as he worked out of this novel with a lot belongs to a class of 'novels fictitious history.' Margaret Drabble comments that 'sepoys are never shown as people at all.'

The novel opens with description of the illusory topography of Krishnapur and its cantonment: "Any one who has journey a few miles sooner than he expected" (*Siege* 9). In this novel he proceeds to debunk the myth of the imperial civilization by strictly maintaining the ironic distance and introducing characters which clearly express his conflicting views of historicity. Fluery, romantic young Englishman, comes to India with a commission to write a book on the "advances that civilization had made in India under the company rule." Here, he finds his own people, being blinded by the dazzling sunlight of an alien land. Hopkins, the Collector, is another possible protagonist who proudly propounds the theory of "superior culture" of the empire-builders. To justify his ideological stand he collects a huge "bric-a-brac" from the Great Exhibition in England and arranges them for a show in his bungalow. Hari, the anglicized Indian prince contacts the imperial disease. Throughout the novel he remains a biased Indian whose English education has brainwashed that his culture is not superior to that of the British. Often he involves in his habits of eating boiled eggs and reading the *Blackwood's Magazine*. Fleury says that the only real progress would be to make man's heart sensitive to love, to Nature, to his fellowmen and to the world of spiritual joy. So, he thinks him to be "frightfully backward." Although Fleury considers the reforms of abolishing *suttee* and digging up irrigational canals are evidence of improvements. They appear to him as deadly symptoms of the disease of civilization. The delineation of the actual historical event is made, thus, thematically less important.

Farrell's depiction from the British point of view is unique in the sense that they could not see through the disaster in advance. Amidst the brewing up of the turmoil, the white community is self-complacently engaged in a lengthy discussion on the causes of the Cholera. At the thematic level the Cholera and the Mutiny are bound up. Just as the beleaguered community inside the Residency fights against the disease; the Indian sepoys fight against their disease from which they have been suffering. Farrell holds a parallel between the two events and interprets the disastrous situation in a humorous way. The two doctors, Dr. Dunstaple and Dr. McNab whimsically differ in their diagnosis and its medical remedy to be treated. As the time passes the disease also attacks the collector and Dr. McNab misdiagnoses it as erysipelas. Soon after recovery the collector abandons his land preserved belief in the "Superior Culture" and civilization of the empire. His physical illness cures his mental illness. The medical debate continues in a state of acute uncertainty and indecision during damage and disaster of the siege. The diagnostic rift between the doctors aggravates the progress of the disease and of the siege. Farrell, instead of limiting himself only to the imaginative recreation of the historical event, attempts also to present it as a larger problem of the imperial civilization. Only the Magistrate, being too rational in the eyes of his fellowmen, escapes into the hill-station to die. The collector sends his ailing wife back to England when his baby dies. Mrs. Scott and Mrs. Porter die miserably. In a larger symbolic perspective the Sepoy Mutiny becomes a life and death question to the British in India. Irony, wit and wry humour pervade the whole novel.

Set in Singapore, *Singapore Grip* (1979) is more experimental in anti-realistic mode than *The Siege of Krishnapur*. It is anti-realistic in the sense that the historical fact has the narrative basis. The theme is the great historical surrender of the British to the Japanese at the end of the war. The fall of Singapore is the particular loss of Britain's grip over its colonies. The novelist gives more attention to the impact of the economic imperialism than to its political consequences.

The story is of Walter Blackett, a rubber tycoon, who, like Dickens's Josaiah Bounderby, believes in the mercenary aspects of his business. In contrast to him, is Matthew Webb, a friend, who recognizes the harsh reality of the capitalist system and its disastrous impact on the morale of the working class. As he considers his daughter, Joan, as a business proposition. He moves far and wide to find her a husband who, like him, can expand his business. Her mother is disturbed by her daughter's "romantic non-sense." He argues that imperialism is a law of Nature: "The weak nations go to the wall—that has always been the way of the worked and always will be" (*Singapore* 140). The collector of *The Siege of Krishnapur*, he gathers the artistic "bric-a-brac" and proudly exhibits them as the marks of his "superior culture." As the World War II looms large over the horizon he unerringly goes ahead with his plan of celebrating the company's silver jubilee for with the slogan "Continuity in Prosperity." Behind his lofty goal of improving the native workers standard of life, lies his hidden motive of giving a face-life to his business. It is highly ridiculous on his part to run the show even under the thick clouds of the war. Parallel to this is still more curious decision of the cricket club "not to put off its match" (*Singapore* 224). His son, Monty, also disagrees with Matthew's view that the British miserably failed in this imperial mission. Taking Matthew to the local brothel he arranges a meeting between him and Vera Chang, a girl prostitute. There he realizes the horror of the imperial exploitation of the natives. Against this dreary background of red-light area both nonchalantly discuss over the purity of colonial enterprise and its dehumanizing process. Within no time Matthew's idealism melts away. Thematically more significant scene in this novel is his visit to the house of dying wherein some aged moribund wait in a state of dejection and helplessness for death. Matthew is still more shocked to hear sarcastic comment on the British by one of the ailing. By this ghastly scene of humanity in its most degrading form, Farrell unravels yet another dimension of capitalism. Also he uses two symbolic acts—Duping's futile attempt to kill a cockroach by a book and Major Perceival's effort of shaving his hard beard in a haphazard manner. Both these acts suggest the strategic defeat of the British in World War II.

The Hill-Station (1981), the third volume of the "empire trilogy" remains in complete piece of fictive imagination. Farrell humourously parodies the adventure fiction in postmodernist way, presenting a love of Teddy and Emily, an English pair.

The beginning is as significant as that of *The Siege of Krishnapur*. "Nowadays railway all the way to Simla, but before the turn of the century it stopped at Kalka." Thus, the novelist juxtaposes the remote times of 1870s and the present. Corollary to the main theme of love is the theme of ethical dichotomy over which the ranging debate takes place between tubercular clergyman named Kingston and his Bishop. Such controversy shakes the moral foundation even in the distant Simla. Dr. McNab, on his tour to Simla with his wife and niece, Emily, finds Kingston reading Keble's *Christian Year*, Lowrie, the owner of the hotels in Simla and Kalka, passes over the details of the clergyman's debate to Dr. McNab. Farrell introduces a character called Mrs. Forester, "a fallen woman" like Lucy, to point out the resemblance between the rigid class-system of Anglo-India and the caste-system of Indian society. The doctor is quite surprised to know that Mrs. Forester has invited Miss Emily. Mrs. Clareworthy, a typical "pure woman" snubs the fallen state of Mrs. Forester. Binns says: "The real thrust of *The Hill Station*, seemingly, could have been less concerned with either religious or social satire than with the development of Farrell's interest in the theme of sickness" (Binns 68). In an arms-wrestling match the Bishop wins over Revered Grenville. Dr. McNab feels that "physical strength is some way concerned with moral strength" (Hill 69). Like Farrell's other novels this novel succeeds in recognizing a close thematic link between the inner illness and the external reality. However, this novel is left incomplete because of the author's accidental death.

The Indian Diary, Farrell's beautiful account of his travel in India, conveys a strong sense of the country and its people. Elaborately he describes the major cities of Delhi, Bombay, Calcutta, Patna, Banaras and Haridwar. His poetic descriptions of men and manners has some catchy phrases—'streets constantly rammed,' 'the swarm of bicycles,' 'tongas and betel nut juices,' 'the dogs on the roads,' and 'deformed beggars.' Nonetheless, this wonderful travelogue is also his spiritual journey through the heart of India with greater sympathy, understanding and alacrity.

WORKS CITED

Binns, Ronald. *J.G. Farrell.* London: Methuen, 1986.

Waynes, Davis. *A Guide to English Literature.* London: Bloomsbury Publishing Limited, 1989.

5

Pinter and Twentieth-Century Drama

Ronald Knowles

In 1956 Harold Pinter trod the boards In Bournemouth and Torquay in over thirty thrillers and comedies, the standard repertory company staple of the pre- and post-war periods,[1] while J.B. Priestley, Noel Coward and Terence Rattigan dominated the West End theatre with comforting spiritualism, stylish comedy of manner and sentimentalised social problem play, all designed to reassure the self-applauding middle-class patrons, through laughter or tears. Alternatively, by the early 1950s, the plays of Arthur Miller and Tennessee Williams with their contrasting realistic modes of incidental expressionism (*Death of a Salesman*, 1949) and passionate naturalism (*A Streetcar Named Desire*, 1947) were quite free from the all-constructive self-censorship of the British class system dominated by virtual terror of the vulgar and lower class. Along with changing post-war social conditions the seeming freedom signalled by the Americans provided an impetus for the rise of the Angry Young Men (pre-eminently John Osborne, Arnold Wesker and John Arden) at the Royal Court Theatre, from the *annus mirabilis* in 1956. Of equal importance, but less sensational in immediate impact was the translation of French absurdism, most famously Samuel Beckett and Eugene Ionesco, to London productions at the Arts Theatre (respective, *Waiting for Godot*, 1955; *The New Tenant*, 1956).

With his outstanding success by the early 1960s, Pinter was frequently associated with the social realism of the Angry Young Men and with the absurdism of Beckett and Ionesco. Furthermore, it is probably safe to say that there Is not a single dramatist of the twentieth century with whom Pinter has not been compared or contrasted, from Ibsen to David Mamet.

Beginning with the question of 1950s realism, this chapter then looks at Ionesco and associated—namely Chekhov, Strindberg, Pirandello, Eliot, Joyce—and, as far as space allows, assesses Pinter's debts, affinities or differences, to gain thereby a sharper recognition of his individual contribution to twentieth-century theatre.

Plays like Osborne's *Look Back in Anger* (1956), Wesker's *Chicken Soup with Barley* (1958) and Arden's *Live Like Pigs* (1958) displaced the middle-class drawing room with the lower-class *mise-en-scene* of 'kitchen sink' realism and without condescension faithfully represented ordinary lives. Each had an implicit left-wing agenda deriving from concept for the dominant middle-class values of past and present conservatism. Plays like Pinter's *The Room, The Birthday Party* and *The Caretaker*[2] with their realistic sets and hyper-real demotic dialogue seemed part of this movement, but only at first glance: 'I'd say that what goes on in my plays is realistic, but what I'm doing is not realism,'[3] Pinter recorded. In comparison with the realists Pinter did not speak from a recognisable political platform. In contrast, he deconstructs social realism by divorcing the identification of character and environment, defamiliarising the pedestrian and destabilising the audience with ultimately self-recriminating laughter. For the realists the accurate presentation of the material conditions of persons in society was a didactic end in itself.

An exception in Pinter's work was *A Night Out*, which he contributed to Sydney Newman's 'Armchair Theatre' series for ABC television of the late 1950s, early 1960s. Newman, a Canadian, had been deeply influenced by the social realism of American television drama. *A Night Out* presents the social entrapment of Albert, an office clerk: intimidated by his mother, he takes out all his resentments and frustrations on a genteel prostitute before returning to the confinement of home. The often-made comparison with *The Birthday Party* brings out the essential difference. Practically everything in *A Night Out* is explicit. Character and motivation are generally unambiguous, the circular plot supplying if not the satisfying resolution of the well-made play, a significance which is clear. Quite the opposite to the numbing circularity of *The Birthday Party* which leaves us aghast, asking where? how? when? why? 'If I'm being explicit I'm failing,'[4] Pinter said. *A Night Out* was highly successful, bet its adherence to 'kitchen sink' realism meant that it lacked that 'core of our living...this ambiguity'[5] which Pinter saw as his main dramatic concern.

Alternatively, the ambiguity of such plays as *The Birthday Party* and *The Caretaker* prompted comparison with the absurdists. Ionesco founded his anarchic, surrealist drama on a premise: the 'Absurd is that which is devoid of purpose.... Cut off from his religious, metaphysical, and transcendental roots, man is lost; all his actions become senseless, absurd, useless.'[6] Consequently the tragic is mixed with the comic, which ultimately liberates through recognition of the confining morality of society. Ionesco's basic technique was a radical estrangement by literalising the metaphorical in concrete stage objects, and by defamiliarization and deformation of language.

The origin of *The Bald Prima Donna* (1950) derived from Ionesco's discovery of an English phrase book which reduced all life to the social repetition of banal, indicative propositions. His parody of this led to comparison of *The Birthday Party* to the 'inconsequential gabble...of Ionesco.'[7] However, the realism of *The Caretaker* prompted another reviewer to claim in *The Room* and *The Dumb Waiter.*[8] A significant distinction was made in another review, comparing *The Caretaker* to Ionesco's *The Chairs*: 'nowhere does Mr. Pinter treat non-communications as an extraneous, rather banal "point" to be made.'[9] The major contrast was made in the most perceptive of all early reviews of The Birthday Party, 'Mr. Pinter's world is one of fantasy; not however of the Ionesco school with its formalism of swelling corpses, piling furniture and gathering chairs,'[10] referring to the externalised stage symbols of, respectively, *Amedee or How to Get Rid of it* (1953), *The New Tenant* (1953) and *The Chairs* (1951). The implicit allegory of Ionesco's theatre appeared most overtly in *Rhinoceros* (1960).

In this play, all but one in a small provincial town turn into a rhinoceros. The allegory of conformist fascism is very clear, heavily so in places: 'Good men make good rhinoceroses, unfortunately. It's because they are so good that they get taken in.'[11] At one point a character turns into a rhinoceros before our eyes. The visual power is stunning but reflection shows that the originality of theatre is incommensurate with the orthodoxy of thought. Compare *The Birthday Party*—to what extent is Goldberg and McCann's abduction of Stanley analogous to fascist atrocity? Pinter's multi-levelled theatrically thwarts a simple allegorical reading.

Pinter denied the influence of Ionesco, claiming that he had never heard of him until after his early plays. Yet in 1959 he acknowledged seeing *The New Tenant*[12] (which had been produced with *The Bald Prima Donna* in London 1956) and there does seem to be a likeness between the garrulous concierge and Rose in *The Room.* Moreover, Ionesco's theatre provided a public debate in 1958.[13] With the realism of *The Caretaker*

Pinter moved on from the absurdism of the 1950s, but his name was still to be associated with that of Beckett.

In 1970 Pinter declared Beckett to be 'the greatest writer of our time.'[14] A forceful indication of his respect survives in a brief letter of 1954: 'I don't want philosophers, tracts, dogmas, creeds, way outs, truths, answers, *nothing from the bargain basement*. [Beckett] is the most courageous, remorseless writer going.'[15] At this point, just before the first London production of *Godot*, Pinter is responding to the artistic integrity of Beckett's fiction. 'I didn't read a play of Beckett's for a long time' Pinter recorded in 1963.[16] Michael Billington gives an account of Pinter's discovery of *Godot*. In Ireland during 1955, Pinter learned of Peter Hall's forthcoming production, obtained a copy of *Godot* in French which he worked through, translating with friends, and then saw the play in London.[17] In another interview Pinter mentioned hearing Beckett's *All That Fall* (1957), which demonstrated 'a certain uniqueness about radio,'[18] namely a complete imaginative absorption not possible in the theatre. We may assume that, correspondingly, this is what Pinter hoped to achieve in the original radio production of *A Slight Ache*, some of the dialogue of which L.A.C. Dobrez acutely compares to the prose reveries of Beckett's *Watt*.[19]

Reviewers of *The Birthday Party* occasionally linked Beckett and Ionesco's names, but Beckett's name was regularly invoked with *The Caretaker*—for praise or blame. Mac Davies, the prevaricating tramp, along with the procrastinating Aston, immediately prompted comparison with Estragon and Vladimir of *Godot*. At an unsympathetic extreme it was suggested that 'this is the way in which all original visions are reduced by inadequate imitation into conventional realism.'[20] Robert Brustein made an analytic distinction: though Pinter may have borrowed some Beckettian techniques, 'the comparison is more misleading than illuming.... In *The Caretaker* it is denotative and specific.'[21] My own view is that Beckett and Pinter use theatricality to quite opposite ends. (Godot dismantles religion and philosophy to reveal the emptiness of teleological truth, whereas *The Caretaker* ultimately transcends theatricality by realising arguably the only truth we have, existence itself.)

Still further indebtedness was claimed with the production of *Landscape* and *Silence* in comparison with Beckett's *Play* (1964). Beckett's work had three figures buried in notorious urns speaking in cross-cut monologues, alternately illuminated by a spotlight. To some extent this minimalist immobility is reflected in Pinter's plays as, indeed, is the content of failed love. *Silence*, it may be conceded, is the most Beckettian of all of Pinter's plays particularly in its use of past and present voices in relation to the fragmentary arbitrariness of memory, as can be found in such plays as *Krapp's Last Tape* (1958) and *Embers* (1959). And yet it possibly anticipates *That Time* (1976). Let a reviewer of 1960 have the last word here: *The Caretaker* 'stands up with full stature to the comparison' with *Godot*, 'it savours of Chekhov, Beckett and Ionesco but, still more, of life itself.'[22]

Life for Pinter's great predecessor, Anton Chekhov, was pedestrian: 'life...as it really is,' that is, not life 'on stilts' of nineteenth-century melodrama.[23] Pinter said something similar in considering 'Life with a capital L, which is help up to be very different to life with a small I, I mean the life we in fact live.'[24] The two, dramatists have been compared many times and, indeed, there are several common factors in their work.

Chekhov and Pinter wrote for a proscenium arch theatre; strong curtain lines are found in both. Chekhov favoured the exposition of the well-made play, which Pinter abhorred as false. However, Chekhov replaced the catastrophe-denouement with the long drawn out coda of the last act. In spite of Stanislavsky's emphasis on the realism and tragedy, Chekhov insisted that the comedy of his plays should be stressed. Conversely, while Pinter is always enjoyed in the theatre as a distinguished writer of comedy, it is very rare for any criticism to take this into account. Each uses comedy to preempt the audience from slipping into a consolatory emotional response of pathos and sentiment. Realism is thereby compromised by theatricality of speech, situation and character. In Chekhov some characters hide their pain behind a comic mask, whereas Pinter uses laughter to induce a retroactive guilt as audience insecurity parallels that of his characters.

Stanislavsky defined the Chekhovian subtext as 'the manifest, the inwardly felt expression of a human being in a part, which flows uninterruptedly beneath the words of a text, giving them life and a basis for existing.'[25] Comparably, Pinter writer '[t]here] are two silences. One when no word is spoken. The other when perhaps a torrent of language is being employed. This speech is speaking of a language locked beneath it. That is its continual reference. The speech we hear is an indication of that which we don't hear.'[26] Typical of Chekhov's dialogue is the way that characters will occasionally talk across each other, as if encapsulated in private worlds. In contrast, evasion of communication characterises Pinter's dialogue. As John Russell Brown points out, one of the striking features of Chekhov's and Pinter's plays is the way in which the most profound expression of feeling is through silence, as at the close of *Uncle Vanya* and

The Caretaker, for example.[27] Chekhov is famous for his 'orchestration' of detail as if his dialogue were composed like a musical score. Again, his promotion of ensemble acting, as opposed to the somewhat operatic star system, often drew comparisons with chamber music. Comparably, a reviewer of *The Caretaker* praised Donald McWhinnie for directing 'with melodic perfection'[28] and the interweaving allusions to 'shoes,' 'Sidcup' and 'papers,' 'shed,' 'saws' and 'roof' indeed suggest the contrapuntal augmentation of musical composition. But such likenesses should not blind us to the differences, which some examples will bring out.

The last words of Toozenbach to Irena, in *The Three Sisters*, before going off to possible death in a duel, are 'I didn't have any coffee this morning. Will you tell them to get some ready for me?'[29] In Act One of *The Caretaker*, having been told by Aston that the gas stove does not work, Davies asks 'What do you do for a cup of tea?'[30]

Because of the crucial situation Toozenbach's celebrated lines, in spite of their banality, give expression to the subtextual emotional impasse that has just been admitted—he is passionately in love with Irena who has agreed to marry him, although she does not love him. Therefore, Toozenbach cannot make a certain kind of romantic appeal because he knows it cannot truly be reciprocated. The psychological truth is recognisable, but so is Chekhov's anti-conventional agenda. As an ironic consequence the lines cannot escape melodrama, albeit of an inverted kind.

Davies's question could be taken literally and the lines simply accepted as an incidental example of Pinter's superb ear for colloquial accuracy. But the inflexible self-interest created by a tramp's way of life suggests that Davies, once more the hard-done-by victim, is indirectly protesting 'Ain't I even going to get a cup of tea?' The first of a number of references to the stove is made here, which subsequently show that Davies just cannot get it into his head that the appliance is unconnected. Thus the question can be taken in terms of Davies's fears of leaking gas as one more example of a malevolent world: 'I don't believe that stove's not working [since you must make a cup of tea].' Alternatively, the question can be read as revealing the basic imperative of a way of life which keeps complete deprivation one symbolic cup of tea away, with the added irony that all that it represents—sustenance, warmth, society—have already been precluded by Davies's habitual repugnance. With Toozenbach's words we know exactly where we are: with examples like that of Davies, which are characteristic of Pinter on the whole, we are drawn into the endless permutations of possibility.

In comparing Chekhov's and Pinter's plays generally, consider the conventional pattern of arrival-disruption-departure as it is found in *Uncle Vanya* and *The Homecoming*. In the Chekhov, individual psychology and emotion are coordinated and conditioned by class structure. Thus Yeliena and Serebriakov start a chain reaction of cause and effect on the other characters according to status, age and position within a determining social microcosm. In *The Homecoming* all cultural values are deconstructed by the visceral, atavistic animality revealed by the reaction to Ruth. Thus for Chekhov existence is always measured against the domestic sphere of social reality, but here Pinter's almost anthropological insight reveals a reality beneath the social.

Chekhov, Ibsen and Strindberg are commonly regarded as the founding fathers of twentieth-century drama. Though Pinter is infrequently compared to Ibsen, a general and a highly specific case for influence can be made. Thomas Postlewait sees Ibsen as bequeathing the conventional characterisation of women in terms of sexual identity, desire and power in the male-dominated home, and builds a fascinating comparison between Hedda, of *Hedda Gabler*, and Nora, of *A Doll's House*, with Ruth, in *The Homecoming*.[31] The specific case is an unusual one, as I shall show below in arguing that the direct influence of Ibsen in James Joyce's *Exiles* reappears in Pinter's *Betrayal*.

August Strindberg's restless dramatic experimentalism anticipates the major developments of the twentieth century. Pinter's plays are occasionally compared with Strindberg, particularly *The Collection*, which featured in a double bill with Strindberg's *Playing With Fire* (1982), directed by Peter Hall in 1962. In one way this was a curiously prescient choice since its concern with a husband abetting his own adulterous betrayal by a friend anticipates Pinter's *Betrayal*. Recently Michael Billington paired *The Lover* with Strindberg's *The Stranger* (1889), a monologue in which a wife addresses her husband's former lover. In his review Adrian Noble called Pinter 'Strindberg's natural heir.'[32] Looking at Strindberg's realist period, in plays like *The Father* (1887) and *The Creditors* (1888), it is possible to identify the power-straggles of sexual politics, outright misogyny and the fixation with the male's impotent defeat by the female, with those in such plays as *The Lover, The Collection* and *The Homecoming*.

More specific influence is difficult to argue, but it can be said that Pinter is the heir to some of Strindberg's theoretical innovations, namely his pause/silence technique, and his concept of dialogue in relation to the exploration of musical form. 'Silence cannot hide anything—which is more than you can say for words'[33] says Hummel just before the 'ghost supper' of *The Ghost Sonata* (1907) which is, indeed, structured around pauses, silences and long silences. Probably by way of Beckett, Pinter became notorious for this technique, which Strindberg developed before Chekhov. Eventually, Pinter structured a whole play by the feature that was to provide its title, *Silence*. In the preface to *Miss Julie* (1888) Strindberg stressed the irregular, haphazard nature of his realistic dialogue in contrast to the mechanistic symmetries of French drama. Strindberg's aleatory dialogue 'is worked over, picked up again, repeated, expounded, and built up like the theme in a musical composition,'[34] which sounds exactly like a description of Pinter's dialogue in *The Caretaker*, that Irving Wardle characterised as like a 'sonata movement', 'undergoing development and combination.'[35] Another influential experimentalist and theorist was Luigi Pirandello.

In 1980, when Pinter received the 'Premio Pirandello' in Palermo, he remarked that he was surprised as he felt that his plays were 'at the other end of the telescope' from those of Pirandello himself.[36] Pieter probably had in mind the metadrama of a philosophy of life and art as found in *Six Characters in Search of an Author* (1921) and *Henry IV* (1922). None of Pinter's plays are self-reflexive or cerebral in the same way, but Pirandello's mixture of the comic and tragic, his dislike of symbolism and abstraction, and above all his destabilisation of the audience, are all common to Pinter's drama. One of the principal modes of promoting audience instability in both is to frustrate the need for verification. In this respect Pirandello's *Right You Are (If You Think So)* (1917), is usually compared with *The Collection*.

Both plays are concerned with the problem of verification where two conflicting versions of a situation are given and a third party has to decide on which may be true. Pirandello is seemingly concerned with revealing the social snobbery of the bourgeoisie in a comedy of manners, but the existential twist at the close raises the psychological and philosophical question of the relativity of the truth and the alienation of identity. In *The Collection* James pursues the truth of apparent adultery in the conflicting stories of his wife and Bill, who use fictions to reposition themselves in the powerstruggles of domestic relationships. But it emerges that James is possibly as much in flight from the truth of his own situation, from heterosexual rejection and homosexuality. Elsewhere, among several interesting allusions to Pirandello, L.A.C. Dobrez compares the Matchseller of *A Slight Ache* as object of Edward's and Flora's fantasies to the veiled figure at the end of *Right You Are*, who declares 'I am the one you believe me to be.'[37]

Pirandello paradoxically entitled his collected plays 'naked masks.' Comparably, a major aspect of Pinter's drama is to disclose the verbal 'stratagem to cover nakedness.'[38] A significant difference, however, is that for Pirandello identity is deeply subjective and incommunicable—the 'private world' of the Father in *Six Characters*, the 'impenetrable world' of *Henry IV*[39]—whereas Pinter's characters evade communication to resist 'being known.'[40] As a consequence, for each dramatist to discover a character is to encounter an autonomous otherness rather than each creating a fiction out of omniscient imagination. In his famous preface to *Six Characters* Pirandello described how his maidservant, Fantasy, admitted the insistent characters to his study. Similarly, in his speech on accepting the Hamburg Shakespeare prize, Pinter recorded 'I am aware, sometimes, of an insistence in my mind. Images, characters insisting upon being written.'[41]

There is a further area of common ground, that of Pirandello's theory of 'l'umorismo,' or humourism,[42] which is related both to character and dramatic structure. For Pirandello humour is much more profound than the mere laughter of comedy, or the moral indignation of satire. The core concept is expounded in Pirandello's example of a grotesquely made-up old lady with an appalling hair-do, attempting to look like a young girl. In fact she looks like an "exotic parrot,' he tells us. The incongruity creates an 'awareness of the opposite'—what a respectable old lady should look like—which gives rise to comic laughter. But when a deeper 'reflection' arises in the viewer it makes us aware of the possible underlying cause of such an appearance (attempting to keep the love of a much younger husband, for example). Then we can no longer laugh. 'Reflection' has made us shift to a 'feeling of the opposite' which makes us respond with compassion, even though elements of the initial comic response may remain.[43]

Consider *The Birthday Party* and *The Caretaker* in the light of this. In Act Two of the former Meg enters for the party '*in evening dress*,'[44] which is immediately stressed in the subsequent exchange. Incongruously, Meg claims that her father gave it to her. The shift in action from Stanley's interrogation creates the laughter of relief which is increased by Meg's garish appearance: 'like a Gladiola,'[45] as Goldberg says. In Pirandello's terms, we laugh from an 'awareness of the opposite,' the disparity between intention and appearance, yet 'reflection' gives rise to the 'feeling of the opposite.' Meg's simple-minded delusion reminds us of the father who seemingly abandoned her as a child, and of her hope to please Stanley, the surrogate of her thwarted maternal longings. Comedy is deepened by the latent compassion of 'humourism.'

Again, consider the figure of Davies in Act Two of *The Caretaker*, trying on the '*deep-red velvet smoking jacket*,' 'You ain't got a mirror here, have you?'[46] The 'awareness of the opposite' is hilarious: the smoking jacket as synecdoche for that pre-war world of the sophisticated gentleman, glamour and romance—and Dawes the tramp. Bur the inevitable 'reflection' gives rise to 'feeling of the opposite' by which the smoking jacket symbolizes all that Davies is denied—status, friendship, love, comfort and so on. We still laugh at Davies as a stereotype of comic affectation here but this is ultimately displaced by the residual compassion for the plight of a human being at the dose.

For Pirandello, as for Pieter, '[t]he humourist... treasures... ordinary events and common details...all [of] which may appear trivial and vulgar'[47] but humourism allows these to shape the artistic structure. What Roger W. Oliver says of Pirandello, '[t]his conflict [of humourism] between surface appearance and deeper realities becomes the basis for both subject matter and dramatic technique,'[48] is also true of Pinter.

Pirandello's work made a major contribution to modernism. Two other leading modernists, T.S. Eliot and James Joyce, directly influenced two of Pinter's plays, respectively *No Man's Land* and *Betrayal*.

T.S. Eliot 'I admire extremely,' Pinter recorded.[49] In the early 1950s he joined a group touring London with a production of the choruses from Eliot's *The Rock* (1934).[50] Eliot's 'Aristophanic fragment' of the 1920s, *Sweeney Agonistes*, was regularly compared with the early Pinter for the common qualities of menace and banality, music-hall stylisation and the demotic. Eliot's Dusty and Doris exchanges are often compared with those at the opening of *The Birthday Party*; they make an even stronger parallel with those of Annie and Millie in *Night School*. Eliot speculated that perhaps the music-hall comedian would make the 'best material' to transform 'entertainment' to a 'form of art,' but it was Pinter who fully realised this with such echoes of the cross-talk double-act of Goldberg and McCann in *The Birthday Party*. Similarly, the 'new form' which might be devised out of 'colloquial speech' that Eliot experimented with, for example at the opening of *The Cocktail Party*, is the celebrated hallmark of Pinter's whole *oeuvre*.[51] Goldberg and McCann's pursuit of Stanley to the seaside boarding-house has often been linked to the Eumenides' pursuit of Harry to the security of his family seat in *The Family Reunion* (1939). Again, an Unidentified Guest at *The Cocktail Party* (1949) leads to the jungle martyrdom of another guest: we do not know the precise fate of Stanley following his birthday party.

Pinter's blind Negro, Riley, in *The Room*, is arguably a burlesque of Eliot's Unidentified Guest who sings the music-hall song of the 'one-eyed

Riley' and turns our to be Sir Henry Harcourt-Reilly. Pinter's Riley also brings a form of revelation, but it is existential rather than Christian. Elsewhere, as Katherine Burkman has hinted, *A Slight Ache* can be considered from one point of view—given Edward's displacement and the seasonal vegetative references—as a burlesque of fertility ritual as found in J.G. Frazer's *The Golden Bough* (abridged 1922).[52] But it was not until *No Man's Land* that Pinter indirectly confronted the informing beliefs of Eliot's dramatic world. For all the upper-class ennui of those conventional drawing rooms, Eliot is concerned with atonement and salvation.

Spooner overtly identifies himself with Prufrock, by repeatedly alluding to his lines—'For I have known them all already...' And I have known.'[53] The epigraph of 'Prufrock'[54] from Dante's Inferno, Spooner's allusion to 'terza rima'[55] and the significance of Dante in *The Waste Land*, suggest a loosely parodic relationship between Spooner-Hirst as a mock Virgil-Dante, and the waste land of Bolsover Street as reflecting Dante's third canto, but there are more direct correspondences to Eliot's dramatic work. Russell Davies has justly paralleled the drinks exchange between the Unidentified Guest and Edward in *The Cocktail Party*[56] but the greater correlation is between *The Elder Statesman* (1958) and *No Man's Land.*

In *The Elder Statesman*, after changing his name to Gomez, Culverwell returns to Lord Claverton's home where, as he knocks back the drink, he reveals his intention to pursue friendship, while at the same time reminding his host of the guilty secret of Oxford days: quite precise analogues for Spooner and Hirst in Act One. Again, Hirst's loneliness is kept at bay by his photograph album whereas Claverton's loneliness is exacerbated by his symbolic engagement book. In great contrast, Hirst at the close remains in his particular alcoholic circle of hell, Pinter thereby effectively rejecting any parallel to the epiphany of love vouchsafed to Claverton, just as Briggs and Foster's mock-antiphony parodies Eliot's liturgical mode.

In Pinter's next play we find a similar structural relationship: Acts One and Two of Joyce's Ibsenesque *Exiles* provide the genesis for scenes one and two of *Betrayal*. The direction of *Exiles* in 1970, a few years before writing *Betrayal*, not only demonstrated Pinter's lifelong admiration for all Joyce's work but also brought into focus the preoccupation with male friendship and betrayal common to both writers is reflected in the central conflict of each play. There are very many correspondences in verbal detail and dramatic situation. A few from each category are examined here, as further demonstration may be considered elsewhere.[57]

In *Exiles* Richard and Bertha return to Dublin and meet Robert and Beatrice once again, after nine years. Pinter's Emma admits to Jerry that she has confessed her adultery to Robert nine years after the affair began. Towards the end of Act One of *Exiles*, following the love overtures of Robert, Bertha is interrogated by her husband and reveals all that took place in the flirtation. In scene one of *Betrayal* the ex-lovers Jerry and Emma meet up in a pub and Emma reveals that not only are she and Robert about to separate, but that she revealed to him 'last night'[58] her affair with his oldest friend. In Act Two of *Exiles* Richard makes his way to Robert's cottage and confronts him with the betrayal: 'I know everything. I have known for some time.... Since it began between you and her.'[59] Robert assumes that Richard was told 'This afternoon,' but Richard has to disabuse him, 'No. Time after time; as it happened.'[60] In scene two of *Betrayal*, at Jerry's request Robert has arrived at his house, where he acknowledges that Emma 'didn't tell me about you and her last night. She told me about you and her four years ago.'[61] Robert expostulates with Richard, 'And you never spoke! You had only to speak a word.'[62] Jerry remonstrates with Robert, 'Why didn't you tell me?'[63] Richard leaves Robert with Bertha after the confrontation in Act Two. Eventually Robert hesitatingly asks, 'Did you tell him—everything?' 'Everything,'[64] Bertha replies. Correspondingly, in scene one of *Betrayal* it eventually occurs to Jerry to ask, 'You didn't tell Robert about me last night, did you?' 'He told me everything. I told him everything,' Emma answers, Staggered, Jerry asks twice, 'You told him everything?'[65]

In Act Three of *Exiles* Bertha expostulates with Richard, 'You are a stranger.... A stranger! I am living with a stranger!'[66] In the longest speech of *Betrayal* Robert plays on relationship, title and names, and the idea of being a 'stranger': 'We could be, and in fact are most vastly likely to be, total strangers.... I could very easily be a total stranger.'[67] At an early stage Joyce's Robert appeals to Richard 'for the sake of...our friendship, our life-long friendship.'[68] Your husband is my oldest friend,'[69] Jerry reminds Emma.

Finally, all that is implicit in the buried homoerotic psychology of the men in *Betrayal*, is arguably made explicit in *Exiles*: You are so strong that you attract me even through her,'[70] Robert says to Richard, who later acknowledges 'I longed to be betrayed by you and by her.'[71]

In conclusion, we can see the likely influence of Beckett, and the direct influence of Eliot and Joyce, on the genesis of specific plays, and the indirect influence of realist and experimental dramatic traditions. In some cases, Pinter's technique bears a fascinating resemblance to his predecessors. However, on closer analysis we find that each of Pinter's plays has its own character and accomplishment, and the totality of his drama, over nearly half a century, is of unique, unrivalled distinction.

NOTES

1. See David T. Thompson, *Pinter: the Player's Playwright* (London and New York: Macmillan, 1985), 131-35.
2. All references to Pinter's plays are to the four-volume Faber edition (London, 1991), as follows: *The Room, The Birthday Party, A Night Out, The Dumb Waiter, A Slight Ache* (Plays One); *The Caretaker, The Collection, The Lover, Night School* (Plays Two); *The Homecoming, Landscape, Silence* (Plays Three); *No Man's Land, Betrayal* (Plays four).
3. Pinter, '*Writing for Myself,*' Plays Two, ix.
4. *The Daily Mail*, 7 March, 1964, 8.
5. '*New Comment*,' interview with Laurence Kitchin, 8 October 1963, BBC transcript, 10.
6. Quoted by Martin Esslin, *The Theatre of the Absurd* (Harmondsworth: Penguin, 1968), 23.
7. *The Financial Times*, 20 May 1958, 15.
8. *Plays and Players*, 7, 10 (July I960), 15.
9. *The Manchester Guardian*, 29 April I960.
10. *The Isis Review*, 14 May 1958, 27.
11. Eugene Ionesco, *Rhinoceros. The Chairs. The Lesson* (Harmondsworth: Penguin, 1976), 104.
12. *The Times*, 16 November 1959, 4.
13. See Eugene Ionesco, '*The London Controversy*,' Notes and Counter-Notes (London: John Calder, 1964), 90-112.
14. *New Theatre Magazine* 11, pt. 3 (May-June 1971), 3.
15. Harold Pinter, *Beckett at Sixty* (London: Calder and Boyars, 1967), 86.
16. '*New Comment*', interview with Laurence Kitchin, 8 October 1963, BBC transcript.
17. Michael Billington, *The Life and Work of Harold Pinter* (London: Faber, 1996), 51.
18. '*Talking of Theatre*,' a joint interview with Donald McWhinnie, with Carl Wildman, 7 March 1961, BBC transcript, 9-10.
19. L.A.C. Dobrez, *The Existential and Its Exits: Literary and Philosophical Perspectives in the Work of Beckett, Ionesco, Genet, and Pinter* (London and New York: Athlone Press, St Martin's Press, 1985), 333.

20. Nigel Dennis, '*Optical Delusion*,' Encounter, 15 (July 1960), 64.
21. Robert Brustein, '*A Naturalism of the Grotesque*,' Seasons of Discontent (London: Jonathan Cape, 1966), 182.
22. *Theatre World*, 56, 425 (June 1960), 8-9.
23. Robert W. Corrigan, '*The Drama of Anton Chekhov*,' in Modern Drama. Essays in Criticism, ed. Travis Bogard and William I. Oliver (London, Oxford, New York: Oxford University Press, 1965), 79.
24. Pinter, '*Writing for the Theatre*,' Plays One, xi.
25. Constantin Stanislavsky, *Building a Character* (London: Methuen, 1968), 113.
26. Pinter, '*Writing for the Theatre*,' Plays One, xiii.
27. John Russell Brown, '*Dialogue in Pinter and Others*,' in Modern British Dramatists, ed. John Russell Brown (Englewood Cliffs, NJ: Prentice Hall, 1968), 140.
28. John Mortimer, *The Evening Standard*, 31 May 1960, 12.
29. Anton Chekhov, *Plays*, trans. Elisaveta Fen (Harmondsworth: Penguin, 1982), 321.
30. *The Caretaker*, Plays Two, 15.
31. Thomas Postlewait, '*Pinter's The Homecoming: Displacing and Repeating Ibsen*,' Comparative drama, 15 (1981), 195-212.
32. Adrian Noble, *The Guardian*, 12 April 1977 'The Week,' 7.
33. August Strindberg, *The Chamber Plays*, trans. Evert Sprinchorn, Seabury Quinn Jr, and Kenneth Petersen (New York: E.P. Dutton, 1961), 136.
34. August Strindberg, *Seven Plays*, trans. Arvid Paulson (New York, Toronto, London: Bantam Books, 1964), 70.
35. Irving Wardle, 'There's Music in that Room,' in *New Theatre of the Fifties and Sixties*, ed. Charles Marowitz, Tom Milne, Owen Hale (London: Eyre Methuen, 1981), 131.
36. *The Independent*, 26 November 1993, 14.
37. Dobrez, *The Existential and Its Exits*, 333.
38. Pinter, '*Writing for the Theatre*,' Plays One, 13.
39. Luigi Pirandello, *Three Plays* (London: Methuen, 1985), pp. 85,187.
40. 'Harold Pinter: An Interview' (with Lawrence M. Bensky) in *Harold Pinter: A Collection of Critical Essays*, ed. Arthur Ganz (Englewood Cliffs, NJ: Prentice Hall, 1972), 26.
41. 'Speech: Hamburg 1970,' *Theatre Quarterly*, 1 (1971), 4.
42. Pirandello, *On Humour*, trans. Antonio Illiano and Daniel P. Testa (Chapel Hill, NC: University of North Carolina Press, 1974).

43. *Ibid.*, 113.
44. *The Birthday Party*, Plays One, 47.
45. *Ibid.*, 48.
46. *The Caretaker*, Plays Two, 40.
47. Pirandello, *On Humour*, 144.
48. Roger W. Oliver, *Dreams of Passion*. The Theatre of Luigi Pirandello (New York and London: New York University Press, 1979), 4.
49. Pinter, *Talking of Theatre*, 7.
50. See Billington, *The Life and Work of Harold Pinter*, 21.
51. For these and the following Eliot references I am indebted to Andrew K. Kennedy's helpful discussion in his Six Dramatists in Search of a Language (Cambridge: Cambridge University Press, 1975), 108-15.
52. Katherine Burkman, *The Dramatic World of Harold Pinter: Its Basis in Ritual* (Colombus: University of Ohio Press, 1971), 47-64.
53. T.S. Eliot, '*The Love Song of J. Alfred Prufrock,*' Collected Poems 1909-1935 (London: Faber and Faber, 1961), 12-13.
54. No *Man's Land*, Plays Four, 78, 121.
55. *Ibid.*, 139.
56. Russell Davies, '*Pinter Land*,' The New York Review of Books, 25, 21/22 (25 January 1979).
57. See Ronald Knowles, '*Joyce and Pinter: Exiles and Betrayal*,' Barcelona English Language and Literature Studies, 9 (1998), 183-91.
58. *Betrayal*, Plays Four, 179.
59. James Joyce, *Exiles* (London: New English Library, 1962), 73-74.
60. *Ibid.*, 74.
61. *Betrayal*, 185.
62. *Exiles*, 75.
63. *Betrayal*, 188.
64. *Exiles*, 97-8.
65. *Betrayal*, 179.
66. *Exiles*, 136.
67. *Betrayal*, 222.
68. *Exiles*, 45.
69. *Betrayal*, 198.
70. *Exiles*, 78.
71. *Ibid.*, 87.

PART - B

6

The Sixth Dimension in *The Woman and the Sea* and *The Old Man and the Sea*

O.P. Bhatnagar

Although P.D. Ouspensky talked of the 'Fifth Dimension' in his new model of the universe in 1931, the creative writers in America were well ahead of it in achieving the 'Sixth Dimension' in their writing. *The Woman and the Sea* by Mary Ellen Chase appeared in 1934 and *The Old Man and the Sea* by Ernest Hemingway in 1952. The controversial statement prose has already been long debated by Joseph Warren Beach, Malcolm Cowley and Hary Levin. But surprisingly enough, Hemingway had already done with it after *For Whom the Bell Tolls* was imperceptibly evolving the sixth dimension culminating in *The Old Man and the Sea.* What Hemingway had done with such labour and persistence Mary Ellen Chase had achieved it without any emotional or aesthetic violence.

The question that first needs clarification here is, what may we mean by the term 'Sixth Dimension.' As in our Lord's Houses there are many mansions so in our artist's works there are many dimensions. The founding of dimensions is not merely a prerogative of science but of men of imagination also. If the 'Fourth Dimension' can be described as 'Time' and the 'Fifth Dimension' as 'A Line of Perpetual Now,' the 'Sixth Dimension' may be described as the 'State of Merging the Conscious with the Unconscious,' the order beyond and the non-human world. It may also be described as the process of non-being. It is the self and clash of self with beings, things and environment that sends a man remote from his state of harmony and sets him apart as a conscious independent identity in opposition. This consciousness derives its existence and image from the fights it is able to pout up as a part of heroism and rebellion. The history of American literature is full of such fighting and rebel heroes asserting and establishing their self as a distinct identity of note. Mr, Maurice Friedman has classified such characters into Modern Prometheus, Modern Job, Modern Abraham or Modern Exile in his reputed book *Problematic Rebel.* The contending forces in this drama may comprise the individual, the society, the nature, some principle or non-human being. Of all the contending forces, sea has occupied a key position in conflict with man in American fiction. But the two novels. *The Woman and the Sea* and *The Old Man and the Sea*, I propose to deal with here do not put up man as a rebel or in fight against the power of the sea but as one making peace with it, becoming a part of it, merging the self with the larger being or non-being and even accepting sea as a guide to humble and harmonious living.

The present line of thinking has nothing to do with the theories of Carl Jung, Kirkegard, Proust or Marcel. It emerges from the striking change one notices in Hemingway's mood, mode and style of writing in The *Old Man and the Sea.* In this novel there is an attempt at silencing the tumult, the turmoil and all agitation. The will, which manifests the conscious, is relaxed. Violence and killings are not rebelled or revolted against but reconciled as natural order. There is no remorse at the biological trap or the ironic turn of events and things. This process is more pronounced in Hemingway than in Mary Ellen Chase. In *The Woman and the Sea* the will and the conscious make attempts at breaking loose from the events, men and environment but it is held in check by the wisdom distilled into Mary by sea. To Mary "her father's ship was to her as safe and strong as her father's big house. The great waters on which it sailed were like the green fields around that house" (11). Her entire life was permeated with sea and "Perhaps the first and clearest things she was remember from life arose from the sea itself and from those changeable forces of weather that governed it. She learned something of winds too, which were so important. As she grew older, she became less fearful of them and their mighty power. She learned not to fear that sudden shaking from every part of the ship caused by a great force of wind. She knew the feeling of a ship throwing itself around like some fearful animal until the sails could he controlled. She knew well too the days when there was no wind at all and the ship rolled on a quiet sea commanded by the strange movements of the water below. And as she grew older, understanding passed into her mind almost without being noticed. It was becoming so much a part of her that it could not even be called a thought—the outstanding that they were a part of the forces of nature in which they moved. Their world, self-contained and directed as it was also contained and directed by a world of sky and wind and water. The ship took her movement from the great heartbeat of the sea. It sent a shaking from the deep water into them—now slowing, now quickening according to its wish, with which they must agree. They talked surprisingly little of things ashore. Fear of storm or wind seemed of small importance when it was past. And so the matters of the world that they had left behind them seemed of small importance" (12-13).

'Mary was sensitive, intelligent and curious.' She began to understand that people who did business in the great waters not only had a great need for them but also, in a larger way, were part of them, following the laws that they followed, moving as they moved more and more clearly she understood that she herself was only a very small part of things that moved needlessly on and on wherever they must. The wind increased and they moved before it, or by the quick use of all their mind and strength, they followed its command. When it died, they waited as quietly as they could until the next one came" (13). She was a part of the sea and "loved to work with a feeling that was more than joy" (51).

In this ever moving, turbulent but closed world of Mary comes a young sailor, Jim Pendleton, the son of a one-time lover of her mother Sarah. Mr. James Pendleton who had promised to marry Sarah, before going on sea, never returned to do so. Instead he married a Frenchwoman and from Sarah she learnt that it was nothing unusual but like a wave on the sea. The young Jim proves a success and makes himself likeable to Mary. But the sea in him makes him act a truant. He starts winning Hester, the friend of Mary and the beloved of John Peters. Then all of a sudden Jim disappears leaving Hester pregnant from him. The coming summer Hester dies while delivering the baby. Nor does the baby survive. Everybody is grievously hurt but Sarah smoothens out things in the following words:

> "You are thinking that some hurt Hester badly—that she paid too much for another person's wrongdoing. The first is wrong and so is the last. I will not say she had not paid too much. She has. But in this world things are not often done alone, and people sometimes have to pay with all they have. And John, you are thinking that this trouble was caused only by Jim Pendleton. You would like to kill him for it. You are wrong too. The sooner you get that

> thought out of your head, John, the better for you all your life. I would know you were wrong the better for you all your life. I would know you were wrong even if Hester hadn't told me herself this afternoon. She told me things before you brought her mother, but she didn't have to. I knew them anyway. There are forces in this world and throw them along before they know that are taken. There are forces that beat them, and people cannot stop them. I am not saying they ought not to know or that they ought to be beaten. I just say they don't know and they are beaten! And sometimes even when they do know, they know too late. And all sorts of things decide what those forces will be-father and mother and family history and the way one is helped to grow up. These are things a person cannot decide for himself." (69)

On the question of transgression and causing hurt to the loved one she learns from Sarah "that he should have guarded Hester against being hurt. You are probably right; he should have. But when another person is thrown by the same force as you are, guarding is not very important in what you think and do" (70). Mary understands that life is more a play of several invisible forces than mere human will. And, therefore, things in life must not be allowed to unsettle, disappoint and frustrate a man and "the best way to take care of such marks, after you have understood them is to remember things strong enough to destroy them. That is the only way I know to stay on one's course in this world. And we have been face to face with big things—things so big that remembering them should leave no room for small thoughts" (71).

And all this training and wisdom in patience had come to them from their life on the sea—"Remember those days when we waited and waited for a wind to fill our sails? It came, didn't it? After we had waited until we thought we couldn't wait any longer? It came, and we went forward again. You will go forward against too if you just put your thoughts straight and wait long enough" (71-72).

As years rolled by Sarah became weak and ill and Jim was sent for on her request. When Jim arrived Mary had an experience like that which her mother had had years before on the sea, facing the father of Jim. "At the sight of Jim Pendleton she had expected to feel pain, even anger, but she felt neither. If sadness were present it was a part of all sadness of the world. In place of the strong feelings she had expected, she had the strange idea that it was right for him to stand there. She did not speak to him or answer his question in words. But he knew that she was glad he had come and that the shyness he had feared was suddenly gone" (85).

Gradually Mary forgot the past and responded to the love of Jim and got married to him. John, her brother, too got married to Ellen to settle things well for Mary. But all this victory over circumstances and the consequent happiness was short-lived. Jim had taken to his old tricks of running after women and fooling them with his promises of warm love. To make matters worse he even took Ellen secretly out for the night to some amorous jaunt but died while returning home in the dark of the night as the coach overturned. John and Mary were struck with pain and desolation but "The long, free thoughts of their families, who had sailed all the oceans for two hundred years, added belief to their own belief" (88). There was nothing more frustrating for Mary to see in life. The current of her feelings was running deep like the undercurrents in the sea. She had lived a life of utter misery and misfortune never bowing to defeat. Even after happiness seemed so close at hand she lost it like a wave disappearing in the vast sea. The irony of her life was that the man she loved most with all her warmth of innocence tricked her again and again. Yet she never felt shaken. She bore everything like sea. Along with Sarah, "Instead she had an understanding that things were not kind. She felt there was a certain necessary sadness and loneliness in human life. It was there in the manner in. which men had always lived their lives. She felt sorry for John and Ellen, for herself, for all other souls throughout the world. Since things were this way, this great warmth, this gentle feeling for all people, produced a sureness, a belief. Without this belief men and woman could not live, though they might not notice that it lessed their problems every moment" (95). She had learnt to be humble and sympathetic and accept the course of events and life as it presented itself before her from time to time. She could stand all these miseries because she had relaxed her will in acceptance of things. She had assimilated everything into herself like the huge sea. She had neither anger nor remorse or repentance. She knew she must endure and yet not make a pride of this virtue. She knew that life was wayward like sea and that she must always be humble, ready and willing to face life with patient and pleasant equanimity. She lived to face the death of John, John's baby, Mrs. Kimball and Sarah Peters with quiet, ageless fortitude. Even the people who had driven quickly through the early morning to tell the sad news of Jim's death "said they had never seen a woman like her. They found her up and working around her house at six in the morning. If she was nervous about the face that her husband and not returned the night before, she did not show it. Nor did she appear surprised when they told her what they had to tell" (116). She was deep, dense, serene and majestic like sea. She still looked towards sea and "A large ship was lying there, all her sails set for her show course toward shore. The last lines of sunlight caught them, and they burned for some moments on the quiet sea" (123) providing the brilliant image of life as a short journey on sea, and giving the necessary detachment of the will, and the consciousness with the self as a separate identity. She rose above the status of a matador, a crusader and the crucified to acquire the sixth dimension in which consciousness merges itself with the great unconscious that controls life as a part of the big process enervating existence.

The basic structure of *The Woman and the Sea* is the same as that of *The Old Man and the Sea*—a whole life time spent on sea, braving the perils and challenges of both life and sea, bowing before the might of nature in all humanity and majesty of surrender. Like Mary, about whom Jim used to say "You're old, Mary. There is nothing new about you. That is why you are different from everybody else. You are full of old places and old thoughts. That is why you can't be touched or—or be afraid of new things not yet tried" (106). Santiago—"was old except his eyes and they were the same colour as the sea and were cheerful and undefeated" (6). He had "strange shoulders, still powerful although very old, and the neck was still strong too and the creases did not show so much when the old man was asleep and his head fallen forward. His shirt had been patched so many times that it was like the sail and the patches were faded to many different shades by the sun. The old man's head was very old though and with his eyes closed there was no life in his face" (14-15) and yet he was full of the memories of sea:

> "He dreamed of Africa when he was a boy and the long, golden beaches and the white beaches, so white they hurt yours,—and the high capes and the great brown mountains. He lived along that cost now every night and in his dreams he heard the surf roar and saw the native boats come riding thought it. He smelled the tar and oakum of the deck as he slept and he smelled the smell of Africa that the land breeze brought and morning. Usually when he smelled the land breeze he woke up and dressed to go and wake the boy. But tonight the smell of the land breeze came very early and he knew it was too early in his dream and went on dreaming to see the white peaks of the Islands rising from the sea and then he dreamed of the different harbours and roadsteads of the Canary Islands." (21)

He was acquainted with the whole sea like a dweller in the house and "He saw the phosphorescence of the Gulf weed in the water as he rowed over the part of the ocean that the fishermen called the great well because there was a sudden deep of seven hundred fathoms where all sort of fish congregated because of the swirl the current made against the steep walls of the floor of the ocean. Here there were concentrations of shrimp and bait fish and sometimes schools of squid in the deepest holes and these rose close to the surface at night where all the wandering fish fed on them" (25).

He not only knew the sea but was emotionally involved in it. The sea had special meaning for him. He "always thought of her as feminine and as something that gave or withheld great favours, and if she did wild or wicked things it was because she could not help them. The moon affects her as it does a woman he thought" (27). He, knew, of the compulsions of sea life and even perhaps of life. He therefore saw not only the necessity of killing as part of sea life but of sustaining oneself at the cost of life of another being "Remember, no matter how little you want to, that you must eat him in the morning" (45). He knew it was a sad thing killing but he could do nothing except beg "her pardon" and "butcher her promptly" (47). In his incessant talking to Marlin, birds and his body he seems to attain a kind of detachment which enables him to become one with the non-human world and merge the consciousness of his separate identity with the greater world of the unconscious, where everything is governed by a natural order permeating the universe and existence, culminating in the most philosophical writing in the novel:

> "'Be patient, hand,' he said. 'I do this for you! I wish I could feed the fish, he thought. He is my brother. But I must kill him and keep strong to do it." (57)

And:

> "There are three things that are brothers: the fish and my two hands." (62)

After he had killed the great Marlin he felt great compassion, for it and said to himself "I want to see him, he thought, and to touch and feel him. He is my fortune, he thought. But that is not why I wish to feel him. I think I felt his heart, he thought. When I pushed on the harpoon shaft the second time" (95).

Santiago wondered whether it was right killing someone whom one loved:

> "Perhaps it was a sin to kill the fish. I suppose it was even though I did it to keep me alive and feed many people. But then everything is a sin. Do not think about sin. It is much too late for that and

> there are people who are paid to do it. Let them think about it. You were born to be a fisherman as the fish was born to be a fish. San Pedro was a fisherman as was the father of the great DiMaggio."
>
> "You loved him when he was alive and you loved him after. If you love him, it is not a sin to kill him."
>
> "He lives on the live fish as you do."
>
> "Besides, he thought, everything kills everything else in someway." (105-06)

He then lets his boat sail at rest led by the fighting life current in the Marlin. But when the sharks set themselves on the Marlin he feels "Maybe I'll have the luck to bring the forward half in. I should have some luck" (117). And "He knew he was beaten now finally and without remedy" (120). But there was no reason for him to be frustrated or agitated. He had to settle with his predicament and make friends with his existence and environment and he feels "The wind is our friend, anyway, he thought. Then he added, sometimes. And the great sea with our friends and our enemies" (121). As Santiago forgets the existence of his self as a separate identity, the mental turmoil and the struggle, in which he had involved himself, subsides and he finds absolute peace in merging his consciousness with the elements that govern that entire universe and existence.

Like Mary, Santiago's life was full of trials and tribulations on sea. He had gradually learnt that exerting self and will was not the right way of overpowering the forces governing life and existence. It was merely staging an Arabic heroic drama. In fact more could be mastered by surrendering the will and resolution and accepting life and events as they unfolded themselves before the conscious self. If the conscious self did not create any resistance to the happenings in the outside world affecting it, it could hope to share in the bigger order of existence in peace and tranquillity. In *The Woman and the Sea* such an attitude is already implicit in the structure and the heroine of the novel. Mary, therefore, is not rent with serious mental and emotional struggles. She goes on imbibing whatever is revealed to her by her expanding vision of her place and relation in the wider order of existence. There are, therefore, no soliloquies or long conversations with the self. Things are resolved as if in a preexisting wisdom in Mary. The style of the novel, therefore, has a certain compactness and serenity of rhythm and majesty of the tragically playful acceptance of life.

There are certain common strands which run both these novels. Both novels recognize the existence of forces beyond human control.

It is this which produces irony against human will and presents before man the need of assessing one's position in life and existence in the right perspective. It does not necessarily impose defeat on man but introduces the need of developing patience, endurance, humility and acceptance as the proper mode of courage, valour and fortitude. Both the novels do this even stylistically well. Despite man's courage there are certain things strong enough to destroy them" (71) and apprehending defeat Santiago remembers of DiMaggio and Lions on beaches. The two contradictory images of DiMaggio and the Lion in the novel have been variously interpreted by Philip Young, Leo Gurko, Carlos Baker, Clinton S. Burhans, Jr. Keichv Harada, L. Contton W.M. Frohock, Nikolaus Happel, Mark Schorer and Robert D. Spector to drive home the fact that the two images are complementary and point in the direction of absolute supremacy of the champion of the game and the king of the forest. To my mind these images do not coalesce to strengthen the supremacy of Santiago on sea but present two conflicting aspects of man's personality—the playful and the resolute. The entire trend of events and adventure takes the novel towards the general relaxation of resolution and the surrender of will to forces outside the self. The novel moves more towards acquiring humility than the lone pride and majesty of the lion. If the final image of the crucified, so vehemently suggested by Melvin Buckman, has to have any significance in the novel then the image of lion gains no such significance. Acceptance, surrender and humility alone are the prize virtues which the competitors in any game take home and the winner takes nothing. Strangely enough both the novelists exhibit a remarkable absence of strong feelings in the works under discussion. Nor do the protagonists ever enter into any display of strong feelings. A serenity flowing from the sea pervades their tempers and actions and they view changes in life with equanimity. Both Chase and Hemingway discuss the problem of right and wrong, sin and virtue and recommend a practical view out of them. Both Mary and Santiago refuse to sweat by the absolutes. Death, misery and defeat are used for bringing clarity of sight into the self and the visible and invisible world around and join in emphasizing the fact that man's basic divinity and majesty lies in identifying oneself not only with the collective being but with the entire non-human world existing around him. For this purpose, both the novelists have used sea as a contending and guiding factor representing the non-human world. And both of these novels provide extremely illuminating images of life as a journey on sea. As the narrative of *The Woman and the Sea* comes to an end it reveals "A Large sailing ship was lying there, all her sails set for her slow course towards shore. The last lines of sunlight caught them, and they burned for some moments on the quiet sea" (123), and *The Old Man and the Sea* begins with the most symbolical description "His shirt had been patched so many times that it was like the sail and the patches were faded to many different shades by the sun" (25).

Both the novels aim at breaking the ego of the being and make consciousness neutral enough to sail into the wider world of the unconscious where things are related to one another in a unique order beyond the questionings of human mind and the conceptual time dimension of the mind. If the disintegration of the three-way time dimension is possible into one dimension then the disintegration of the perpetual now is also possible through relating it to a cosmic process of timelessness like Santiago's journey far out into the sea beyond the trappings of time. The entire case of narration and the relaxed style of expression and exposition and the serenity of syntax speak of the sixth dimension to which Mary Ellen chase and Hemingway had reached in their novels. Both trace not 'the now' but 'the ever' of things which is what the sixth dimension is.

WORKS CITED

Mary Ellen Chase. *The Woman and the Sea*. Bantam, 1934.

Ernest Hemingway. *The Old Man and the Sea*. Dutton, 1952.

7

The Underpinnings of Life's Terrors and the Restored Balance in Edward Albee's *A Delicate Balance*

R. Saraswathi

> For the first time Rieux found that he could give a name to the family likeness that for several months he had detected in the faces in the streets... Once plagues had shut the gates of the town, they had settled down to a life of separation, debarred from the living wrath that gives forgetfulness of all. In different degrees, in every part of the town, men and women had been yearning for a reunion, not of the same kind for all, but for all alike ruled out. Most of them had longed intensely for an absent one, for the wrath of a body, for love, or merely for a life that habit had endeared. Some, often without knowing it, suffered from being deprived of the company of friends and from their inability to get in touch with them through the usual channels of friendship—letters, trains, and boats. Others, fewer those—Tarron may have been one of them—had desired reunion with something they couldn't have defined, but which seemed to them the only desirable thing on earth. For want of a better name, they sometimes called it peace.
>
> —*The Plague*, Albert Camus

Agnes (Unperturbed)

Yes, the terror. Or, the plague—they're both the same. Edna and Harry have come to us—dear friends, our very best...have come to us and brought the plague. Now, poor tobias has sat up all night and wrestled with the moral problem.

Tobias (Frustration, anger)

I've not been...wrestling with some...abstract problem! These are people! Harry and Edna! These are our friends, God damn it!

Agnes

Yes, but they've brought the plague with them, and that's another matter. Let me tell you something about disease...mortal illness; you either are immune to it...or you fight it. If you are immune, you made right in, you treat the patient until he lives, or dies of it. But if you are not immune, you risk infection. The centuries ago—and even less—the treatment was quite simple...burn them. Burn their bodies, burn their houses, burn their clothes—and move to another town, if you were enlightened. But now with modern medicine, we merely isolate, we quarantine, we ostracize—if we are not immune ourselves, or unless we are saints. So, your nightlong vigil, darling, your reasoning in the cold, pure hours, has been over patient and not the illness. It is not Edna and Harry who have come to us—our friends—it is a disease.

—*A Delicate Balance*, Edward Albee (155)

In the above passage from *A Delicate Balance* Agnes, the wife, describes the couple who invade their home not as people but as representatives of the alienating disease of modern times. This example of blending "ideas into people"[1] aptly suggests the allegorical nature of this play, which deals with the need for personal moral responsibility to counteract the destructive nature of individual isolation. "Disease" or "plague" is illustrated and symbolized in Harry and Edna, a man and wife who become afflicted with terror after glimpsing the vacuity of their lives and come as children to the house of a friend for sanctuary.

Harry

We were scared....

(Silence; Agnes comforting Edne, Harry stock still. Quite innocent, almost childlike.)

It was like being lost; very young again, with the dark, and lost. There was no...thing.

Edna

We were Frightened.... And There was Nothing. (55)

Although Albee's play deals with disease as an abstraction, Camus' *The Plague* and Albee's *A Delicate Balance* bear a thematic resemblance.

Camus explores alienation as a residual effect of a real epidemic of disease which, although it ends, does not eradicate the persistent human urge for communication. In *A Delicate Balance*, the plague is fear itself as the impetus which has brought the two people into the friends' house where each discovers his own need. Like the disease, the presence of the couple within the family causes each person to suffer a removal of fragile protective tissue, exposing the raw sore beneath. Following the trauma of exposure and the admission of terror underlying the surface comes a realization of the need for shared love and the will to shape co-existence of people in community.

This play, despite its surface realism, continues Albee's use of the allegorical genre of *Tiny Alice* as a technique for examining disruptions in contemporary society. Albee integrates the private world of dis-ease into the general social outlook here as in *Tiny Alice* where personae are multiple facets of Julian who, as victim of the world around him, "is walking on the edge of the abyss but is balancing." Although the setting, an upper middle class living room, is realistic as in *Who's Afraid of Virginia Woolf*? it provides, like the seemingly "normal" life of its vaguely identified characters, only a surface over a substructure of violence, guilt and terror.[2]

Agnes and Tobias (no surname given) are a married couple in their late fifties who live with Claire, Agnes' alcoholic sister, in a "large and well-appointed suburban house" (no locale given). Agnes muses about "becoming a stranger in the world." Losing her mind and "drifting" into madness "some autumn dusk;" she wonders if she is "the only one of you to admit to it; not that I may go mad, but that each of you wonders if each of you might not...." Tobias is apathetic, uninvolved, resigned only, of growing even older than yon are in the company of you steady wife, your alcoholic sister-in-law and occasional visits from their daughter Julia returning regularly from the failure of her many marriages.

In a scene between Claire and Tobias, Claire suggests that perhaps, for excitement, the seemingly emotionless Tobias ought to kill Agnes—in fact, all of them, including Julia. Tobias remonstrates, "But it would have to be an act of passion—out of my head and all that." As Agnes later states, they are all living in a "demise of intensity, the private preoccupations, the substitutions" (90).

In a reminiscent mood, Claire launches into a parable-like recollection of a one-time search for personal meaning and place. It is connected in reality and in metaphor to the departure of Claire from the house and family. It happened "the spring I moved out," she says. She equates her drunken state to a fall into the depths of animosity, despair and illness, and wandering child searching for a substitute family among Alcoholics Anonymous. Even though she received a kind of parental praise approval from them, she knew she did not belong and had returned to the curiously dispassionate group, dwelling in the "nest." The general state of all the characters is aptly described by Nelvin Vos as person who with the exception of Claire, may be compared to autumn leaves have forgotten how to cling.[3]

Agnes enters with the news that Julia is returning home again after the failure of her fourth marriage—as was expected. Despite her latest failure, Agnes says "...it is her home, we are her parents, the two of us, and we have our obligations to her," the term "obligation" parable about his love for a cat, its death, and his repentance. He had found that his love for the animal was not being returned by the cat despite all his overtures. In retaliation he at first beat the animal, his own love turning into vengeful hate. In a description of a former state of high emotionalism from which he has now retreated, he says, he "resented having...being judged." Being betrayed, and he had the cat killed—"put away," corrects Agnes. Now, in retrospect, Tobias repents his failure to accept the responsibilities in the situation: "I might have tried longer. I might have gone on, as long as cats live, the house with her, done penance. For something. For what, God knows." In the course of the parable the "she" of the cat becomes almost human.

Intruders arrive. Harry and Edna, good friends of Agnes and Tobias, described as being "very much like them," have become suddenly frightened like "lost children in their own home" and have come for safety to their friend's house. By the beginning of Act II on Saturday evening, Julia the daughter has also returned. She finds that the intruders are occupying her room and becomes emotionally distraught at having been displaced. Rivalry for the possession of her room and jealousy of Harry and Edna who are newcomers into the family become Julia's dominating impulses. Reverting to a "little girl," she complains bitterly of her new secondly role. From this point, as the placidity and balance of the house becomes disturbed, multiple disruptions in relationships among members of the family are revealed beneath the surface amenities. Identities of the parents become confused as "disease" of fright spreads during the dark hours. Agnes, confronting Julia, begins to examine her role as mother and gradually undergoes a curious wishful transformation into a male; the ineffectual Tobias is shaken into the role of "mother" by a seemingly playful but serious Agnes; the intruders paradoxically become usurpers of the parents role while acting also as children in the family, the daughter Julia reverts farther and farther into childhood as her security of place and parent become increasingly shaken on all sides.

The Saturday night which follows becomes, as characterized by Claire, a "festive" night in which realities and unrealities of the group situation are suspended or recalled in time. The central event of the night's ritual is Julia's appearance with a gun, threatening to shoot Harry and Edna whom she regards as usurpers of her rightful place in the family. Her motivation for revenge is a hysterical effort to gain passage to her room like Jerry in *The Zoo Story*. In a strangely calm reception of her violent actions, Tobias and Agnes subdue her and she is led away. The outburst has characteristics of the replay of a performance familiar to Agnes, Claire and Tobias.

In this context of a replay, usurpation of Julia's place by Harry and Edna becomes a repetitive situation, recollecting an earlier displacement by an earlier intruder: Teddy, a younger child of Agnes and Tobias who is now dead. The circumstances of Teddy's death are never made clear. But we do know that Julia was intensely jealous of him and that after he died, she did "penance" on her bloody knees. Teddy's death—an odd parallel to the death of the cat in his parable—has also had a profoundly alienating effect on Tobias; Tobias had refused after that time to consummate sexual relations with Agnes, fearing the responsibility of the fruits of love: another birth, another death. According to Agnes, "fearing the responsibility of the string" which had pulled their marital relationship awry causing Tobias's retreat into himself. A parallel disruption is now present in Harry and Edna, and the question of his reaction is open.

Act III takes place on Sunday morning. Tobias has spent most of the night alone in the living room in a "Godlike" introspection of the situation where "the house is not in order". He and Agnes had been forced to share a room and because of their proximity had begun some restoration of physical contact with each other—to Agnes a hopeful sign for the future. But for Tobias, the night "watch" has resulted in a decision which reverses his former attitude: to take in the intruders permanently as an obligation—even though he does not love them. This constitutes metamorphosis in Tobias's thinking from the time of the cat parable as well as the beginning of the play. The strangers have also had their restorative balance in the night. Forced by the sharing of a room to reestablish some weak communication, they have come to the realization that the safety of another's house will not bring them love. They must find it—with its original members plus Julia, spent by the ravages of the night's "disease" but with a deeper realization of need for each other and responsibility to others. As Cohn has stated, the delicate balance of the home is preserved.[4]

II

In *A Delicate Balance* Albee continues his probe into the underpinnings of life's terrors, employing thematic materials already familiar from past plays; association of terror and the "lost" child, displacement from home as a metaphor for alienation and loss of love, and the family context as theatre for the real and symbolic struggles of man. He concentrates intensely on states of childhood within the sanctuary of the home. Harry and Edna and the returning Julia all come to the home as frightened children.

Julia

What...what do they want? Harry and Edna... ... ...

Claire

Comfort.

Wrath. A special room with a night light, or the door ajar so you can look down the hall from the bed and see that Monay's door is open.

***Julia* (no anger; loss)**

But that's my room.

Claire

It's...the room. Happens you were in it. You're a visitor as much as anyone, now. (99)

Albee deals with a complex series of mirror-like reflections of the child in past and present times and as dead and living. To Julia, the dead Teddy and the intruders become facets of each other as she struggles against her replacement by the couple as she might have intruders but in a curious psychodramatic replay of the past. The violence of the pretended shooting in this play is reminiscent of the phantasmagoria of verbal violence and ritual in *Virginia Woolf* when the memory of an illusory child is exorcised and the confusion of identity of the boy is in question. Here, the ritual is subsumed by dramatic action as recollection of childhood fear and as revelation of inner psychological state. In addition, we have multiple views of the characters in their separate returns to the state of childhood fears: Claire, Harry and Edna, as well as Julia.

Tobias's parable covers up his mental and psychological fears, while revealing his current state of mind and soul. Albee is employing the familiar roster of characters in the deep probe into personal fears. But, although they retain some characteristics still of the earlier domineering Mommy and the arid Daddy, Agnes and Tobias are more mature in years, warmer and more responsible. Probably the single most important method of character portrayal developed by Albee in this play is the revelation of self by means of introspection expressed in dialogue or monologue. In this way, the viewable interior of each character is extended, revealing in the flow of memory and the thought the basic ambivalence of his position in respect to the outer world. This method of exposition of self marks the beginning of Albee's technique of psychodrama which is to flower in subsequent plays. Extending his, probe of the inner psyche of his characters, Albee has come a long way from the direct statements of the earlier, flatly conceived Mommy and Daddy, the exaggerated and farcical characters in *Sandbox* and *American Dream*. The continuously innovative techniques of Albee are exemplified in this play's method of exposition while employing essentially the same members of the family.[5]

Dramaturgical devices of role-playing and the "surrogate" character, as means of revealing hidden truths, continue from *Virginia Woolf* and *Tiny Alice*. In pirandellian shifts of character between the real and the pretended, superficial personal characters dissolve in sex changes, confusions and mergings of identity, all occurring in the climatic scene which takes on the coloration of a performance—a ritual ceremony of death, which is the central scene of the play.

The character most overlooked by critics of this play[6] is the dead child Teddy. His progenitors are the dead twin of *The American Dream* and the illusory child of *Virginia Woolf*. If the play is seen as a Strindbergian exposure in depth rather than a linear development in time, the character of Teddy resides at the centre—in the depths of jealousy, guilt and alienation suffered by Julia, Agnes and Tobias. He may be seen as the earlier counterpart of Julia's current jealousies of the instructing Harry and Edna. We know that his death caused a separation between Agnes and Tobias and after the crucial scene enacted in the night, Tobias changes his view of self as giver rather than received, involved rather than alienated, as if his guilt had finally been expiated. Expiation, as an exorcism of sin, is the motivating force of change in his attitude. Behind the change lies a complex of interrelations which Albee has manipulated within a structure of balances and parallels, where the doubling of identities and repetition of parallel situations predominate.

III

The play's movement may be seen as describing a course of balances and imbalances, going from precarious balance to imbalance to ordered balance. Within the outer form, the inner rhythm of each character reflects a similar path, exposing superficialities by their opposites. The action of the play is provoked in a system of antithesis activated by the intrusion of Harry and Edna. The disease brought by them afflicts all others except Claire and they are caused to strip away their "balanced" emptiness in a series of memories, fears, and desires linked to terror and reality. In time, both actual and metaphoric, we go from the beginnings of a night—a dusk of temous balances—into the darkness of agonizing revelations or disorder and again into the daylight when evils depart and an acceptance of new order begins. Although *A Delicate Balance* can hardly be classified as a tragedy, its movement is not structurally dissimilar from classic drama as revelation rather than story. Proof of the insights gained by Agnes and Tobias lies in the opening and closing speeches of Agnes.

Although at the opening Agnes has desires, in a vague and undefined way, to go gently into madness "some autumn dusk" when "...it is not beyond happening: some gentle loosening of the moorings, seeding the balloon adrift..." (13), at the end of the desire for happiness is spent:

> What I find most astonishing—aside from my belief that I will, one day...lose my mind—but when? Never, I began to think, as the years go by, or that I'll not know if it happens, or may be even has—what I find most astonishing, I think, is the wonder of daylight, of the sun. All the centuries, millenniums—all the history—I wonder if that's why eve sleep at eight, because the darkness still-frightened us? They say we sleep to let the demons out—to let the mind go raving mad, or dreams and nightmares, all our logic gone away, the dark side of our reason. And when daylight comes again...comes order with it.... Come now; we can begin the day. (174)

Agnes's concluding attitude is quite opposite from the opening: it is an affirmation of hope. The play's form describes the course traversed—perhaps a course of madness in the time between—an ordering of life after all the characters have survived the disease of the night's purging experience. This is a good distance from the opening of doubtful balance of reason and the suppression of love at the first sight.

Of all the characters, Claire remains outside, one who has already experienced insight. Judging by her parable of exile and return from the outside and her position in the family as objective viewer, she stands like Agatha in T.S. Eliot's *A Family Reunion*, a choral figure of truth during the dark experience of others.

Agnes (Eyes closed)

I am merely assaying that there is disease here!

And I ask you who in this family is immune?

Claire (Weary statement of fact)

I am. I've had it. I'm still alive, I think.

Agnes

Claire is the strongest of us all.... (157)

Claire exists outside because she has previously inscribed the rhythmic course of departure from the family in search for protection by a surrogate family and has now returned, enlightened about her own self. Her childlike desire for approval and sanctuary in her journey outside the house parallels the search for Harry and Edna who come there as children; the motif of departure and return also foreshadows the movement of Julia and her ultimate acceptance of sad realities. In a masterful extension of the importance of Claire as "clairyovant," Albee makes Claire's self-knowledge prototypical of the emergence of all into final understanding of self. The impelling force behind the change, the metamorphosis—or recognition— is exemplified in Agnes.

Agnes describes her precarious and uneasy familial situation in terms of an artificiality of order and superficiality of love at the beginning of the play. "There are no mountains in my life... nor chasm here"(15). Claire describes the state of their emotions, sardonically. "*Love* is not the problem. You love Agnes, and Agees loves Julia and Julia loves me and I love you. We all love each other; yeas we do. We love each other.... To the depths of our self-pity and greed" (44).

The play unfolds to reveal that beneath the surface of the false exterior, the opposite is true. Harry and Edna play double roles in precipitating crises; they come as children to Agnes and Tobias. "We may go to bed now?" (56); they also usurp the familial hierarchy by assuming a place of authority in the family structure, even though Agnes states that she is the "fulcrum" (89). Edna wants to be the Mommy and refurbish the room (102), and later assumes authority over Julia, as godmother. The couple have become surrogate children and surrogate parents at one time, a state which throws everything off balance—especially for Julia who finds her world in turmoil. The lines for her resistance are drawn. The first act ends with Claire's announcement (with a small chuckle, "that she had been wondering when it would begin") (58).

The two scenes in Act II expose and mature the hidden imbalances of Agnes's "madness," Tobias's guilt, Julia's need for love and home which she has been unable to find in pursuance of her marriages away from home. At the beginning of the night, in the "dusk" forecast by Agnes at the time of her possible onset of madness, unrealities and realities begin to merge in a chiaroscuro which does not wholly reveal nor wholly obscure. Albee creates a Chekhovian ambience in that household of secrets and yearnings. But unlike Chekhov, Albee deals with an element which extends the uncertainties: he plays with sex-changes and confusions of identities which in a perverse way reveal inner psychological states. By means of exposing ambivalence in sex, he erases accepted realities and disorders the superficial status of male and female parenthood, intensifying the trauma suffered by child. The changes and remissions in sex by Agnes and Tobias become dramatic devices for upsetting the balances. Agnes slides almost imperceptibly from female to male and back again; Tobias subsides into a female, as the superficial cohesion of the first act family is shaken from the inside.

"I shall try to hear you out," says Agnes to Julia, "but if I feel my voice changing in the middle of your...rant...you will have to forgive my male prerogative, if I become uncomfortable. Look at my watch or jiggle the change in my pocket" (66). As Agnes becomes masculine, a "pope" to Julia (87), Tobias's feminity is described to Julia by Agnes as he enters, "your mother has arrived. Talk to him" (67). These switches in parental role add to the increasing loosening of Julia's hold on her family and are proportional to her own view of loss of position as child in the house.

Authority in the household vacillates between the two sets, Agnes-Tobias and Harry Edna, adding to Julia's instability. Bigsby sees the intruders as "expressions of the suppressed fears of Agees and Tobias" and as the other half of the schizophrenic couple.[7] This view takes cognizance of the merging of the roles, but does not relate to Julia's situation in respect to the change in parental rank and authority. "They have come in her and ordered" says Julia (120), a play on the word which illustrates the importance to her of the accepted order and custom in the house. The presence of the intruders provokes an increasing instability in the house, as they assume dominance over the familiar situation. In this erosion of established hierarchy, identities are confused so that—as with the quarter in Beckett's *Waiting for Godot*—individual distinctions merge, another way of erasing the realities of outward appearance, throwing customary rank within the group out of balance. As the insidious and pervading presence of societal disease, the force and impulse for familiar disintegration, Harry and Edna take on a timeless existence—as if these evil forces are always present. Tobias calls them "passers-through," to which Claire responds, "As they have been all these years" (96). In structural as well as thematic function, Harry and Edna have brought to the surface the inner disorder existing in the house and like Nick and Honey in *Virginia Woolf*, having provoked the display, they become the audience for a bitter ritual of exorcism.

The night begins as a "festive" one, according to Claire—"from the smell of it, and sister Claire wants to do her part" (92). In preparation for the performance, she has armsingly appeared with her preparation for the performance, she has amusingly with her accordion. Claire describes the preliminary atmosphere as one of "waiting" for a show or waiting in a doctor's office for a "Bi-op-see," a probe of interior cells which may reveal the hidden depths of a cancerous disease (94).

Genet, in *The Balcony*, employs role-playing as a device for revealing the inner nature of the play's personae, staging ritualized ceremonies, each of which is centred on the sexual suppressions of the characters. In a similar vein, Albee stages a curious ceremony of Julia's attempted shooting, in which the major actors seem to know their parts and where (as in *Virginia Woolf*) the violence of the leading character is received by all but Harry and Edna in an attitude of calm expectancy. The scene builds on the example and symbolic replay of Julia's displacement from her room and rank in the house.

After the arrival of Harry and Edna who have gone to get their clothes, the scene is ready and the audience at hand. Time is suspended and goes backward as Agnes prepares Edna, informing her that Julia's present condition is like her highly emotional state at the time of her brother Teddy's death, "if he ever lived at all" (109). Agnes thus sets the stage for a series of "unreal" (108) associated with Teddy and his death. A distinct parallel emerges her between the earlier intruder teddy and the present intruders, both usurpers of Julia's place, both objects of her jealousy; events which are about to transpire seem known and familiar to the players. In a forecast of what is later to come, Agnes says to Julia:

Agnes

> Well, why don't you ran upstairs and claim your goddam room back! Barricade yourself in there! Push a bureau in front of the

door! Take Tobias's pistol while you're at it! Arm yourself! ("A burst From an accordion."

Claire appears in the archway wearing it.)

Claire

Barricades? Pistols? Really, So soon? (91)

Those actions do occur. Tobias enters and describes Julia upstairs as backed against a wall, eyes wide, in hysteria. Most significantly, in a Genet-like mirrored reversion in time, Tobias augments the Teddy-Julia dream as replay, describing Julia's actions as if they were those of an androgynous child-lover coming to the mother's bed. The actual replay of the shooting occurs like a dramatic spectacle in which each person knows his part. Julia enters, carrying Tobias's pistol "not pointed; awkwardly and facing down" (119). "That's my cue," says Claire who launches into an overture on the accordion, a humorous background of yodels and an "ump-pah base" which seems oddly incongruous with the seriousness of Julia's melodramatic action. Julia screams to her Daddy to "get them out of here get them out of here." Her actions her met with a peculiar calm, the word "calm" appearing consistently as stage direction throughout the scene. Julia continues to act our her hysterical jealousy: "HAVE YOU COME TO STAY FOREVER?" she shouts. In the end she is made to accept the fact that the intruders are there to stay, that "you must...what is the word?, co-exist, my dear," says Edna. Julia, a "confused child" calls on her "M-mother" as she is led to bed by Agnes who will "soothe and solve...and fall to sleep" (123).

Again, as in *Virginia Woolf*, we have the exorcism, the playing out of fears as in a cultic rite which purifies—with the child as instrument. The scene employs the Albee reflecting technique of the child as the scapegoat in the family with his/hers fears violently exposed, and death or threatened death as purgative. The purification extends to a new vision for everybody in the play (except Claire). Julia's exposure of fear suggests a wider reference than her own, extending towards a view of imbalances below the protective colouring worn by all. Bigsby recognizes the symbolic nature of the personae[8] in this ritual which describes the whole of their lives until as he says, they are forced to "wake to the nightmare and face their true image in the mirror."[9]

The ceremony has been a kind of confessional exposing the truths which, as Claire says, "lay on the grassy bottoms" (100), where guilt and death mingle, where sex-patterns undergo sea changes, and the established hierarchy of authority is washed away. Change in Tobias caused by the cleansing exposure of the night, signals the metamorphosis of all others. In his change of view, Tobias who has been "racked with guilt" spends a night in agony and comes from the "nightwatch" into daylight. His literal and physical withdrawal from Agnes has been symbolic and symptomatic of his avoidance of responsibility as displayed in the cat parable; in his agony of thought during the night, he comes to realize that he has an obligation to become involved with his fellow humans even though he cannot love them.

The three-point structural progression from the extremes of imbalance to final order lies more simply in the separate visions of the others, with the exception of Claire who has already found her substitute for love in alcohol. For Harry and Edna, there has come a glimpse of truth which enables them to exist outside protection of the "house" of Tobias. But their philosophy represents a complete antithesis to Tobias's and Agnes's; although they become capable of leaving that "nest," their self-examination in the night leads to the conviction that outsiders such as they cannot really belong to the "family". The intruders depart; they march out of the home as that "house" becomes cleansed of the alienation disease.

As for the others, irony and paradox surround Julia; a failure in love coming home to find love, she must fight for it and fight for place. She is restored to her position with the correction of the balances. As for Agnes, who could be considered as the chief spokesman of the play,[10] the peace achieved at the end is not a utopian order. Agnes has gone from the artificiality of her married life as "rolling, pleasant land" through a complete upheaval of that terrain. Bigsby argues that Agnes rejects her insight and retreats into illusion, contrasted with Tobias's emergence. On the contrary, Agnes, having glimpsed the truth experienced in herself and in company with the others, is willing like George and Martha in *Virginia Woolf* to continue with the acceptance of illusion as an ingredient of the only order man can know. The drawn of the new day, allegorically and realistically, for Agnes is to be lived knowingly, in possession of the facts, recognizing like Prufrock in T.S. Eliot's poem that "time happens. When you do you, sword shield...finally...there's nothing there...save rust; bones'; and the wind" (169). In face of this, her resolute "come now; we can begin the day," is an affirmation of the triumph of spirit over the knowledge of emptiness, a continuing of life accepted as it is. If Agnes is the ultimate spokesman, then the conclusion of this play is that order in human affairs is achievable even in the face of desperate realities because the individual, coming through agony and madness, possesses with himself the capacity to main a balance—delicate though it may be.

NOTES

All quotations from the text are references to Edward Albee, *A Delicate Balance* (New York: Pocket Books, 1967) edition.

1. Ruby Cohn, *Edward Albee*, Univ. of Minnesota, Pamphlets on American Writers, No. 77 (Minneapolis: Univ. of Minnesota Press, 1969), 44.
2. Concerning the metaphoric setting, Gerald Weales observes, "They live in an obvious and unspecified affluence, a mansion in the suburbs of hell, that existential present so dear to contemporary writers in which life is measured in terms of loss, love by its failure, connection by its absence." Gerald Weales, "Stop the Balance, I want to Get Off," *Reporter*, 35, No. 6 (1966) 52.
3. Nelvin Vos. *Eugene Ionesco*; *Edward Albee: A Critical Essay*. (Grand Rapids, Mich. Eerdmans, 1968) 26.
4. Cohn, 37.
5. Michael E. Rutenberg, *Edward Albee: Playwright in Protest* (New York: DBS Publications, 1969), 150.
6. Vos states that the presence of Teddy "haunts the stage, but the topic is avoided." Vos., 27.
7. C.W.E. Bigsby, *Edward Albee* (Edinburgh: Oliver and Boyd, 1969), 100.
8. *Ibid.*, 97.
9. *Ibid.*, 98.
10. This is a position which neither Bigsby nor Cohn takes. Neither gives full consideration to the fact that the play begins and ends with Agnes, the mother.

8

Centrality of the Marginal: New Horizons in Ethnic American Women's Poetry

Shikha Misra

America has from the very beginning been a nation of immigrants. Except perhaps for the Native American Indians, all people living in the United States are either immigrants or others who descended from them. Dominant American culture has, in fact, always been the culture of the outsider. Ethnicity, and hence otherness, has very often been the rule rather than the exception in a multicultural American where today an ethnic woman may forge her own identity and construct her own language.

But, it was not always so. Adopting the language of mainstream culture was an important part of attempts made by ethnic immigrants of the 19th and the 20th century (as opposed to those who arrived with the founding fathers) to gain an American identity and become part of the great American family. The resultant schizophrenic mixture of disparate ethnic discourses, ideologies, languages and cultures is tellingly portrayed in Mary Antin's *They Who Knock at Heaven's Gate* (1914) and Mourning Dove's *Cogewea* (1927). These works anticipate the double consciousness which was to characterize much of later ethnic writing especially that of the Harlem Renaissance of the 1920s and 1930s. Also known as the New Negro Movement, the Harlem Renaissance was the first assertion of a specific Black identity. The women, however, were less successful than the men caught between the passionate desire to be true to themselves, yet lacking the courage to challenge the debilitating stereotype of black woman as loose and wanton, African American women chose the path of least resistance. They wrote on genteel themes, used conservative diction and overall failed to impress an America interested at the time in modernist tropes and experimental techniques.

Yet writers such as Zora Neale Hurston were comfortable with their marginality. Reviled during her own time, her classic work *Their Eyes were Watching God* (1937) assures her a permanent place in the ethnic woman's history. She fearlessly explores the dimensions of ethnic double consciousness, the relation between cultures and discourses—black and white, women and men—conflicts that she portrays and creates a world of her own. She continues to be the source of inspiration for contemporary writers such as Alice Walker and Toni Morrison, who, resisting the pull of assimilation, have carved out a central place in the dominant canon by accepting, celebrating and glorying in their difference.

Ethnicity in America may have found credibility but the fame an ethnic American found herself in a unique position. She was an outsider twice over. She was an ethnic and she was a woman. Now, nearly all American culture—even that which is mainstream—has till recently been seen as occupying an essentially peripheral position *vis à vis* the European center. Thus, the experience of marginality—which has been central to the American nation itself—is best recorded in the writings of the ethnic female. The lot which fell to her was not hers alone but had been that of all Americans at one time or another. Her feelings, her sufferings, her narratives reflected the feelings, sufferings and stories of all peoples of United States. She came to be representational in the true sense.

Convinced that writing is neither a gender-neutral nor race-neutral site the ethnic woman's voice found cogent expression in the convention bound realm of poetry. Employing an experimental, radical and subversive style she undertook to storm, disrupt and dismantle the traditional and hence patriarchal bastion of poetry, for long regarded as a predominantly male dominion. In so doing she aimed at recovering lost ground in order to construct a new order where she could be at the center.

1993 was a landmark for African American Women writers. Toni Morrison was awarded the coveted Nobel Prize for Literature. Rita Dove was officially declared Poet Laureate of the United States and Maya Angelou was chosen to recite the celebratory poem, *On the Pulse of the Morning*, on President Clinton's Inauguration Day. Twenty years earlier, in 1974, poets Adrienne Rich, Audre Lord and Alice Walker accepted the National Book Award "in the name of all the women whose voices have gone and still go unheard in a patriarchal world," with special attention to the "self-determination of all women, of every colour, identification or derived class."[1] These signal honours marked the end of a long day's journey into night as Black women writers finally won for themselves a place in the American sun.

The first known poetic composition by an African American is 'Bars Fight.' Composed by Lucy Terry, a Black slave woman (1730-1821), it was handed down orally for more than a century and is known today for its historic value rather than for any literary reasons. Phyllis Wheatley (1753-1784) was the first African American to publish a book of verse, *Poems in Various Subjects, Religious and Moral* (1773) in which she speaks of her love of freedom and protests against the plight of slaves. Frances Ellen Watkins Harper (1825-1911) was the most important African American woman writer of the 19th century. Adopting the language, conventions and verse forms of the American masters these early women poets appeared to pay due homage to their white rulers. Contemporary critics however see in this mimicking an attempt to subvert and overthrow the master/slave hierarchy even while seeming to pay lip service to the then dominant cultural forms.

The beginning of the 20th century saw the emergency of Harlem, New York as the center of African American resistance to white domination. Nella Larsen (1891-1964), Zora Neale Hurston (1891-1960) and Jussie Fauset (1888-1961) were well-known women of the period for their best work in the field of drama and fiction. Poets Angeline Weld Grimke (1880-1966), Alice Dunbar Nelson (1875-1935), Georgia Douglas Johnson (1886-1966) were writing during this time, yet none of them received the acclaim which their male counterparts commanded.

The contemporary period in African American literature is marked by some significant poetic achievement. Margaret Walker's *For My People* was published in 1942 in the Yale Series of Younger Poets—a signal honour for a Black poet at the start of her career. Gwendolyn Brooks, arguably the most important African American poet, published her first collection *A Street in Bronzeville* in 1945. She won the coveted Pulitzer Prize with her second volume *Annie Allen* (1949) and was the first woman to be elected to the National Institute of Arts and Letters. By the time her third volume *The Bean Eaters* (1960) appeared, Brooks had graduated from being a merely literary person to one with political 'savvy.' She chose to record the miserable lot of her African sisters and metamorphosed from what she calls a 'Negro' poet to a radically aware 'new Black' poet.

Maya Angelou, poet, educator, actress, dancer is an important voice in contemporary African American poetry *Just Give Me a Cool Drink of Water Before I Diiie* (1971), *And Still I Rise* (1978), *I Shall Not Be Moved* (1990) are among her publications. Audre Lord, a prolific writer, published six volumes of poetry between 1968-78. Using a traditional modernist style she talks about many African women in America—and their preoccupation with the themes of violence, oppression, and differences in status. Alice Walker perhaps the most significant poet of the post' 50s is also an internationally acclaimed writer of fiction. Her first volume of poetry *Once* was published in 1970. Written on a trip to Africa when she was pregnant, miserable, it is autobiographical in that each poem is a record of a day successfully lived through. *Revolution Petunias* (1973), *Earthling Poems* (1991) are her other volumes. Others making a mark include Pinkie Gordon Lane's *Mystic Female* (1978), *Girl at the Window*, (1991), Carolyn Rodgers' *How I Got Ovah: New and Selected Poems*, (1976), *Morning Glory: Poems* (1989), and Rica Dove's *Thomas and Beulah*.

*

Asian American women writers are a heterogeneous group comprising Japanese, Chinese, and Filipinos as also Indians, Pakistanis, Koreans, Vietnamese and Hawaiians. Much of Japanese ethnic poetry is riddled with the angst which was the direct result of the holocaust in Peal Harbour. Refusing to separate the literary from the political Toyo Suyemoto, the first published Japanese poet, wrote during her internment in America in the Second World War (1941-1944). She preferred to employ the economical Japanese forms of haiku, hokku, and tanka. Mitsuye Yamada's poetry is the record of the struggle to come to terms with her Japanese cultural identity in a hostile American society. Her volumes of poetry include *Camp Notes* (1976) and *Desert Run* (1988). Janice Mirikitani's work *Awake in River* (1978), *Shedding Silence* (1987), often oral in quality, contains the raw passion of rage at the patriarchal abuse of women and rampant US militarism in Vietnam. Kimiko Hahn's *Air Pocket* (1989) protests US militarism in Nicaragua; in 'Resistance: A Poem on Ikat Cloth' she desires the global manifestations of patriarchy. One more aspect of identity retrieval employed by these poets is the drive to rescue cultural materials from memory and to emphasize a past that is different from Anglo American history. Patricia Ikeda writes poems praising familial values of love, loyalty and stability. Implicit is the ironic undercurrent criticizing a hostile counter-society, which makes of the family a necessary sanctuary.

Chinese women poets have also made their presence felt. In their poems they explore such issues as an ethnic community's nostalgia for the past through modernist and postmodernist experiments with language, reflexivity, allusiveness and opaqueness. An interesting variety of styles inform Chinese poetry: there is the simple, referential, transparent language of Nellie Wong in *Dreams in Harrison Railroad Park* (1977) and the *Death of a Long Stem Lady* (1986), in contrast to Mei-mei Berssenbrugge's vivid diction to depicting ironical, unstable, interior states of mind *Summits Move with the Tide* (1974), and *Random Possession* (1979). Diana Chang uses a post-modernist style delineating how language constructs the very subject it claims to explore (*The Horizon is Definitely Speaking*, 1982; *What Matisse is After*, 1984; *Earth Water Light*, 1991). Poets like Fay Chiang (*In the City of Contradictions*, 1979), Marily Chin (*Dwarf Bamboo*, 1987), Caroilyn Lau (*Wode Shofa*, 1989), Hilary Tham (*Bad Names for Women*, 1989), Genny Lim (*Winter Place*, 1989) deal with intra-ethnic problems, oppressed women characters and fragmented female identities.

Variety of style is what distinguishes Filipina writing as well. There is Jessica Hagedron (*Dangerous Music*, 1975; *Pet Food and Tropical Apparitions*, 1981) whose poetry is marked by experimental, jazzy language, and Brechtian images. Fellow Filipina Virginia Cerenis (*Trespassing Innocence*, 1989) on the other hand uses a style which can best be described as a kind of socially realistic sentimental moralizing. Korean poet Theresa Hak Kyung Cha's *Dictee* (1982) is a rich postmodernist work which employs a condensed, highly allusive vocabulary of French, Korean and English and has been read as both novel and poetry. The text achieves that rare feat of being inseparable from the language—a work where signifier and signified are inextricably woven together to become one. The poetry of Hawaiian Cathy Song (*Picture Bride*, 1983; *Frameless Windows, Squares of Light*, 1988) is grounded in the sonorous pastoral depiction of the natural beauties of the island of Oahu while Juliet S. Krow (*Hilo Rains*, 1988) shifts her attention to her native Hawaii. *Malama* (1985), *Bamboo Ridge* and *Sister Stew* (1991) are publications which show that the recent move has been to exploit the rhythm and colour of pidgin, the dialect spoken on the island and hitherto dismissed as the language of the illiterate.

*

Latina writing in America includes the poems of Chicana (Mexican American Women), Puerto Rican, South American, Central American as well as Hispanic women writers. Chicana writers believe that sex, gender, race and ethnicity are intertwining issues. Besides the usual ethnic problems a recurrent theme is the tension which arises from confrontation with social inequities which are not necessarily gender oriented. Other central motifs are Aztlan (the legendary homeland of Mesoamerican Indian declared a Chicano/a political space during the Chican Rights Movements of the 1960s) and mestizaje (the Spanish/Indian racial and culture syncretism which is basic to Chicana consciousness). Much of their poetry is also inspired by the historical icon La Malinche and the mythical icon La Llorona—both archetypes of woman, sexuality, power and culture.

Powerful Chicana poets include Ana Castillo who has been one of the first poets to offer a woman-oriented alternative to the traditional machismo of early Chicano nationalism. Besides books of poetry (*Zero Makes Me Hungry*, 1975; *I Close My Eyes* (*to See*), 1976; *My Father Was a Toltec*, 1988) she has also written an award winning novel *The Mixquiahuala Letters* (1986). Probably one of the best Chicana poets active today is Lorna Dee Cervantes. Her volume *Emplumada* (1981) has been reprinted several times. Through a complex procedure the fleeting temporal aspect of life signified by the bird plumage (plumado) that moults and is shed with the passing of the seasons is sought to be captured and immortalized by the pen (pluma) and its permanent inscriptions.

Aztlan as concrete space and symbolic presence is dealt with in the poems of Bernice Zamora (*Restless Serpent*, 1976), Sandra Cisneros (*My Wicked, Wicked Ways*, 1987) and Lucha Corpi in 'Veraruz' and 'San Potosi' (1980). In her narrative poem Marina cycle Corpi reinterprets the history of the Spanish conquest through the eyes of Dona Marina. Dismissed as a whore by writers such as Octavio Paz, Marina, the infamous mistress of Cortes, has been reinstated as an important feminist figure—the key foremother of "herstory."

Cherrie Moraga gained national recognition for her anthology *The Bridge Called My Back: Writing by Radical Women of Colour* co-edited with Gloria Anzaldua. Her autobiographical prose poem *Loving in the War Years* (1983) is a successful weaving of techniques and genres (essay, poetry, personal narrative) and a celebration of mestizaje through a bold flouting of literary conventions. Also exploiting *mestizaje* is Carmen Taffola in *Get Your Tortillas Together* (1978) and *Sonnets to Human Beings* (1992),

Puerto Rican writing is an important element of Latina literature. *Nuyorican* or Puerto Rican writers in English, along with other ethnic groups, face the common problem of racial and social discrimination. Early poets include Amewlia Agostini de Del Rio (*Vignettes of Puerto Rico*, 1965; *Song to San Juan, Puerto Rico and Other Poems*, 1974) who uses the technique of *costumbrismo* (regionalism) to evoke childhood memories of her native Yauco and Julia de Burgos (six books of poetry in life span of 39 years, including *Poems in Twenty Furrows*, 1938) who uses modernist modes to explore the female psyche. Sandra Maria Esteves (*Yerba Buena*, 1980; *Bluestown Mockingbird Mambom*, 1990) has spoken up for the urban Latina who has to battle with stereotypical female roles within Hispanic patriarchal culture on the one hand and Anglo-American cultural discrimination on the other. A bicultural practice of switching effortlessly from English to Spanish, sometimes within the same poem, led to the work of these poets being dismissed as 'Spanish.' But in the face of their persistence bilingual poetry has become a popular vehicle for expressing the concerns of a Puerto Rican community hitherto excluded from traditional literature. Boricua, (like Aztlan for the Chicana), has become the indigenous pre-Hispanic, pre-American, idealized space of Puerto Rican dreams.

Cuban American poets Mireya Robles (*Artisan Time*, 1973; *In This Dawn*, 1976), Nancy Morejon, Achy Obejas, Carolina Hospital have explored the texture of a split (island verses mainland) consciousness while dealing with immigrant motifs and life in ethnic ghettos.

Native American writing of comparatively recent origin, since its literature has been chiefly oral, forms a link with the past of America—both native and non-Native. It records the Indian American preoccupation with the all-pervasive and ever-present Spirits which permeate the animate and inanimate universe so that not only humans but rocks, trees, clouds are seen as kith and kin to all. The Western world with its tendency to analyse and fragment fails to grasp the distinctive uniqueness of this magical bonding the exact nature of which is narrated through myth, legend and ritual of the native peoples. The modern Chickasaw poet Linda Hogan (*Winged Words*, 1990) has described how the strong oral tradition of song and poetry has inspired and strengthened her imagination to the point where she feels she can hear the voices of her ancestry talking to her and guiding her in her writing.

Laguna Pueblo, poet Leslie Mormon Silko (*Laguna Woman*, 1972) and Paula Gunna Allen (*Spider Women's Granddaughter*, 1990) perform the role of culture bearers who rework the ancient oral stories and myths into contemporary tales of cultural survival. Thus, Mary Tallmountain in her poem 'Ggaal Comes Upriver' (1991) uses the ggaal (King Salmon) as the symbol of continuation and survival of the Koyukan in the face of colonial oppression.

Other oft-used themes are the honoured place held by women in tribal societies; the organic cycle of female birth, life, and death; woman's unique ability to bestow life and health. Native writers working with such traditional material skillfully transform them into contemporary poems. In 'Rainy Day' (1990) Joy Harjo celebrates the birth of her daughter seeing in her the link between the old and new as she inherits the memories of her ancestors in order to fulfill the dreams of their future. The ancient and powerful American Indian tradition thus written and recorded is an integral feature of contemporary Native American poetry.

*

To sum up, we can say that America, which was once an overtly racist nation is now a more tolerant and inclusive society—a phenomenon especially evident after the African American rebellion against assimilation, and the subsequent Civil Rights Movement which began in the 1950s and lasted for a span of about two decades. In the wake of changing social conditions and due also to the powerful feminist movement of the 1960s women, as members of society, were not only willing to be seen but determined to be heard as well. A new spirit, a new awareness, a new boldness and urgency characterizes the ethnic women poets of the contemporary period and the literary output as a result has been powerful and energetic. The themes they explore range from a desire to confront the cultural contradictions of an immigrant community, to coming to terms with subject positions *vis à vis* a dominant culture, to making sure with the feminists that their voices are heard, dignity restored and traditions preserved.

Although much has been achieved much remains to be achieved. Not irrelevant even today is the feminist outrage of Alice Walker's—

> And the word
> 'sister'
> hissed by snakes
> belly low,
> poisonous,
> in the grass.
> Waiting with sex
> or tongue
> to strike.
> Behold the brothers!

(*Revolutionary Petunias*, 1973)

Ethnic women have laboured under two layers of oppression. Having had lesser choices than their men they often shocked the unwary reader with brutal, often heart-rending, accounts of reality as they saw it. But, according to Walker, the blame does not lie with them. Speaking of the iconic Zora Neale Hurston she comments—

> I can't remember all the times that I would be appalled by some of the views that she (Hurston) held. But it wasn't her fault she had to report things a certain way. That was what *she* found.[2]

Undergoing a trial of fire where pain was the norm rather than the exception these remarkable writers—both ethnic and women—resolutely forged ahead. It was as if the horror and bitterness of their personal angst fuelled them inexorably in a direction which led centerstage. Dauntless they stand today at the threshold of a new millennium waiting to reclaim their legacy and to rewrite history on their own terms.

NOTES

1. Quoted in Rachel Blau DuPlessi's 'Contemporary Women's Poetry,' *The Oxford Companion to Women's Writing in the United States* ed. Cathy N. Davidson and Linda Wagner-Martin (New York: OUP, 1995), 674.
2. David Bradley, 'Novelist Alice Walker: Telling the Black Woman's Story', *The New York Times Magazine*, Jan. 8, 1984.

9

Sex, Violence and Disguise: Postmodernist Problematics in Jerzy Kosinski's *Passion Play* and *Pinball*

Satnam Kour Raina

In 1960, Kosinski made his English publishing debut: *The Future is Ours, Comrade*, a socio-political analysis of Russian life, publishing under the pen-name of Joseph Novak. In this regard, the novelist later remarked "a pen name allows you the fun of remaining anonymous and to openly recommend your books."[1] Such a behaviour became consistent with Kosinski's chosen motto: *Larvatus Predeo*—'I *go forth disguised*.' Disguise becomes marked and repetitive quality among the author's fictional protagonists. Coupled with sex and violence, disguise also constitutes a prominent postmodernist existential motif.

Twentieth century American fiction celebrates and eulogizes the anti-hero, a man thoroughly at odds with the times and imprisoned by them, yet Kosinski's heroes outgrow even this concept of despair. The anti-heroes at least proclaimed their own specific dimensions being either rebels or renegades, possessing substance in their own psychological and social, or anti-social definitions. It became possible to identify them; they carried with them their specific 'tags' their own social reality and historical awareness. Compared to this the self or 'hero' in Kosinski's novels has been stripped completely of such dimensions. It is very difficult to grasp the shape of these men, for they tend to exist only in their separate actions, in their public events and in their private fantasies. Kosinski heroes are formed only by the formlessness of the events and actions that seem to imprison them totally. An unorthodox, experimental and inventive genius of a true disciple and practitioner of postmodernist art and ideology gets exhibited through the depiction of such protagonistic situations. There is nothing in his fiction, which does not happen in postmodernism society. The novels are full of violence, sex and disguise, the main ingredients of postmodernist society to create in our minds "a mode of postmodernism, a particular typology of culture and imagination."[2] In the fictional narratives of Jerzy Kosinski, sex is projected as a vehicle for an intimate encounter, as well as opportunity for self-understanding. Every sexual encounter of the Kosinski fictional hero becomes an important episode in the evolutionary process of the hero's self-awareness, besides symbolizing the "paradoxical postmodernism of complicity and critique, of reflexivity,"[3] besides inscribing and subverting the "conventions and ideologies of the dominant cultural and social forces of the twentieth century Western World."[4]

Sex, violence, and disguise, as intrinsic components of the postmodernist ecstasy in Kosinski's novels are the reminder of the disruptionist, anti-formal and anarchic impact that postmodern culture has wrought upon fictional forms and narratives. When we go in the detailed study of Kosinski's *Passion Play* (1979) and *Pinball* (1982), we will try to analyze how the protagonists of these two fictional works go all out in true maverick style to attain a detotalizing totalized self, by means of sexual aggrandizement, deception, disguise and even libidinal force, which is perfectly in tune with the postmodern problematics.

Passion Play depicts the existential saga of Fabian, the Central protagonist, who undergoes a quest, search of narcissist in pursuit of his image. Fabian is a polo-player who writes books about what it means to be a rider. He lives in his Van Home, a huge vehicle with room for his two horses in the back. Fabian has never been a team man, he makes his living playing one-on-one for stakes, and makes a small amount of money from his books, from lecturing, and from training young girls in horsemanship, as he travels about the country. As an equestrian with expertise in horsemanship, Fabian prefers to teach beautiful high-school-age girls who have an aptitude for the Sport. He not only teaches them riding, but initiates the girls sexually as well. The training he imparts in riding and sex, follows an identical philosophical pattern. In both cases, Fabian aims to tap and extract the total potential latent in his students. Such a choice on part of the hero, symbolizes in postmodernist ethics what has been termed as, "experience of limits.... Of subjectivity, of sexual identity...of systematization and uniformation."[5] Fabian's best student is Vanessa Stanhope, niece of Stanhope, the man who lost his life in the Polo match with the hero. Vanessa becomes the most willing and talented learner in Fabian's twin spheres of instruction, but because she is a minor, and he does not want to be caught and charged with statutory rape, the duo carefully preserve her technical virginity, doing everything they can think of sexually, but always preserving her hymen. Such a paradox from the world of dehumanization, conforms again to the essence of deculture which postmodernist culture breeds.

In the fictional present of the novel Fabian stages a comeback to claim Vanessa who is now a beautiful heiress, in the prime of her youth. He is old and gaunt—older than her father, almost penniless and desperately in need of a job. She has remained a virgin for him; and when he hesitates, she literally forces herself on him, using him to launch her into womanhood. Interestingly, Vanessa is the only person he has really loved and avoided all these years, the final sexual consummation. Having finally launched her into a fast paced existence, he would feel he had fulfilled his role as a teacher. Fabian never wanted to lose Vanessa, but at a later stage now, he prepares his mind to leave her. The woman does all she can to keep him, even presenting him with a no-strings-attached gift of one million dollars, so that Fabian could be independent, and money wouldn't become an obstacle between them. But he recognizes that what she is asking for, is a kind of possession of hi, robbing him of the stern independence and solitude of his nomadic life. He refuses her gift and leaves.

The title of the novel is deliberately ambiguous, referring to the passion of play, the passion of competition in one-on-one field play; but it also signifies Fabian's suffering, his own passion and the play of passion in the hero, that neither horses nor women can satisfy. When Fabian envisions himself in decay, he muses: "Once only the expression of his spirit, had become a form for ageing, nature's own expression."[6] He wants to transcend this physical decay through the passion of poloplaying and the play of the sexual passion. Even as the death's head grins in the mirror, Fabian guides his Van Home in to the heart of still another nameless city, which is for him a "place of deliverance...the habitat of Sex" (8). In these familiar streets where "flesh was only feet away from flesh" (8) the death's head in the mirror could be temporarily ignored, so that Fabian found it easy to allow his sexual desire to romp and play, in the same way as he frees his two polo ponies from the confines of their stalls in the Van Home for exercise and training. Human sex, especially exotic contacts with pubescent girls, trans-sexuals and partners as transient and avid as himself, renews Fabian's belief in not only his sexual potency but his capacity to create his own destiny, to fashion it into his own

existence. Sexual expression, Fabian sees as directly related to the vitality of his own sense of language: "Sex liberated him, giving language to an urgent vocabulary of need, mood, signal, gesture, glance a language truly human, universally available" (8). Real postmodernist essence is created, since instinct or simply intelligence can no longer be trusted as a guide to feeling and conduct. In postmodernist fiction, a questioning takes place, a probing of the "totalizing impulse," which has its roots in some kind of "a late romantic need to privilege free, unconditioned experience."[7] In case of Fabian, the past is demolished and detotalized in order to enjoy an "unconditioned experience." The precedent of the past is considered an inhibition from which the hero is struggling to escape. An infallible technique, by which the hero asserts his self-reflexivity, is of course "the... sexual technique," and it is in this sphere that "protagonists' narcissistic preoccupations have become concentrated."[8]

Fabian finds the young girls he requires by reaching through the pages of the "Saddle Bride," a trade journal of the horse—world. Glossy pictures debutantes of the horse set, are there in this journal, with all their best points listed, almost as if the girls were horses to be offered to the highest bidder. The double-entendre of the journal's title suggesting a play on horseback riding and sexual intercourse, is exploited fully. In true postmodernist fashion, Kosinski is "obsessed with Sex to the extent that opportunities for extra-sexual levels of relationship have died our."[9] Women and horses, Sex and riding, have identical connotations, having double meaning. The favourite mounts of the young girls are also given in the "Saddle Bride." Of Stella, for instance, we learn that she earned a championship award in the "Plantation Pleasure Competition," besides being accomplished in the "Breeders Futurity event for young riders" (175).

While Fabian is teaching the girls horsemanship the analogy between coaching girls in equestrian art and training horses is explicit. Fabian tells that he wishes to put his "brand" on the young high-school girls: "He knew that if Vanessa were to come to him as he willed, it must be to imprint him in her memory; like a colt, she was to be schooled, he at the lead, she following at liberty, without rigs, harness, reigns" (221) when they make love, Fabian mounts the girl according to innovations on mounting horses. Things come to their fullest expression when the hero is with Stella, as sometime he makes love to her wearing spurs and at other times he puts bridles and other gear on her. Sometimes he presses her up against a horse's backside, as if he were actually mating with the horse. Such animalistic and repulsive degeneration of the human world to the animal world, symbolizes the influence of perverted deculture of human actions, a common feature of the postmodernist demonic civilization. Fabian's action of combining and making synonymous, horse-riding and equestrian training and sexual baptism of girls, also signifies the straddling "of the border between the imaginary/fantastic... and the realistic...."[10]

For a while, Fabian had been a friend and sort of paid partner to Eugene Stanhope, a millionaire who played polo as a hobby. But then, the hero got seduced one night by Stanhope's girl friend, Alexandra. The next day, Alexandra claimed that Fabian had attempted to force himself on her and she had necessarily to run out. Stanhope, in a fury, had challenged Fabian to a one-on-one match, and during the match it became clear that Stanhope, was going directly for his adversary, with the intention to murder him. Ironically, with a fluke hit, Fabian hits the ball into Stanhope's head, killing him. A few years later, Alexandra has her new boy friend, a rich South American professional polo player. She seems to have an intention of humiliating Fabian and as such makes her boy friend challenge the former for money, Fabian pools as much money as he can to beg against the South American. The opponent is injured in the rough play and has to concede defeat. Like sex, violence too seems to be pervading the very atmosphere of the novel in a true postmodernist fashion.

As a player of polo, Fabian resists the notion of team-play, and sees the game as "essentially a one-on-one Contest" (33). Gradually, he becomes a "menace to the collective soul of the game," and is dropped pointedly from one team after another, slipping gradually into the "notoriety of isolation, a maverick" (34). Fabian sees polo as a form of dueling, and his victims are not only his mastered ponies and the mounted team opponents but his own team members as well. The hard, wooden ball is a weapon, an instrument of Fabian's personal vengeance. Since Polo involves only establishment people, the hero's touchstones become the extraordinary wealthy, such as the Stanhope and several such people enter and re-enter Fabian's life, even after he kills one of them, Eugene, in contest which denotes revenge rather than a game of Polo. During one match, Fabian imagines a former lover, Alexandra, who once betrayed him, being hit by the ball he is about to strike with his mallet: "Then he saw the ball pounding into Alexandra's head, leveling her ear, the ruptured veins spurting blood, her jaw fallen away" (96). This is only a fantasy, a pleasant conjuring up of a desired act. Yet, the imaging of the acts as a vicarious killing, envisions the polo ball as a weapon to execute revenges. This imagined and real violence goes exactly intune with the postmodernist problematics. Thus, *Passion Play* through the portraiture of Fabian, as a real practitioner of violence and orgiastic sex, becomes a perfect example of the postmodernist problematic individual who virtually plays havoc with people's lives. Like any other Kosinski hero, Fabian in hawk-like fashion, preys upon as well as encroaches into the lives of others, especially women.

Kosinski's *Pinball* (1982) is another typical example of Postmodernist problematics, where sex, violence and disguise constitute the very matrix of the novel, to depict "the emergence of new formal features in culture with the emergence of a new type of social life...."[11] Like his creator, Jerzy Kosinski, the hero of *Pinball*, James Osten, assumes a false identity, the identity of Goddard in order to combat an expected intrusion of society upon the self. Structurally and thematically, the novel reflects the illusory security of wealth and the mirage of success. The action, as the narrative unfolds, is presented in four parts. In the first part we have Patrick Domostroy, once a celebrity as a composer of music and as a performer, and Andrea Gwynplaine, a voluptuous enchantress who indulges in sexual orgies with Domostroy. Andrea is determined to use Domostroy in order to execute a game plan for entrapping Goddard in order to expose the real identity of this singer and composer, who has already become a living legend. Domostroy initiates the action by writing letters to Goddard in the name of a lady who dotes upon the enigmatic celebrity and his music. As Goddard reads these letters, which are written on stolen White House stationery, his relationship to Domostroy is unknowingly established. The second part of the book reveals that Goddard is Jimmy Osten, an unremarkable youth whose public image is that of a literature student but who secretly writes and records the bestselling songs of Goddard. Osten's hiding place, the counterpart to Domostroy's own (an abandoned ball room in the South Bronx called "Old Glory"), is his ranch in California which he calls "The New Atlantis." Here, in the seclusion of his State-of-the-art recording centre, his "House of Sound," Goddard composes his music in a safe, secure and secretive manner. Soon Domostroy's letters penetrate Osten's House of Sound, intervening the mysterious celebrity with the very matrix of the plot that Domostroy has written for him.

In the novel's third part, Domostroy becomes involved with Osten's former girl-friend, Donna Downes, a black pianist also studying at the Julliard School, a school of music aspirants. Domostroy eventually succeeds Osten as Donna's lover, forming still another tie between himself and Goddard. In the fourth and final part, predator and prey finally meet in a bizarre shootout in the empty ball-room of the Old Glory, Domostroy's dwelling place. Here, with the burned out South Bronx as a backdrop, Domostroy finds that he is a victim of a larger plot hatched by Andrea and her boy-friend, Chick Mercurio, a disgruntled and failed rock star, when the shoot out is over, only Domostroy and Osten, now allied in their common status as victims, survive. Each has come to know the other's true identity, and each has been given a singular glimpse into other's wellspring of creativity. The two depart, Osten back to his life as Goddard, Domostroy to brood over his inability to compose.

Domostroy once created an audience that now has turned against him. His listeners are no longer captivated by his music, and as a consequence, he avoids contact even with former fans, knowing that their roles have changed. He plays an organ at Kreutzer's, a rather garish night club in the Bronx, complete with pinball games and a bevy of call girls, works only as an accompanist, preferring not to play alone because "it made the break with his past—as a solo performer—clean and complete."[12] Domostroy's playing at Kreutzer's parallels prior compositions: Bethoven's *Kreutzer Sonata* and Tolstoy's *The Kreutzer Sonata* (1989). Tolstoy's book addresses itself to the power of music and its relation to human sexuality. The main character, Pozdnyshev, relates his long tale of sexual anguish, marital hypocrisy and eventual wife-murdering to a sympathetic fellow passenger on a train ride. Both music and sex are terrible things to Pozdnyshev, precisely because they "transfer" the Self, as he says, into another condition, another perspective Marriage is a hypocritical arrangement, a trap. Pozdnyshev's outbursts against men's lust, women's entrapments and current moral standards, are played off in Tolstoy's book against "The Domostroy," a sixteenth century Russian treatise on moral behaviour which revered marriage as a "mystery." The discarding of "The Domostroy" by modern Russian Society and Pozdnyshev's frantic search for a moral code that confronts honestly the reality of human sexuality, are themes from Tolstoy's novel that reverberate and resound in Pinball. Like "The Domostroy," Patrick Domostroy has been discarded, made to seem old-fashioned: like Pozdnyshev, Domostroy understands that social conventions surrounding human sexuality, are often hypocritical. Domostroy's solution, however, is poles away from Pozdnyshev's. In fact, Pozdnyshev argues for continence before marriage and self-restraint during it. Domostroy seeks out the very qualities of consciousness which horrified Pozdnyshev: unpredictable transformations of himself by means of the power of sex and music, combined. As he says to Donna, who is about to play chopin for him, music is meant to give pleasure,

8. John Aldridge, *The American Novel and the Way We Live Now* (New York: Oxford University Press, 1983), 14.
9. — *The American Novel and the Way We Live Now*, 14.
10. Linda Hutcheon, *A Poetic of Postmodernism*, 61.
11. Fredric Jameson, *Postmodernism and Consumer Society*, Foster (1983), 111.
12. Jerzy Kosinski, *Pinball* (New York: Bantam Books, Inc., 1982), 8. All further references have been incorporated as PB.
13. Linda Hutcheon, *A Poetics of Postmodernism: History, Theory, Fiction*, 40.
14. Ihab Hassan, *The Culture of Postmodernism*, 12.
15. David Daiches, *Politics and the Literary Imagination*, in Ihab Hassan's ed. *Liberations: New Essays on the Humanities in Revolution* (Middletown, Conn.: Wesleyan University Press, 1971), 100-16.
16. Christopher Lasch, *The Culture of Narcissism: American Life in an age of Diminishing Expectations* (New York: W.W. Norton and Company, Inc: 1978), 69.
17. Jonathan Baumbach, *The Landscape of Nightmare: Studies in the Contemporary American Novel* (New York: New York University Press, 1965), 2.

10

Cultural Politics: Experiments in Two Recent Native American Novels

Ms. Nila Das

In last two decades the analytical debates over culture have largely centred around culture as a crucial terrain of power and struggle. Some recent American intellectuals theorize culture in terms that markedly differ from both the modernist macropolitical and the postmodernist micro-political positions, the familiar combat zone. Staked out as a mode to meet the challenges of the rapidly expanding cultural industry of transnational techno-capitalism, the standpoint demands attention.

A serious post-postmodernist reaction to totalitarian culture control is that it de-sensitizes the community towards history, heritage, memory no less than towards the socio-economic-political imbalances within the status quo.

In early seventies, accentuating the necessity of a survival ideology, Herbert Marcuse wrote of opening to "the new dimensions in history" (1972: 71-72). A section of recent theorists of cultural political stress on socio-cultural paradigm shift, and sequential systemic transformation of the political power network. "It is culture that moulds the sensibilities and thus cultural politics attempts to undo the talking and being" (Dauglas Kellner and Steven Best, 1999: 6). Some foundationalist futurists define the "new way of seeing" in terms of its (re)emphasis on basic human values, the quality of life, the structural integrity of personality and relations, a cultural wholeness, without which, they postulate, no civilization can long endure (Ref. Berton 1998). The trend of thought, evidently, expands cultural politics beyond the boundaries of exclusionary group, class, race, gendered counter-culture collisions. In the context, contemporary Native American thoughts on cultural identity as a world-view and basis of a broader political orientation, stand out heralding a therapeutic ideology, an integrating vision that in itself counter-balances if not decentres politico-cultural imperialism.

Explicating the Native American world-view, Scott Momaday, the renowned Pueblo novelist, poet, painter said in an interview, "the whole world-view of the Indians is predicated upon a principle of harmony in the universe. You can't tinker much with that, it has the look of an absolute" (Bruchac 1987: 180). Peter Blue Cloud, the Torquois poet, novelist, story writer speaks the similar way: "there is an essence in us, our own... mystery, which is the power...and this is passed on to the other people" (*Ibidem* 210). Blue Cloud identifies the "power" with the Native American organic/circular perception of existence: "to live is to live in the past, in the present, and in the future. It is a continuous thing...going back to the circle" (*Ibidem* 39). To many contemporary Native American writers reverting to the "circle" is a matrix for creating consciousness against the "warp speeded" technocratic civilization given over to the "power of now."

Utilizing literature as a site for political socialization is not new. Development of a cultural paradigm and/or apparatus for socio-political analysis open possibilities of going for new aesthetic forms. For the recent Native writers, restrained by historical contingencies and commercial vernacular as they are, it is a challenging venture to find a machinery of meaning that makes political sense, and can validate their socio-cultural paradigm as a viable if not vital part of the envisioned renewal of the commodified civilization.

A number of recent Native American novels are experiments in living through the Native world-view or ideology as an inroad to cultural politics. Mostly the novelists incorporate the view through history and lore. For this, they often revert to making wide use of culture specific images. Preservation and communication of knowledge, cultural history, value and belief systems through stereotypical images have been an age old device in Native American oral literature. Specially folktales developed an entire technology of using images so that the community could memorize them, and retain the values through them.

Conscious, as they are, that the immediate identification of the culture specific images is no longer easy for the present readers or the characters, the contemporary novelists often develop the narratives over the initial distance, at times critical distance between the receiver and the received image or the concept evoked by it. In course of the novels, sometimes the received image is recognized as a culture ideal, and the receiver resists counter-pressures to attune him/herself to it. Sometimes the distance between the image and the receiver widens, plunging the receiver into an irreprievable marginality. In some novels the distance initiates the character to a dialectical experience, with the antithetical perspectives, value polarities, complex interacting relations finally shaping up a co-ordinated body of ideas about living in society. In some novels the readers rather than the teachers, attain the dialectical perspective. Expectedly, the novels are resistant to conventional narrative patterns. Time jumps back and forth. Some novels are but a collage of memories, reflections, dreams, facts and fiction.

Let us read two Native American experimental novels and trace the pattern the aesthetic forms relate to cultural-political implications. The random choice is self-explanatory.

We begin with Thomas King's *Green Grass Running Water* (1993). King, a Charokee-German-Greek professor of American Indians Studies, chooses for the novel an intricately textured multi-perspectival plot that blends cross-cultural mythology, oral history, literary allusion, symbolism, lived experience, fantasy. The novel, divided into four parts (four, a unifying number in Native tradition) is woven in and out of several apparently disparate individual stories that actually mirror a variety of socio-cultural-political attitudes. The attitudes predominate the novel. The short chapters frequently shift the point of view, diverting the reader's polemical participation.

The title of the novel refers to a standard phrase in the nineteenth century land treaties protecting Indian rights in perpetuity. In the novel, the phrase also stands for the Native perception of life as an originative fluidity, a resurging vitality that opens to unconstrained possibilities. The novel begins with the image of the water, the primeval life-source: "In the beginning there was nothing. Just the water." Throughout the novel, the image is recurrently used as a cultural critical optic.

A major storyline moves around the construction of a massive hydroelectric dam tied up in litigation suit over Indian treaty rights. The dam, erected over a sacred tribal river, betokens the hegemonic techno-capitalist version of reality ("Government built it to help Indians.... We are all supposed to be millionaires" 449). To Eli stands Alone, the university professor who fights the suit, the actual combat is ideational: "It's the idea of the dam that's dangerous" (206). Eli's small ancestral property ("green grass") including a cabin, blocks the dam's spillway, keeping it from operating. In the context, the "green grass" counter-balances the adamantine scheme of things. Expectedly, doubts are raised over the outcome of Eli's anti-regime suit. "As long as the grass is green, and the waters run," replies Eli, himself all-too-aware that the phrase is but a metaphor. "Treaties were hardly sacred documents." In a novel of ideas, however, metaphor has its own strength.

Ideational and social resistance to hyper culture's power and control is registered in the other stories too, although the cultural-political front line is not always sharply drawn for the Native characters themselves. The five Blackfoot Indians living on or near Blackfoot reserve, on whose life-narrative the novel develops, are adrift in time as barely observable parts of the overbearing, hierarchical racist and resistant socio-political machinery. All have careers that range from T.V. salesman, tourist trap operator to lawyer and university professor. All find it hard to "accept the concept that lay at the heart of business and Western civilization" (330), yet none can do without it. In their own respective ways they search for a theme, a life-plot that truly includes them.

The immediate stories of the Blackfoot Indians are rotationally intersected by a surreal account of four aged Native shamans, the escapes from a mental institution or institutionalized power structure. Driven by a cosmic purpose, Lone Ranger, Hawkeye, Ishmael, Robinson Crusoe (names make them a cross-cultural group) observe, comment on, at times help determining earthbound action. In each part of the novel, one of the four, takes turn as a narrator of a feminocentric Native myth of creation. Sometimes the storyteller de/re-constructs the original tale, making it parallel, collide with and act the catalyst of the stories of the present time. The legendary Coyote, the mischievous trickster of the Native lores, who sings and dances the world into existence, occasionally intervenes. His benign humour defuses the ideational collisions to gentle resistance and tolerant hope.

In part I, the Lone Ranger's tale of the First Woman who made the Garden and lived with Ahdamn, cuts across the American frontier history as the mystical characters encounter "live rangers" pointing their guns at both. The story trails off with the pair catching a train to Florida, with a bunch of Indians having chains in their legs. The First Woman and Ahdamn also have chains in their own legs. "Is this a puzzle?" asks Coyote. "We are going to set it right," says the storyteller. The de-/re-constructed myth can be read as a socio-political metaphor, if the reader is prepared to accept it.

In Ishmael's story of the Changing Woman, who falls down from the sky on the "White" canoe, the core character herself turns into a listener, and eventually into a participant in the Moby Dick adventure. "Why are you killing the whales?" she asks Ahab. "Oil, perfume too.... We kill things that are useful, or thing we do not like," replies the captain, the mastermind of oppressive utilitarianism. The Changing Woman insists on identifying the whale as the black whale Moby Jane. The whale punches a large hole in Ahab's ship. "What happens to Ahab?" asks the Changing Woman. "He will be back. He always comes back," replies the whole. The recurrence, in the context, acts its own critique.

The novel ends with the Blackfoot Indians and the four shamans preparing to gather for the Blackfoot Sun Dance ritual for renewal of life. An earthquake breaks out. The dam gives way, so does Eli's cabin. The land rises around like waves, the water rolls on "as it had been for eternity" (455). The novel returns to the starting point with image of water as the primeval life force. The aged four return to the asylum. "They always come back" comments an attending staff. "It is spring again. Everything is green. Everything alive" (461) celebrates the relived asylum in-charge. The images denoting apocalyptic, reversal, renewal, continuity, eternity appear unconvincing in the socio-political context. The imposed celebration invites more doubt than assurance. Throughout the novel the both/and logicality, the tolerant hope, the literary jugglery with mixed myths and metaphors fail to integrate the basically oppositional paradigms of the Native and Euro-American cultures into a richer life-story for both.

Returning to myths necessitates re-entering another history of human spirit, another concept of the structure of human existence. The a-temporal transpersonal view of human situation in terms of renewal can counter-balance historical tensions and frame a healing ideology if the mind is oriented towards it. In *The Woman Who Owned the Shadows* (1982), the second novel of our choice, Paula Allen, the Laguna-Lacota-Lebanese American poet, novelist, critic, cultural theoretician, probes the issue through a close focus on the experience, thoughts, memory imaginings and realizations of Iphanie Atencio, a mixed-blood class Western educated Native American woman. Ephanic represents the Native generation caught between the none-too-familiar tribal past and the none-too-aculturated Euro-American present, mostly in terms of mutual confrontation.

In her theories Allen prescribes a dialogue with the past as a way to reach beyond the limit situation of the present, and a better mode of coping with it: "The tribes seek through... sacred stories...to embody, circulate and share reality, to bring the isolated private self into harmony and balance with this reality" (1975: 112-13). In *The Woman Who Owned the Shadows* she uses a large number of Native myths and legends, projecting every sacred myth as a symbolic process. The novel experiments whether a contemporary Native American Woman (in Native myths woman is the harbinger, and preserver of life, race and society) can own the multifarious socio-cultural-political "shadows" in her life and outlook, as she lives through contacts/confrontations with the mainstream culture as well as with the other ethnic groups. In the context, absorbing the contraries synchronises a larger ideological orientation.

Allen's novel too runs into four parts, each part introduced with a feminocentric myth of creation and preservation. The myths mirror the organic wholeness of Native American life, sensibility and culture. Ephanie's own life-story sharply contrasts the mythical tales.

The first part begins with Ephanie recovering a severe psychic breakdown. She tries to sort the parts of her dislocated self through process of remembering, half hoping that memory would act the catalyst. The recollection of her childhood aspiration to be tall and serene (her name itself was for "someone tall and serene. Someone filled with grace"), and the reversed reality in course of her contact/confrontation with the dominant culture and its value system, stimulates her to reaffirm herself through her Native cultural roots.

Back at her village, Ephanie meets her White American grandfather, who opted the Native life ways, shared joy, grief, life and death with the tribal community. The Native and the mainstream cultures did meet at the elementary level. "Maybe their bonds were more important. Who knows?" Ephanie ponders. The basic human values, the integrity of relations need restitution as foundations of cultural-political ideology, enunciate the recent theoreticians. Ephanie, however, cannot readily attune herself to the guiding principle.

The mythical story in the second part is on the rite of exorcism. In pursuit of psychic exorcism for herself, Ephanie makes for the north-west urban life, imitates the money-status-success oriented white American life pattern. The Euro-American community does not own her: "she was not extoric." A college-read woman, who had involved herself in the struggle for Civil Rights, had smoked dope. Worn mini-skirts, Ephanie contradicts the stereotypical image of the Native female, created and fostered by the mainstream culture.

Ephanie's second marriage to a Japanese American, who himself suffers from identity dislocation, presents another dimension of the socio-cultural-political situation. The marriage collapses as Ephanie refuses to seek any entry point to the Japanese-American community and culture. Nor does her husband to hers. The sickness remains in her mind. The psychic rite of exorcism remains unperformed. Incapable of owning or resisting the paradoxes in her life, the rebel-compromiser attempts to commit suicide, but stops at the last moment as she remembers her grandmother Shimanna, who had brought the "shadows" of two seemingly discreet cultures into accord in her life. She had waited all her life through, waiting being her way of coming to terms with the society and the self. It is a motto the granddaughter has failed to inherit. In Native belief, kinship bond ties succeedingly generations to the core of cultural tradition. Ephanie accepts the responsibility of continuity. The unexpected stance makes one wonder if physical continuity guarantees the continuity of tribal spirit of vision.

REFERENCES

Allen, Paula Gunn, 1975. "The Sacred Hoop: A Contemporary Indian Perspective on American Indian Literature," *Literature of the American Indians*. Ed. Chapman Abraham. New American Library.

— 1982. *The Woman Who Owned the Shadows*. San Francisco: Spinsters/Aunt Lute.

Bertman, Stephen, 1998. "Hyper Culture." *The Futurist*. Dec. 18-23.

Bruchac Joseph, 1987. *Survival This Way: Interview with American Indian Poets*. Tuscan: University of Arizona Press.

Eliade, Mircea, 1960. *Myths, Dreams and Mysteries: The Encounter Between Contemporary Faiths and Archaic Realities*. Trans. Philip Mairet. New York: Harper Torchbooks.

Killner, Dauglas, 1999. "Postmodern Politics and Battle for the Future."

Best, Steven *Illuminations*. 1-13. C:/WIN95/DESKTOP.

King, Thomas, 1993. *Green Grass Running Water*. Boston: Houghton Mifflin Company.

Marcuse, Herbert, 1972. *Counter Revolution and Revolt*. Boston: Beacon Press.

11

Postmodernism as Feminine Text: A Study of Toni Morrison's *Sula*

Deepsheekha Kotwal

By undermining the master narratives postmodernism creates new space for pluralism, marginality and difference, values also stressed by feminists. Black feminist writing is a desperate, act of self-definition and find a 'room of one's own' by the wilful occupation of the marginal space. It is a gendered fight against invisibility and inaudibility, challenging authority, icons, stereotypes and sexist values. Writing as a feminist inevitably makes one a postmodernist because it is a political act which involves decolonization, decanonization and the creation of alternative worlds of private powers.

The postmodernist feminine writer does not merely play with concepts, she deconstructs in order to reconstruct. Her writing is open-ended text rather than work fragmented. Multiple narrative voices are heard, in fact there is a possibility of multiplicity of narratees. She does not topple the phallocratic order but disrupts and modifies it from outside. Helene Cixous defines feminist practice of writing as something that cannot be theorized or coded and is only written by subjects who are 'breakers of automatisms; by peripheral figures that no authority can ever subjugate,' Elaine Showalter, has called it the 'wild zone' of feminine space. It is mapped by the 'double-voiced discourse' of feminist-writing, double voiced, because it voices the social, literary and cultural heritages of both the muted and the dominant.

French theorists like Luce Irigaray, Julia Kristeva, Helen Cixous and Monique Wittig say women write the "difference" that subverts many basic assumptions of Western humanism. Female art is conceived as a "Dark Continent" beyond the laws of white patriarchy. It is translated from blackness, like a new way of communicating rather than an already formed language. Post-structural feminism has emerged as a powerful alternative discourse to the void left by the deconstruction of humanism.

Toni Morison is a dominant voice of this alternative discourse. She reflects a consciousness that writes both from and about a 'wild zone' that is outside of literary convention and disrupts traditional norms of sexism, racism and classicism. She debunks hegemonic critical theory that mystifies rather than clarifies Afro-American feminine texts. Her work is historical, political and artistic but it defies the critical strait jacket of traditional critical theory. She defines her text as "difference," "I am not *like* Faulkner, I am not *like* in that sense."[1] The very concept of canonicity is subverted by Morison because she represents language as difference rather than as cohesive discourse. She debunks western literary cannon by speaking what it considers unspeakable. Barbara Hill Rigney states: Morrison "does write the feminine text; she does compose a literature that is distinctly African American; her works do constitute a contribution to postmodernism; she is a deconstructionist. Or, she is none of these things because she is all of them—and more. She writes in the difference, in the spaces and margins from the vantage of otherness which then becomes the familiar."[2]

On the surface Morrison's second novel *Sula* delineates the experiences of the Black community of Bottom, but its central focus is on Sula and Shadrack who subvert all accepted norms of conventional society. The Bottomites, always, wondered what Sula and Shadrack were all about. Black historically signifies a lack in Western discourse. In Morison's novel by a process of reinterpretation it becomes "is" from "not." Sula is motivated by a strong sense of Me-ness and she looks at life not as something to be blindly accepted rather as something to be challenged. To explore Sula's quest for authentic self-hood Morrison develops her character in relation to the other, her community, her family, the Peace women and her soulmate Nel.

Though the novel is named after *Sula*, she is not the sole focus of the novel like Jane Austen's *Emma* or Charlotte Brontë's *Jane Eyre* are in the novels named for them. Sula shares the quest for a black identity with Nel, Shadrack, Eva and the community at large. Her identity is multiple, she is both an individual as well as a symbol. Different people see different things in Sula. For the towns people Sula is a witch, for Nel she is a soulmate, for Shadrack she is an ideal communicant. Morrison created Sula from her imagination and then allowed her to craft herself. Sula balances herself with the animate quality of life in the Bottom and connects herself to its past. This ambivalence extends to the portrayal of Sula's character too. Morrison bombards her with a host of negative images, of an alazon, compulsive rebel who cocks a snook at convention, in her destructive events, she is a silent spectator to the deaths of Chicken Little by drowning and Hannah by burning. Sula is allowed to die a lonely death and it seems Morrison hates what she has created a la Frankenstein. Yet on the obverse side Sula is a highly individualized portrait of a strong and unique woman and her quest for authentic selfhood arraigns her against a dormant and conventional community. Sula's kinetic personality subverts the hegemonic social mores of Bottom and shakes the community out of its slumber.

The "death of the self" is characteristic of all postmodern fiction. For the Blacks, who are marginalized by dominant discourse, a sense of identity is constructed through impersonal and social relation of power rather than through the reflection of an inner essence. In Morrison's fiction there are no whole men or women, she subverts traditional Western motions of the unitary self by presenting a fragmented notion of identity. Toril Moi writes:

> As Luck Irigaray and Helene Cixous would argue this integrated self is in fact a phallic self, constructed on the model of the self-contained, powerful phallus. Gloriously autonomous, it banishes from itself all conflict, contradictions and ambiguity. In this humanist ideology the self is the sole author of history and of the literary text; the humanist creator is potent, phallic and male-God in relation to his work, the author in relation to his text. History, or the text becomes nothing but expression of this unique individual all, art becomes autobiography, a mere window to the self and the world, with no reality of its own.[3]

Feminine language is based on the complex biology of women and is inherently multiple as is the feminine self it seeks to express. Therefore, in *Sula* Morrison's characters represent multiple and fragmented selves which are inevitably amorphous always merging with the concept of blackness. Identity is always provisional, there can be no isolated ego striving to define itself as separate from the community. Individual characters are inevitably formed by social constructions of both race and gender.

Shadrack is a lunatic fisherman who had spent a year in a mental asylum after he returned from the War. On witnessing the death of a fellow soldier in an explosion Shadrack was left psychologically and physically impaired, "he saw the face of a soldier near him fly off...the rest of the soldier's face disappeared under the inverted soup bowl of his helmet. But stubbornly taking no direction from the brain, the body of the headless soldier ran on, with energy and grace, ignoring altogether the drip and slide of brain tissue down its back."[4] Shadrack faced with fragmentation of the self seeks to tie "the loose cords of his mind." He has a dream in which "he saw a window that looked out on a river which he knew was full of fish" (10). Morrison's use of Jungian terms indicates Shadrack, like Biblical namesake, is seeking to emerge from the fire of war (act of re-memory). The window symbolizes the conscious that is outwardly seen and the river is symbolic of the Collective Unconscious. The window also refers to his cabin by the river where he caught fish. The twenty-two-year old Shadrack is just twenty-two miles away from his home Medallion which thus becomes synonymous with the self.

When he sees his reflection in a toilet bowel in the prison cell where he is kept he saw "a grave black face. A black so definite, so unequivocal, it admonished him. He had been harbouring a skittish apprehension that he was not real that he didn't exist at all. But when the blackness greeted him with its indisputable presence he wanted nothing more" (13). Shadrack's disorientation is symbolic of the Black community which has lost touch with its historical past. The acceptance of blackness as a positive presence by Shadrack is in stark contrast to Pecola in *Bluest Eye* who sees blackness as an absence and wants to have a presence by desiring a white skin and blue eyes. To overcome his fear of death he institutes January third as National Suicide Day. Initially Shadrack led a solitary parade but slowly he and Suicide Day became part of Bottom Life. Finally the community followed Shadrack in "a pied piper's band" to their death in the tunnel. Shadrack's fragmented personality is aptly set forth in the bedlam he creates on the streets with his disorderly, vulgar and drunken behaviour to the pristine neatness and order of his cabin, "the neatness, the order startled her, but more surprising was the restfulness. Everything was so tiny, so common, so unthreatening. Perhaps this was not the house of the Shad. This sweet old cottage, with its made-up bed? With its ragrug and wooden table?" (61-62).

Similarly Sula is a "Centreless protagonist."

> Hers was an experimental life—She had no center, no speck around which to grow. She was completely free of ambition, with no affection for money, property or things, no greed, no desire to command attention or compliments—no ego. For that reasons

> she felt no compulsion to verify herself—be consistent with herself. (118-19)

During Sula's childhood neither her grandmother Eva nor her mother Hannah served as positive role models of domestic bliss and security. On the contrary the two women in their personal lifestyles exhibited all the characteristics of non-conformism to traditional mores of society. Like them Sula was determined to be accountable to no one but herself for the direction of her life, "I don't want to make somebody else. I want to make myself" (92). To make of one's self a single entity is impossible, for all selves are multiple, divided and part of a greater whole. For instance the rose shaped birthmark on Sula's forehead not only individualises her ambiguous essence. The birth mark represents a variety of images, a tadpole, a snake, a flower and it changes colour as Sula grows older. Morrison employs such emblems like she does blackness not just to distinguish individuals but to symbolize their participation in a greater entity like community or race. Sula is a pariah for Bottom because her promiscuous and shocking lifestyle appals the community. Even in death she is shunned by the community yet in life as well as in death Sula has the power to effect the community substantially.

Nel and Sula are both in search of "Me-ness." Sula considered Nel "the closest thing to both an other and a self" Mbalia says, "Nel and Sula represent two extremes, their surnames are, indicative of each. In Nel Wright's household too many directions are given. Nel's house is incredibly orderly. In Sula Peace's household, none are given. "It is a household of throbbing disorder."[5] To be right (Wright) means to conform to society; to be at peace is to choose your own path. Combined together the two girls would have made a wonderful human being. In childhood they find relief in each other's personality but in adulthood Nel succumbs to the norm while Sula rebels against it. The characterization of Sula and Nel shows the self as something perpetually in process. In the end Sula discovers she and Nel were not one and the same thing. When Sula beds Jude she is simply making a distinction between sex and friendship, while Nel who is playing the conventional role of the betrayed wife sees this as a betrayal of their friendship. Sula who had no sense of ownership or moral responsibility failed to see what all the fuss was about,

> "And you didn't love me enough to leave him alone? To let him love me. You had to take him away."
>
> "What do you mean take him away? I didn't kill him. I just fucked him. If we were such good friends, how come you couldn't get over it." (145)

At the moment of death Sula thinks only of Nel, after her death realization comes to Nel that it is not Jude but Sula she misses in her life. In a cry full of loss and nostalgia she says: "We was girls together.... Lord, Sula...girl, girl, girl" (174). Thus identity remains relational as the kaleidoscope of the self seeks to define itself in relation to the community.

The plots of Toni Morrison's novels are not conventional ones with a distinct beginning, middle and end. A feminine text starts on all sides, all at once, it is endless, and does not stop. The plot of *Sula* is feminized because it represents multiple points of view, theirs is no climax and no resolution in the usual sense. *Sula* as a novel subverts textual unity and defies totalized interpretation. It is named after *Sula* but begins from the perspective of Shadrack. It is interpreted from both points of view, i.e., a double voiced discourse. Eva Peace is the archetypal Great Mother. Abandoned by her shiftless husband Boy Boy, she has no means to support her three children. She disappears from the town and reappears after eighteen months with only one leg. It is rumoured she stuck her leg in front of a train and after it was amputated she claimed welfare money to support her family. When her daughter Hannah catches fire Eva throws herself out of a window and tries to douse the fire with her own body. Hannah who equates loves with play asks Eva about her love for her children. Eva explains she never had time for recreation: "There wasn't no time...soon as I got one day her comes, a night. With you all coughin and me, watching so TB wouldn't take you off...what you talk bout did I love you girl I stayed alive for you can't you get that through your thick head" (69).

If the emphasis here is on the sacrifices Eva has made as a mother Morrison shifts the discourse to Eva as a "Terrible Mother" who has emasculated her son by calling him Sweet Plum. When he returns from the War scared psychologically, he seeks an escape in drugs. Eva feels betrayed as a mother because all the sacrifices she had made seemed to have been in vain, so she burns Plum in order to save him from further degradation. The giver of life becomes the take of life as well. Moreover, the burning of Plum is seen both in terms of the myths of marginalized as well as dominant discourse. It is interpreted in the African concept of eschatology, because the image of whiteness and light signifies the fluid of the uterus and twilight symbolizes rebirth. The "great wing of an eagle pouring a wet lightness over him" (47) refers to the Western myth of death and rebirth as the eagle stands for the phoenix which is born from the same fire in which it dies.

The double voiced narrative is visible in the use of language as Blacks write and speak in a language they do not own. Paradoxically they speak in silence, they are the voice of the voiceless. Sula the central character is defined as "no speck, no center." Her presence is actually an absence. As young girls Sula and Nel are defined more by what they are not than what they are, "neither white nor male." The absence of Eva's leg is responsible for her presence in her family and community. Her sacrifice has bestowed on her a mythic presence which people cannot ignore. When Ajax deserted Sula, she was reminded of his presence by his absence, "she could find nothing, for he had left nothing but his stunning absence. An absence so decorative, so ornate, it was difficult for her to understand how she had ever endured, without falling dead or being consumed, his magnificent presence" (134). As Morrison explains in "The Afro-American presence in American Literature" that "invisible things are not necessarily 'not there,' that a void may be empty, but is not a vacuum. In addition, certain absences are so stressed, so ornate, so planned they call attention to themselves arrest us with intentionally and purpose...."[6] In death Sula remains deathless, a potent presence in the lives of Nel, Shadrack, Eva and even the Bottomites who despised her as an evil witch. As Morrison said, "she doesn't stop existing after she dies. In fact what she has left behind is more powerful after she is dead than when she was alive."[7]

In *Sula* the concept of time is circular and arbitrary rather than chronological and linear. Through this technique of "desubstantification" Morrison seeks to subvert a linear projection of history, by expressing the untold story in fragments and pieces. The plot in *Sula* unfolds in a chronological fashion from 1919 to 1965. Medallion where the whites live and Bottom inhabited by the Blacks constitute the binary opposition of the story. The writer subverts traditional expectations in several non-linear ways. Firstly she deliberately misnames the actants of the plot. Medallion (up) is actually a rich and fertile valley which a white farmer did not want to give to his black slave. He cheated the "nigger" by giving him barren land on the top of the hill (bottom). This transaction becomes a symbol of the relationship between the two communities. The whites destroy Medallion by their rampant commercialization and then look towards the hills (Bottom) for leisure and relaxation so Bottom is torn apart to make place for a lush golf course. The young Blacks shift to the valley in search of better prospects and just the old and poor Blacks are left prospects and just the old and poor Blacks are left behind with the rich white people who have built properties there. Ironically Bottom and

Medallion instead of melting into one another simply change places as opposites. "In an endless quest for happiness, fulfillment and order, like dogs chasing their tails, the white move geographically and intellectually in a whimsical, cyclical fashion, while the blacks react in a desperate attempt to define themselves in a topsy-turvy, fickle world. Chronological time means very little when history repeats itself."

Secondly, Morrison uses nature and setting to serve as a context for the chapters which are divided chronologically. Sula returns to Bottom in 1937 but what the people remember is "the plague of Robins, that accompanied her." The image of Robins shitting on the Bottom community portends Sula's future relationship with Bottom. The novel begins after the First World War in 1919 and ends long after the Second World War, in 1965 which was considered a period of great social progress. The Blacks who moved into the white community have exchanged community values for each value, Material prosperity has brought spiritual death hinting at the unending nature of the exploitation of the Blacks.

Postmodern literature uses fantasy and surreal landscapes because it sees mimetic representations as insufficient to represent reality. In *Sula*, Morrison has used a blend of mimesis and fantasy to awaken readers into an awareness of the harsh reality that daily erodes selfhood. In this novel death is not incidental or natural but seen as resulting from evil or self-neglect Hannah's horrible death by fire is presaged by a number of omens. There was a wind that brought to rain, Hannah's strange question to Eva if she ever loved her children and her dreams of the wedding in the red dress. Sula is perceived as a witch by the community. It was said she was not human because she had a horrible birthmark, drank bear and never belched, mosquitoes never sat on her, she never had chicken pox as a child, and strangely Shadrack was civil to her when he ignored everybody else. To ward off her evil eye Bottomites "laid broomsticks across their doors at night and sprinkled salt on the porch" (113). In order to understand the endless oppression of their lives. Bottomites search for an evil agent, Sula conveniently fits the handle and is made a scapegoat. In lieu of significant political action as an oppressed group they prefer to vent their frustration on Sula.

Toni Morrison is a myth basher and in her work she has laundered one American ideal after another. The traditions of home, family and romantic love are all satirized in *Sula*. The near lesbian relationship of Sula and Nel, the all female household of Eva stand out in stark contrast to the restricting atmosphere of heterosexual relationships and nuclear families.

There are no successful marriages in the novel, no "normal" households and no happy families. Helene Wright maintained the stereotyped image of the middle class domesticated housewife and mother and she attempted to suppress any funky urges her daughter Nel might have, had, "she drove her daughters imagination underground." When she groveled before a white ticket checker on the train and is forced to urinate with Nel in open fields at station stops because of her colour, Nel realizes that her mother cannot survive with any sense of dignity outside Bottom. Stifled by her mother's bourgeois mentality and the oppressive neatness of her house Nel loved the freedom of Sula's disorderly house:

> She preferred Sula's woolly house, where a pot of something was always cooking on the stone, where the mother, Hannah never scolded or gave directions, where all sorts of people dropped in, where newspapers were stacked in the hallway, and dirty dishes left for hours at a time in the sink, where a one legged grandmother named Eva handed you goobers from deep inside her pockets or read you a dream. (29)

Eva is positioned in the text as the embodiment of self-determinism. Unlike the lackluster Helene Wright, Eva is arrogant, domineering, mean spirited and practical. Helen and her neighbours are "frightened," "fearful," "vulnerable" while in the Peace household people are "funky," "fanciful," "sweet" and "spontaneous". Eva, Hannah and Sula represent a dynamic self-sustaining all women family while Helene Wright represents a sterile nuclear family distanced from its Black roots.

From her mother Hannah Sula had learnt that "sex was pleasant and frequent, but otherwise unremarkable." Sula treated men as play things to be used at will and has nothing but contempt for women who cling to their husbands, "the narrower, their lives, the wider their hips." The childhood bonding of Nel and Sula is an example of lesbian jouissance while heterosexual relationships for Sula are nothing more than passing time, "there was this space in front of me, behind me in my head, some space. And Jude filled it up. That's all. He just filled up the space" (144). In having sex with Nel's husband, Jude, Sula strikes at male domination which condemns women to the agony of possessive love, making one women enemy, of the other. The germ of an adult lesbian bonding is there in Nel and Sula's childhood relationship but they fail to bring it fruition, Nel succumbs to the mores by opting to be Jude's wife and the mother of his children while Sula refuses to conform. Sula realizes long before Nel does that "a lover was not a comrade and could never be—for a woman."[8]

In her revisioning enterprise Morrison begins "her search by addressing the black family, and then broadens her scope to the black community, regions of the United States, foreign lands and alien cultures, history and reality."[9] Each novel moves forward to a new concern without completely leaving behind the previous ones. Her writing is a participatory enterprise as she projects a self that invites the reader to identify with this self. Morrison's success as a great American writer is due to two factors:

> Her ability to manipulate her insider/outsider status, for she both subverts and maintains, is exploited by and exploits the literary establishment, and by her recognition that her double consciousness can never be, perhaps never should be, integrated into a single vision. Indeed, she is in the truly remarkable position of being able to articulate with near impunity two cultures, one black, the other white American.[10]

NOTES

1. Barabara Hill Rigney, *The Voices of Toni Morrison* (Columbia: OUP, 1991), 105.
2. Hill Rigney, 105.
3. Toril Moi, *Sexual/Textual Politics: Feminist Literary Theory* (London: Methuen, 1985), 8.
4. Toni Morrison, *Sula* (London: Picador, 1991), 8. (All subsequent references to this edition have been mentioned with page numbers in parenthesis).
5. Doreatha Drummond Mbalia, *Toni . Morrison's Developing Consciousness* (London: AUP, 1991), 41.
6. Hill Rigney, 65.
7. Hill Rigney, 24.
8. Denise Heinze. *The Dilemma of Double-Consciousness: Toni Morrison' Novels* (London: UGP), 127.
9. Heinze, 12.
10. Heinze, 10.

lives of servants and marginal figures. They are unlike their economically sound counterparts in other stories. Questioned as to why she made this choice, Lahiri answers:

> Both of these characters came out of observations of people when I was there (in Calcutta). What drew me to writing about them was partly a projection of my feelings of being marginal when there, of not being of the culture, of feeling foreign even when this was a place my parents call home and refer to in their minds as home, even though they've been away for 30 years.[11]

A *Real Durwan* was written, recalls Lahiri, "soon after returning from a visit to India in 1992, in my bedroom in parents' house in Rhode Island." It is a pathetic but powerful pen-picture of an old lady, Boori Ma, a self-appointed sweeper of the stairwell of a multi-storeyed building. Her services 'came to resemble those of a real durwan' (73) because in exchange for her lodging below the letterboxes, she kept the 'crooked stairwell' spotlessly clean. Apart from this, 'the residence liked that Boori Ma, who slept each night behind the collapsible gate, stood guard between them and the outside world' (73). But the same residents, accusing her of the theft of the basin, throw her out one day because they need a real durwan as 'Boori Ma has endangered the security of the building' (82). The vagaries of material possession plaguing human relationship from the matrix of this story. '*The treatment of Bibi Haldar*' is yet another moving tale of a 29-year orphan, unmarried girl who suffers from a mysterious disease. Staying in a married cousin's house, she has to sleep, initially, on a camp cot downstairs but is, subsequently, forced to stay in the storeroom for ever as her presence, the Haidar couple to get her married, as the doctor in charge of Bibi's case, after performing a series of blood tests 'concluded that a marriage would cure her' (161). The Haldars, reluctant to waste their money on a wedding, finally move off to a new place leaving her in the store. She lapses into a prolonged isolation until one day when the women discover her 'about four months pregnant' (172). Later one evening she delivers a son but would never 'tell us who had done it'. The women help her in raising the child and setting up a small shop in the storeroom. The story ends on a positive note: "for years afterwards, we wondered who in our town had disgraced her.... But there was no point in carrying out an investigation. She was, to the best of our knowledge, cured' (172).

A brief but deeply intimate adulterous relationship constitutes the core of *Sexy*, the fifth story in this collection. Miranda, a young American, falls in the love with Dev, a married Bengali investment banker, whose wife has left for India for a few weeks. They spend every night together, visit shops and theatres, drink sangria and eat pulled pork. One Saturday afternoon Dev takes Miranda to his favourite place in the city called Mapparium, where, standing on a transparent bridge thirty feet apart, Dev wants Miranda to say something. Dev's whisper turns her on, 'she felt it under her skin, under her winter coat, so near and full of warmth that she felt herself go hot.

"Hi," she whispered, unsure of what else to say.

"You are sexy," he whispered back. (91)

Miranda's relationship with Dev begins to lose its passions and warmth after the arrival of Dev's wife. Dev's Sunday afternoon sessions of warming up Miranda does not help her recover from her gnawing loneliness. She offers to look after for a day, Rohin, the unhappy and precocious nephew of her friend Laxmi. Rohin asks Miranda to put on, for his entertainment, the slinky cocktail dress that she had once bought with Dev in mind. When she puts on the dress, Rohin, like Dev in Mapparium, remarks, 'you are sexy' (107). Miranda's heart skipped a beat. Later, forced physically by Miranda to explain the meaning of sexy, Rohin whispers, 'It means loving someone you don't know' (107). "What the classicist and philosopher Martha Nussbaum has called 'Love's knowledge' is her eclipsed by a radical scepticism that is primarily sexual, but must also be implicitly philosophical."[12] The story ends with Miranda's deciding to end the relationship and returning to places where Dev had kissed her.

The poignant realization of the loss of the familiar is well treated in the next story *Mrs. Sen.* Mrs. Sen, the 30-year old wife of a mathematics professor, becomes the baby-sister for the 11-year old Eliot, the son of a single mother who has her own problems to cope with. It is hinted early that Mrs. Sen wants the job for an engagement to fill up her lonely afternoons. The more she tries to connect herself to the new environment, the more she finds herself cut off from her milieu. Eliot gradually becomes Mrs. Sen's companion and confident and discovers that only two things make her happy—letters from home, that is, India and whole fresh fish from the sea. Unfortunately, she does not know how to drive and her husband has no time to drive her to the fish market. 'It is very frustrating,' says Mrs. Sen 'to live so close to the ocean and not to have so much fish' (123). She turns nostalgic and adds that 'in Calcutta people ate fish first thing in the morning, last thing before bed, as a snack after school if they were lucky' (123). Mrs. Sen's acute sense of alienation reaches its climax when she turns philosophical in a conversation with Eliot:

12

Home and Abroad: Jhumpa Lahiri's *Interpreter of Maladies*

Parmanand Jha

A slim looking Jhumpa Lahiri has emerged as a literary heavyweight following the publication of her debut collection of short-stories *Interpreter of Maladies* which won her the prestigious Pulitzer Prize, American's ultimate literary accolade, for the year 2000. Being the first South Asian to win an individual Pulitzer, Lahiri has joined the elite-company of such illustrious winners of Pulitzer as Steinbeck, Norman Mailer, Saul Bellow, Ernest Hemingway, Pearl S. Buck and John Updike. With the stunning success of her very first literary venture, Lahiri has turned out to be the expatriate version of the one and only Arundhati Roy.

Born in 1967 in London to parents who emigrated from Calcutta, and raised in Rhode Island, America, Lahiri has been a precocious child, writing since the age of seven. "The very first stories I wrote, in the second grade during recess," reminisces Lahiri, "were imitations of what I'd learned to read in the classroom. Writing allowed me to observe and make sense of things without having to participate."[1] Her c.v. amply shows her insatiable thirst for academic distinctions—B.A. in English Literature from Barnard College, M.A. in English, M.A. in Creative Writing, M.A. in Comparative Studies and Ph.D. in Renaissance Studies—all from Boston University where she taught creative writing, apart from a short stint as a teacher in the Rhode Island School of Design. She has been a recipient of the Transatlantic Review in 1993 and a fiction prize from the Louisville Review in 1997. In 1999 she was named by the *New Yorker* as 'one of the 20 best writers under the age of 20' alongside Sherman Alexie, David Foster Wallace and Jurot Diaz. Three of the stories in *Interpreter of Maladies* have already been published in the *New Yorker* and the title story has been selected both for the O'Henry Award and the award for the best American short stories.

Lahiri has been shuttling periodically between Boston and Calcutta. She views Calcutta as "a bustling unruly city, so different from the small New England town where she was raised."[2] She has spent a lot of time in Calcutta with her grandmother, reading, writing and observing things and finding solitude in life amidst a crowd of people. Calcutta was the nursery where she learnt to think imaginatively. "Calcutta nourished my mind, my eye as a writer and my interest in seeing things from a different point of view,"[3] reminisces Lahiri.

Interpreter of Maladies, with the sub-title "Stories of Bengal, Boston and Beyond" deals with the problems of the immigrants in an alien land; the yearnings of exile, the emotional confusion, et al. Being an immigrant herself Lahiri deeply felt the importance of family bonds which tie people to their homelands. She has undergone the trauma of failing to find her identity in a world where she could never have a sense of belongingness and so tries to fall back upon the treasured memories of what Rushdie calls 'Imaginary Homeland' which with its vibrant colours and versatility gave life of her starving existence and stimulated her very being. "I went to Calcutta," Lahiri admits "neither as a tourist nor as a former resident—a valuable position, I think as a writer. I learned to observe things as an outsider and yet I also know that as different as Calcutta is from Rhode island, I belong there in some fundamental way, in the ways I didn't seem to belong in the United States."[4] This is rather a problem faced by many others of Indian diaspora. In an interview with the *Newsweek*, just after winning the Pulitzer Prize, Lahiri said, "It's hard to have parents who consider another place 'home'—even after living fully at home here. There's no body in the whole country that we're related to. India was different—our extended family offered real connections. To see my parents as children, as siblings was rare."[5] But the pangs of not growing up in India took its own toll. She further adds, "I wasn't a part of things. We visited often but we didn't have a home. We were clutching at a world that was never fully ours with encouragement."[6]

This dilemma, this sense of emotional exile and the excruciating pain it entails is at the core of the stories in *Interpreter of Maladies* which has not only gleaned rare reviews from countless critics but has also been sold in Germany, the U.K. and in several other countries. Six of the nine stories in the collection have their settings in America and deal with the lives of Indian immigrants who hope to find a better life. But what they flashed across Lahiri's mind following an encounter with an acquaintance in Boston way back in 1991. "I asked him," recalls Lahiri "what he was doing and he said he was working as a translator for a doctor who had a number of Russian patients who had difficulty in explaining their ailments in English. I had never heard of a job like this, but realized that it was a necessity in places where doctors and patients didn't have a common language."[9] It is a complex story about an Indian-American couple—Mr. Das, his wife Mina and their three children—Tina, Ronny and Bobby. They hire the services of one Mr. Kapasi as a tour-guide and chauffeur, to see the famous Sun Temple at Konark. During their conversation en route the couple learn that Mr. Kapasi, besides his part-time job of a tour-guide, works as an interpreter in a doctor's clinic where he translates the Gujarati spoken by some of his patients. Mr. Kapasi who 'found nothing noble in interpreting people's maladies' (51) is flattered to hear Mrs. Das describe it as 'romantic.' Unlike his wife, who 'had little regard for his career as an interpreter' (53), Mrs. Das had 'reminded him of its intellectual challenges' (53). Mrs. Das, whose 'shaved largely bare legs' had tickled Mr. Kapasi earlier, seemed to be interested in him, he thought, and he began to imagine a romantic relationship with her. His fantasy is further fed when the couple invites him to be included in the photographs they take. Mrs. Das even asks him for his address so that she could send him copies from America. The real crisis, however, comes when Mrs. Das discloses to him, in the car, that one of her two sons, Bobby, was conceived from her husband's Punjabi-Indian friend in a mutually agreed sexual encounter in her own house. Mr. Kapasi, the interpreter of people's maladies, fails to offer any remedy to Mrs. Das's malady (which may be her failing marriage and falling out of love for life), which she had vainly hoped, he would offer. All he can utter is, "Is it really pain you feel Mrs. Das or is it guilt?" (66). Mrs. Das's scornful silence shatters the fantasy of Mr. Kapasi and thus puts an abrupt, early end to their strangely intimate relationship. "When I was putting the collection together," writes the author "I knew from the beginning that this had to be the title story because I think it best expresses thematically the predicament at the heard of the book—the dilemma, the difficulty and often the impossibility of communicating emotional pain and affliction to other, as well as expressing it to ourselves. In some sense I view myself as a writer, in so far as I attempt to articulate these emotions as a sort of interpreter as well."[10]

The two other stories with their setting in India are *A Real Durwan* and *The Treatment of Bibi Haldar*. In these two stories Lahiri portrays the

lives of servants and marginal figures. They are unlike their economically sound counterparts in other stories. Questioned as to why she made this choice, Lahiri answers:

> Both of these characters came out of observations of people when I was there (in Calcutta). What drew me to writing about them was partly a projection of my feelings of being marginal when there, of not being of the culture, of feeling foreign even when this was a place my parents call home and refer to in their minds as home, even though they've been away for 30 years.[11]

A *Real Durwan* was written, recalls Lahiri, "soon after returning from a visit to India in 1992, in my bedroom in parents' house in Rhode Island." It is a pathetic but powerful pen-picture of an old lady, Boori Ma, a self-appointed sweeper of the stairwell of a multi-storeyed building. Her services 'came to resemble those of a real durwan' (73) because in exchange for her lodging below the letterboxes, she kept the 'crooked stairwell' spotlessly clean. Apart from this, 'the residence liked that Boori Ma, who slept each night behind the collapsible gate, stood guard between them and the outside world' (73). But the same residents, accusing her of the theft of the basin, throw her out one day because they need a real durwan as 'Boori Ma has endangered the security of the building' (82). The vagaries of material possession plaguing human relationship from the matrix of this story. '*The treatment of Bibi Haldar*' is yet another moving tale of a 29-year orphan, unmarried girl who suffers from a mysterious disease. Staying in a married cousin's house, she has to sleep, initially, on a camp cot downstairs but is, subsequently, forced to stay in the storeroom for ever as her presence, the Haidar couple to get her married, as the doctor in charge of Bibi's case, after performing a series of blood tests 'concluded that a marriage would cure her' (161). The Haldars, reluctant to waste their money on a wedding, finally move off to a new place leaving her in the store. She lapses into a prolonged isolation until one day when the women discover her 'about four months pregnant' (172). Later one evening she delivers a son but would never 'tell us who had done it'. The women help her in raising the child and setting up a small shop in the storeroom. The story ends on a positive note: "for years afterwards, we wondered who in our town had disgraced her.... But there was no point in carrying out an investigation. She was, to the best of our knowledge, cured' (172).

A brief but deeply intimate adulterous relationship constitutes the core of *Sexy*, the fifth story in this collection. Miranda, a young American, falls in the love with Dev, a married Bengali investment banker, whose

wife has left for India for a few weeks. They spend every night together, visit shops and theatres, drink sangria and eat pulled pork. One Saturday afternoon Dev takes Miranda to his favourite place in the city called Mapparium, where, standing on a transparent bridge thirty feet apart, Dev wants Miranda to say something. Dev's whisper turns her on, 'she felt it under her skin, under her winter coat, so near and full of warmth that she felt herself go hot.

"Hi," she whispered, unsure of what else to say.

"You are sexy," he whispered back. (91)

Miranda's relationship with Dev begins to lose its passions and warmth after the arrival of Dev's wife. Dev's Sunday afternoon sessions of warming up Miranda does not help her recover from her gnawing loneliness. She offers to look after for a day, Rohin, the unhappy and precocious nephew of her friend Laxmi. Rohin asks Miranda to put on, for his entertainment, the slinky cocktail dress that she had once bought with Dev in mind. When she puts on the dress, Rohin, like Dev in Mapparium, remarks, 'you are sexy' (107). Miranda's heart skipped a beat. Later, forced physically by Miranda to explain the meaning of sexy, Rohin whispers, 'It means loving someone you don't know' (107). "What the classicist and philosopher Martha Nussbaum has called 'Love's knowledge' is her eclipsed by a radical scepticism that is primarily sexual, but must also be implicitly philosophical."[12] The story ends with Miranda's deciding to end the relationship and returning to places where Dev had kissed her.

The poignant realization of the loss of the familiar is well treated in the next story *Mrs. Sen.* Mrs. Sen, the 30-year old wife of a mathematics professor, becomes the baby-sister for the 11-year old Eliot, the son of a single mother who has her own problems to cope with. It is hinted early that Mrs. Sen wants the job for an engagement to fill up her lonely afternoons. The more she tries to connect herself to the new environment, the more she finds herself cut off from her milieu. Eliot gradually becomes Mrs. Sen's companion and confident and discovers that only two things make her happy—letters from home, that is, India and whole fresh fish from the sea. Unfortunately, she does not know how to drive and her husband has no time to drive her to the fish market. 'It is very frustrating,' says Mrs. Sen 'to live so close to the ocean and not to have so much fish' (123). She turns nostalgic and adds that 'in Calcutta people ate fish first thing in the morning, last thing before bed, as a snack after school if they were lucky' (123). Mrs. Sen's acute sense of alienation reaches its climax when she turns philosophical in a conversation with Eliot:

> 'Eliot,' Mrs. Sen asked him while they were sitting on the bus, 'will you put your mother in a nursing home when she is old?'
>
> 'May be,' he said 'but I would visit her every day.'
>
> 'You say that now, but you will see, when you are a man your life will be in places that you cannot know now.' She counted on her fingers, 'You will have a wife, and children of your own, and they will want to be driven to different places at the same time. No matter how kind they are, one day they will complain about visiting your mother and you will get tired of it too, Eliot. (131-32)

The story presents the difficulties faced by Indian wives in an alien culture, without friends or family, struggling to cope with the new surroundings they can't call their home. Also, it skillfully probes the mixed feelings of an American child fear, astonishment, fascination and awe—toward an Indian abroad. "In this beautifully observed story East meets West in the shared experience of loneliness and the poignancy of Mrs. Sen's situation in handled with utmost delicacy and control unsullied by any hint of mawkishness."[13] The story is partly autobiographical. Lahiri herself admits, "Mrs. Sen is based on my mother who baby sat in our home. I saw her one way but imagined that an American child may see her differently reacting with curiosity, fascination or fear to things I took for granted."[14]

The reasons behind the emotional and spiritual distance between spouses trying to adopt the culture of their new home are excellently explored in the next story *The Blessed House*. Sanjeev, an ambitious corporate vice-president has recently married Twinkle, a 27-year old girl. Their marriage is arranged through their parents who are old friends. They are only in the second month of their marriage and certain things begin to nettle Sanjeev 'the way she (Twinkle) sometimes spat a little when she spoke, or left her undergarments after removing them at night at the foot of their bed' (142). The discovery of a white porcelain Christ, St. Francis postcards and Noah's arc-light switch plates left behind by the previous tenants proves deeply unsettling. While the wife seems fascinated by the discovery, the husband is scornful and dismissive. He underestimates the tenacity of her whim and threatens to dispose of the found only to find her in tearful rage, who shouts at her, 'I hate you' (149). The story, like *A Temporary Matter* ends with a makeshift peace.

The last story *The Third and Final Continent*, is to quote Khushwant Singh, 'perhaps the best in the collection.' It tells us of an Indian immigrant who reminisces about his first few weeks in America thirty years ago. Having studied for four years in London, he makes a short trip to Calcutta for his arranged marriage with Mala. He moves to America only a week after his marriage, to work as a librarian at the MIT. His wife has to wait for her visa for six weeks before she can join her in America. On his arrival in Boston he checks into the local YMCA. The year is 1969, the year of America's landing on the moon. "The timing is more metaphorical than coincidental; the new country the narrator stumbles upon is as foreign to him as the moon."[15] Sometime later, the narrator rents a room in the home of a 103-year old crotchety widow, who lives by herself and is visited infrequently by her 68-year old daughter. The widow is finicky about the class of the renter (he must either be from Harvard or MIT), about punctuality (both in matters of returning time and rent) and about the American Flag on the moon. When the narrator's wife joins him, the lady, Mrs. Croft, puts her through a series of scrutiny and interrogation and finally pronounces 'she is a perfect lady' (195). It is through this scrutiny that the narrator feels empathy for his bride as it reminds him of his own experiences as a confused and bewildered stranger in London. 'I like to think,' says the narrator 'of the moment in Mrs. Croft's parlour as the moment when the distance between Mala and me began to lessen' (196). They later on shift in their new house and come to know one day of Mrs. Croft's death in an obituary column. The narrator grieves over as if he had lost his own mother. The story comes to an end on a positive note as the narrator and his wife reconcile themselves to the new life on the third and final continent.

The nine stories in the collection offer a wonderful variety of experiences gathered from the cultural clashes ripping outward in many directions. The trauma of dislocation, an acute sense of loneliness and the pangs of estrangement suffered by the millions of 'exiled Indians' who try unsuccessfully to balance themselves between 'home' and 'abroad' are the major maladies Lahiri attempts to interpret. Most of her characters keep hanging in limbo—between two identities—non-Indian and Indian, a fact that brings Jhumpa Lahiri fairly close to Bharati Mukherjee, another successful interpreter of 'immigrant angst.' In her attempt to diagnose the discrepancies that exist between 'home' and 'New home' abroad, Lahiri stands in close proximity with Shauna Singh Baldwin and even Amit Choudhury. In interpreting the 'meaning of distance' (as Miranda does in the story *Sexy* Lahiri recalls Amitabh Ghose in *The Shadow Lines*). In writing about the disturbed conjugality and its impact on the young couple (*A Temporary Matter*) she reminds us of Carver. In portraying tour-guides, seduction and subsequent disillusionment (*The Interpreter of Maladies*) she comes close to Hemingway. She even draws obvious parallels with Isherwood when she writes about a landlady scrutinizing her young renter evoking contrary feelings of disgust and tenderness (*The Third and Final Continent*). The octogenarian young man Khushwant Singh likens her to Somerset Maugham: "Without striving to impress, without a witty turn of phrase, Jhumpa manages to hold the readers' interest. She reminded me of Somerset Maugham."[16] Like Bernard Malamud who dealt at length with the Jewish community in America, Lahiri has created a literature revolving around the Indian immigrants in America. Like James Joyce, she displays an insight and a penchant for documentation of details. Her keen awareness of the contours of her craft coupled with the use of direct, clear, elegant and sparkling prose makes *Interpreter of Maladies* a timeless treatise.

NOTES AND REFERENCES

1. Jhumpa Lahiri, "To Heaven Without Dying," FEED (www.feedmag.com. copyright, 2000) 16-1-00 17:2.
2. Lavina Melwani, "Interpreting Exile," *The Hindustan Times*, April 23, 2000.
3. Surabhi Khosla, "Beauty, Brains, Bounce and Bengal," *Swagar*, Nov. 2000, 155.
4. Lavina Melwani, "Interpreting Exile," *HT*.
5. Surabhi Khosla, "Beauty, Brains, Bounce and Bengal."
6. *Ibid.*
7. Jhumpa Lahiri, *Interpreter of Maladies* (Delhi: Harper Collins, 1999), 12.
8. Jhumpa Lahiri, *To Heaven Without Dying.*
9. Naresh Fernandes, "An Interview with Jhumpa Lahiri," *Literature* 13 June, 1999, 18.
10. Lavina Melwani, "Interpreting Exile."
11. Gaiutra Bahadur, *An Interview with jhumpa Lahiri*, Citypaper.net. Sept. 16-23, 1999.
12. Aveek Sen, "Enigmas of Distance," *The Telegraph*, 1-5-2000.
13. Susan Ram, "Chronicle of the Cultural Interface," *Frontline*, Oct. 22, 1999, 71.
14. Vibhuti Patel, "Maladies of Belonging: An Interview with Jhumpa Lahiri," *Newsweek International*, 20-9-1999.
15. Greg Changnon, "Interpreter of Maladies," *The Atlantic Journal Constitution*, ajc.com 1 of 2.
16. Khushwant Singh, "Between Two Continents," *The Telegraph*, 1-5-2000.

PART-C

13

A Dance of the Forests: A Socio-Political Satire

Basavaraj Naikar

A Dance of the Forests is, perhaps, the most difficult and complex among all the plays written by Wole Soyinka on account of its archetypal characters, multiplicity of themes, complicated symbolism and multidimensional technique. Since the play was occasioned by the political event i.e., the Independence Day of Nigeria in 1960, Wole Soyinka had to select a theme to suit the occasion. But being a richly endowed mind, he was not satisfied only with the topical theme, but tried to extend its scope to wider and deeper levels by enriching it with multiple dimensions, symbols and theatrical devices. Because of its complexity of theme and technique, the play is likely to baffle the uninitiated reader and compel the serious critic to indulge in interpretive controversies. It is rather difficult for any critic to decide its meaning equally successfully in all its ramifications. Therefore, a humble attempt has been made in the present article to explain the element of socio-political satire so dominant in the play.

Since *A Dance of the Forests* was meant for the occasion of the Independence of Nigeria, Wole Soyinka had to choose a theme that was relevant to his country at that juncture of time. Whenever a country achieves independence, she has to undergo a transitional period in her history marked by the end of the colonial rule and the beginning of postcolonial freedom. Such an experience can be as thrilling as challenging to a nation. The sudden removal of the colonial rule and oppression results in the acceptance along a progressive path by following some great ideals set by the ancestors and gods etc. In other words, a newly independent nation has to face a dilemma as to whether it has to shape its present in line with the past or to forget the past completely and begin on a blank sheet. It is such a dilemma that is selected by Wole Soyinka for dramatic treatment in *A Dance of the Forests*. But far from expressing it in straightforward and transparent manner, he articulates it through the rich and complex African mythical symbolism.

The characters of the play represent three worlds i.e. human, natural and divine—a feature so common to Greek tragedy and epics of the world. The human world is again divided into the ancient and the contemporary ones. Firstly, the characters like Adenbi, Agboreko, Demoke and Rola represent the contemporary civilians of Nigeria, whereas the Dead Man (Captain of army), the Dead Woman (the Captain's wife), the Child, Mata Kharibu, the Court Historian and the Poet represent the ancient life of Nigeria. Secondly, the characters like Agboreko, Araba, Obaneji the Forest Head, Murete, the tree spirits, the river spirits, the spirits of pachyderms and ants signify the natural world. Thirdly, the characters like Eshuoro, Oro and Ogun etc. represent the divine world. Thus, Soyinka offers a complex picture of the Nigerian life where the human, the natural and the divine world are interrelated symbiotically.

The central event in the play happens to be the ritualistic ceremony called the gathering of the tribes and welcoming of the dead. This event might be taken to symbolize the Nigerians' desire for national solidarity and unification on the one hand and their desire for the pursuit of the high ideals of the past on the other. Such desires are, obviously, motivated by the dream of some sort of golden age in the future. But such ideal is, unfortunately, not easily fulfilled on account of the stark ugliness of reality being in conflict with it. Thus, the central conflict in *A Dance of the Forests* happens to be operative between ideal and reality.

The Nigerians, like all the Africans in general, have great respect for the ancestors who provide them great ideals of life for the modern ones—the truth of which is borne out by their rituals and myths. It is this truth which is symbolized by the typical characters like the Dead Man and the Dead Woman who have risen up from their graves and come to the modern world to attend the gathering of the tribes. But the paradox happens to be the fact that these ancestors instead of being welcomed with pomp and glory are simply cold-shouldered. Instead of attracting the special attention of the hosts, these ancestors are forced by circumstances to request the hosts to consider their cases:

Dead Man:	Will you take my case, sir?
	(Adenbi starts, stares, and runs off.)
Dead Man:	(Shaking his head.) I thought we were expected.
	(They both seem to attempt to sense their surroundings.)
Dead Woman:	This is the place.
Dead Man:	Unless of course I came up too soon. It is such a long time and such a long way.
Dead Woman:	Will you take my case?
	(Obaneji stops and looks thoughtfully at them. The Dead Man, listening hard, goes quickly towards him. Obaneji withdraws, looking back at the pair.)
Dead Man:	I thought he might. He considered it long enough.
	(Demoke enters. He is tearing along.)
Dead Woman:	Will you take my case?
Demoke:	(Stops) Can't you see? I am in a hurry.
Dead Woman:	But you stopped. Will you take my case?
Demoke:	When you see a man hurrying, he has got a load on his back. Do you think I live emptily that I will take another's cause for pay or mercy?
Dead Woman:	And yet we'll meet there.
Demoke:	You say you know. I am merely on my business. (Going.)
Dead Woman:	Stop. I lived here once.
Demoke:	That was before my time. (Going, stops again.) Perhaps we'll meet. But the reveler doesn't buy a cap before he's invited.[1]

The Dead Man and the Dead Woman feel really insulted and begin to wonder if they are wanted at all. The Dead Woman expresses her puzzlement, "I know they told me to come. I know I was summoned. What is to them from whom I descended—if that is why they shun me now? The world is big but the dead are bigger...."[2] Thus, there is no concordance between invitation to the guests and reception by the hosts. The ancestors claim a special attention and respect from the living, but paradoxically the living people do not want them perhaps because of their selfish concerns. Rola, for example, articulates her contempt for the dead, "I can't take anyone who happens to wander in, just because she claims to be my auntie!"[3] The disappointment of the guests is matched by the disappointment of the hosts also. The ancestors who are expected to inspire, and bless the living ones unfortunately do not have those qualities, but they have their own complaints and grievances. The hosts feel that something has gone wrong somewhere and consequently wrong people have been sent. As the old Man expresses, "Well, believe me when I tell you that everything has misfired. These people who have come to claim our hospitality do not wish us well. We were sent the wrong people. We asked for Statesman and we were sent executioners."[4] Thus, there is no proper welcome extended to the dead. But the dead have their own grievances. The overall suggestion of the situation seems to be that there is no proper alignment of interest and expectation between the ancients and moderns. Hence the confusion in their motives. The Dead Woman and the Dead Man have their own grievances. The Dead Woman, for example, is tired of bearing and rearing children eternally, although she has been sent by a wombless woman. Likewise she is also tired of bearing the burden of her pregnancy. She wants to be relieved of the burden, she is delivered of only a half-child. Similarly the Dead Man has been suffering from restlessness both when alive and when dead. The crowning frustration of these ancestors happens to be their realization of their dysfunctionality and irrelevance for the modern people. They are, paradoxically, accused of coming to the mortal world before the scheduled time, in spite of the earlier invitation extended to them. Finally, they realise the futility of their visit to the mortal world and return to their realm of the dead. The welcome to the dead turns out to be an insulting farewell to them. The meaning of the central event of the play appears to be ambivalent and Wole Soyinka seems to suggest that the modern Africans need not depend totally on the past and the ancestors, but accept the responsibility of owning up their actions, improving their life independently and shaping their future properly.

Another paradox in the nature of the ancestors happens to be that the Dead Man and the Dead Woman, though dysfunctional in the present were people with high moral principles in their past lives and that even such principled people had been rendered helpless by the feudal powerstructure prevalent in the past. The preponderance of corruption at various levels in various details is shown through the phantasmagoria of the past invoked by Aroni. Corruption happens to be closely linked with countless other vices. Wole Soyinka seems to be satirizing the past which has a powerful influence on the present life. The misuse of power which entails other vices like exploitation, flippancy, lying, cheating, inhumanity, betrayal is expressed and satirized through the depiction of the proceedings of the Court of Mata Kharibu. Sexual exploitation by political power may be seen illustrated in Mata Kharibu's having snatched away somebody's wife. Soyinka's attack on the high-handed legalisation of illegality, shameless opportunism and selfishness are more than obvious here. The illegally acquired woman has attained the status of a queen and is nicknamed as Madame Tortoise.

> Soyinka satirizes the flippancy and brainlessness of the queen through the same scene. When the court begins, Madame Tortoise is very sad about having lost her canary. Unable to show any serious attention to the court matters, she persists in her desire to recover the lost canary. Similarly she has no brains to think about which task to be assigned to whom. She, therefore, asks the court-poet to follow the novice to the rooftop of the palace and fetch it, "And I order you to follow him. When he has retrieved my canary, bring it here to me, like a servant."[5] Rendered helpless by the queenly command, the court-poet allows the notice to mound the rooftop of the palace. But the novice, in his eagerness to please the queen, falls down from the height and breaks his arm. When the Court-Poet brings the canary to the queen with great difficulty, she has already lost interest in the bird:
>
> (The Court-Poet enters with a golden cage, containing a canary.)
>
> Madame Tortoise: You were late returning, poet.
>
> Court-Poet: Such is the generosity of my lady's smiles, the poet is now indulged, and cannot abide storms. Madame, I waited until sunshine was restored....
>
> Madame Tortoise: Is that my canary? I no longer desire it.
>
> Court-Poet: It is the privilege of Beauty to be capricious.[6]

The abduction of someone's wife is a very blatant violation of ethical ideal which is not appreciated or tolerated by the sensible people including the Warrior (who has appeared as a Dead Man in the present time). Mata Kharibu who has abducted the wife of somebody wants to justify his immoral act and defend his kingdom against the enemies belonging to the kingdom of his wife's earlier husband. He, therefore, asks his Commander (or Warrior) to take the army to fight the enemies. But the Warrior refuses to press his soldiers into service for an unjust cause:

Physician: I am trying to help you. Not only you, but your men, who regard you so much as their leader that they can refuse to fight when you order them not to.

Warrior: It is an unjust war. I cannot lead my men into battle merely to recover the trousseau of any woman.

Physician: Ah! But do you not see? It goes further than that. It is no longer the war of the queen's wardrobe. The war is now an affair of honour.

Warrior: An affair of honour? Since when was it an honourable thing to steal the wife of a brother chieftain?7

The Warrior is a man of sterling character who wants to pursue only the right and public values and shun the wrong and selfish ones. He does not approve of Mata Kharibu's abduction of a brother chieftain's wife and the additional demand of her dowry from her former husband through war. The Warrior rightly feels that such a war is an unjust one and that Mata Kharibu cannot justify one sin with other sins. The Warrior, thus, becomes an embodiment of moral consciousness and provides a sharp contrast Warrior is known for his sophisticated moral thinking about the pros and cons of any action before indulging in it. It is exactly this thinking which is not tolerated by Mata Kharibu:

Mata Kharibu: (Advancing slowly on him): It was you, slave! You it was who dared to think.

Warrior: I plead guilty to the possession of thought. I did not know that it was in me to exercise it, until your Majesty's inhuman commands.

(Mata Kharibu slaps him across the face.)[8]

Mata Kharibu does not like the 'thought cancer' either in the Warrior or in the other civilians of his kingdom. He wants them to be dumb obeyers of his commands. There is, thus, a conflict between opportunism and idealism represented by Mata Kharibu and the Warrior respectively.

The use of political power, especially the military force, for justifying the selfish ends has been very powerfully attacked by Wole Soyinka. War-mongering, thus, happens to be an ally of the political evil. In spite of the prophesy by the soothsayer about the possibility of bloodshed on account of unfavourable stars, Mata Kharibu insists upon the indulgence in war and even goes to the extent of selling away the soldiers who are unwilling to fight in the war as slaves. His unscrupulousness and inhumanity have crossed the limits of shame and decency. There is simply nobody to check his callous exploitation of the helpless subordinates of his kingdom.

Bribery happens to be an evil practice that goes with political power. In the feudal bureaucracy, one evil supports and perpetrates another. For example, when Mata Kharibu high-handedly decides to sell a few soldiers as slaves to a slave dealer, the Historian objects to it on the ground that the slave-dealers' bank is too small to contain the big number of slaves. But when the slave-dealer bribes him profusely, he alters his tone and offers a false testification:

Slave-Dealer: I have no wish to argue that point. Mr. Physician, I assure you more sincerely that you are mistaken. My new vessel is capable of transporting the whole of Kharibu's court to hell—when that time does come. The Honourable Historian here can testify to it. I took him aboard... (Behind his back, he passes a bag of money to the Historian, who takes it, feels it and pockets it.) ...only this afternoon and showed him every plank and rope...ask him yourself.[9]

Such official corruption is not special to African past but happens to be a ubiquitous phenomenon.

The corruption of power goes hand in hand with sexual impurity and immorality. When, for example, the Warrior refuses to fight for the queen of Mata Kharibu, he is chained and brought before her. She threatens to torture him and boasts of her ability to ill-treat him:

Madame Tortoise: Torture! I have cause to torture you. Did you know the one who fell from the roof? The one who leapt to his death, on my account?

Warrior: Madame!

Madame Tortoise: He could not understand that I took him, just as I select a new pin every day. He came back again and could not understand why the door was barred to him. He was such a fool.[10]

The queen, thus, revels in her ability to torture the people who do not oblige her on account of their own high principles. When the Warrior refuses to listen to her, she changes her strategy and begins to tempt him sexually. Her sexuality is marked by a shameless opportunism and treacherousness. She does not show any loyalty to Mata Kharibu who has won (or kidnapped) her from her former husband. Chastity seems to be an irrelevant virtue for her. She is even ready to betray her second husband in favour of a third one:

Madame Tortoise: Mata Kharibu is a fool. You are a man and a leader soldier. Have you no wish to sit where Mata Kharibu sits?

Warrior: I cannot hear you Madame, I cannot hear you!

Madame Tortoise: Call me by my name, Madame Tortoise. I am the one who outlasts you all. Madame Tortoise. You are a man, I swear I must respect you.

Warrior: Guard! Guard!

Madame Tortoise: I can save you. I can save you alone, or with your men. Choose. Choose. Why should a man be wasted? Why must you waste yourself for a fool like Kharibu? Choose, and let me be with you.

Soldier: Guard! Guard!

Madame Tortoise: What are you? Men have killed for me. Men have died for me. Have you flints in your eye? Fool, have you never lived?[11]

The Warrior is so strong in his moral principles that he is not at all tempted by the queen's offer of herself and her position. She feels deeply insulted by his rejection of her love:

Madame Tortoise: (her face breaks into fiendishness): I know it was incredible. It could not be. I, Madame Tortoise, spurred by a common soldier. For that! Was it for that?[12]

Now the feeling of insult awakens vindictiveness in her. She wants to get him castrated into a eunuch to guard the harems:

Madame Tortoise (to the Warrior): You are lost. But have your wish. Warriors are sold as men but eunuchs guard the harems of other Mata Kharibus, drooling on wares that they cannot taste. Choose![13]

But the Warrior does not budge an inch. The phantasmagoria of the past, obviously, reveals a picture of corruption, exploitation, adultery, immorality, opportunism, bribery etc., that go with political power. It holds a picture of the enthronement of Evil and the helplessness of Good. The picture of the African past shows the preponderance of evil and remains unanswered. The Warrior who is an embodiment of unswerving moral principles has now come to the modern world of Africa where he is neither really wanted nor sufficiently attended to. One might easily discern Wole Soyinka's view here which seems to be that the African's reverence for the past happens to be only mechanical and not dynamic and that the good of the past remains irrelevant whereas the evil of the past continues to be perpetrated in diverse forms. As Oyin Ogunba rightly remarks, "the satirical point still comes through, albeit in garbled form. Here are a people gathered to rejoice at the attainment of independence with pomp and revelry. But there is really nothing to rejoice at except past crimes and present treachery. The absurdity of the situation comes to light when one realises that amidst the apparent jollity the shadow of death establishes itself unmistakably. In this play, then, the author is not only being satirical; he is being prophetic as well."[14]

The contemporary African world also seems to be one of conflict and corruption. Agboreko, Adenbi, Demoke, Obaneji and Rola are the five major characters who represent the modern African world. They are all aware of the great function i.e. gathering of the tribes and welcome to the dead, that is going to be celebrated shortly. A part of the forest has been cleared for the said programme and a totem has been ordered to be carved by Demoke. The totem is symbolic of the regeneration of the tribes. But their conversation reveals the picture of the present life which is not a happy one. It is marked by corruption, selfishness and inhumanity. Obaneji, for example, knows too much about corruption of his countrymen to be happy about it. He asks Rola:

Obaneji: Don't misunderstand me. It is just that I work as a filing clerk for the Courts. Senior clerk, mind you. I know about people even before I've met them. Know their whole history sometimes. And against my will, I find that all the time. I am guessing which name belongs to who. You don't know how unnerving that can be, especially when one is so often right.[15]

Further, he illustrates his knowledge of official secrets with some important case histories. For example, he narrates the history of a motor lorry nicknamed as Chimney of Ereko as it smoked like a perpetual volcano and had survived eight crashes. Then he narrates the history of another passenger lorry called the Incinerator which had a capacity of forty, but the clerk took a substantial bribe and changed its capacity from forty to seventy. He further tells how the lorry caught fire and burnt sixty-five passengers to ashes:

Obaneji: Yesterday. That is why they called it the Incinerator since yesterday. Of the seventy people in it, five escaped. It overwhelmed you see, and the body was built of wood.... Dry and brittle in the Harmattan season too. They were all on their way here—to the gathering of the tribes.[16]

Bureaucratic corruption happens to be a rampant phenomenon in the present day Africa and there seems to be no remedy against it.

Rola is another important character who signifies the degeneration of the value of sexual purity. Whereas she was an adulterous wife of Mata Kharibu nicknamed as Madame Tortoise in her past life, she has become a prostitute proper in the present world. Thus, she suggests the logical consequence and progressive degeneration of feminine history from adultery to prostitution. Wole Soyinka's creation of such a character (i.e. of prostitute Rola) seems to be satirical by contrastively suggesting the absence of a character of a 'loyal wife.' Prostitution, thus, happens to be the major role of a woman in the modern Africa. Rola does not believe in the institution of marriage and the joys and responsibilities of motherhood and child-bearing. She is not ashamed of her profession or the gossip about her. She snubs Adenbi when the latter tries to tease her by saying that she considers all her customers responsible for their foolish investment or behaviour. She clearly denies the fact that she is the cause of her customers' ruin:

Rola: I regret nothing. You men are conceited fools. Nothing was ever done on my account. Nothing. What you do is boast yourselves all the time. By every action. When that one killed the other, was it on my account?[17]

She thinks that she is not responsible for the foolish behaviour of her customers. Elsewhere she declares very clearly that "This whole family business sickens me. Let everybody lead their own lives."[18]

A totem was required as a symbol for the gathering of the tribes. So it was ordered to be carved by Demoke. Demoke took three days and three nights to carve to totem from the araba tree. The totem is a symbol of regeneration, recollection and solidarity. But the paradox is that Demoke who carves the totem symbolizing the spiritual regeneration is himself subject to deep envy and causes the death of Oremole. Wole Soyinka seems to satirize the blatant gap between the ugly reality and the high ideal of regeneration. As Eldred Jones points out, "Demoke's Totem in *A Dance of the Forests* towers above both the vandalism of the councilors and his own petty human jealousy. There seems to be a persistent hint that the world could be saved only through the artistic, the creative spirit, but spiritual progress is slow."[19]

The significance of the totem is very great for the nation. It is explained by Adenbi:

> An occasion such as the gathering of the tribes—a great thing... it would happen only once in several lifetimes...only once in centuries of history. It is a whole historical epoch in itself. We resolved to carve a totem, a totem that would reach to the sky.[20]

The gathering of the tribes is motivated by a desire of collecting the great people of the past like Warriors, sages, conquerors, builders, philosophers and mystics in order to resurrect the past glory of the nation.

But the irony is—Soyinka seems to suggest and satirize—that something has gone wrong somewhere and consequently the very purpose of the grand programme has been reversed. As the Old Man, father of Demoke points out to Adenbi:

> Yes, it was a fine speech. But control, at some point was lost to our enemies. The guests we were sent are slaves and lackeys. They have only come to undermine our strength. To preach to us how ignoble we are. They are disgruntled creatures who have come to accuse their tormentors as if this were a court of law.[21]

The disappointingly wide gap between the dream and harsh reality is satirized by the playwright through the character of Adenbi who says:

> I see. I had thought how splendid it would all be. Purple robes. White horses dressed in gold. Processions through the town with communion and service around our symbol...by the way I really ought to tell you how disappointed I was with your son's handiwork. Don't you think it was rather pagan? I should have thought that something more in keeping with our progress would be more appropriate.[22]

The gathering of the tribes happens to be a rather disappointing one. All the dreams and ideals of the people seem to be frustrated by the inimical forces.

The forest dwellers like Eshuoro do not approve of the gathering of the tribes. They feel that this function is going to be conducted only at human insistence and that they are not really interested in it. Nor do they approve of the token either. As Eshuoro says:

> The totem, blind fool, drunk fool, insensitive fool. The totem, my final insult. The final taunt from the human pigs. The tree that is marked down for oro, the tree from which my followers fell to his death, foully or by accident, I have still to discover when we meet at the next wailing. But my body was stopped by the impious hands of Demoke, Ogun's favoured slave of the forege. My hand was hacked off by his axe. Trampled, sweated on, bled on, my body's shame pointed at the sky by the adze of Demoke, will I let this day pass without vengeance claimed blood for sap?[23]

Similarly, they are not happy about the human beings spoiling the atmosphere of the forest with their poisonous gas emitted by petrol. Further, Eshuoro feels insulted to know that he is not properly invited to the gathering of the tribes. He, therefore, wants to take revenge upon those who have slighted him.

But the Forest Father wants to conduct the gathering of the tribes in order to chorus the Future through the lips of earth-beings. Hence the three protagonists are masked and reduced to a state of resigned passivity. The Forest Head sits there supervising the programme of listening to the confessions of earth-creatures like the Spirit of the Palm, the Spirit of Darkness, the Spirit of Precious Stones, the Spirit of the Pachyderms, the Spirit of the Rivers, the Chorus of the Waters, the Spirit of the Sun, the Spirit of Volcanoes, Ants and Ant Leaders who narrate their dilemmas. After the confession from these creatures is over, the three protagonists are unmasked so that they can see the rest of the function with their natural eyes. Now the unmasked triplets begin to express their newly earned wisdom through formulas. The first triplet says that he is the End that will justify the Means. The second triplet confesses that he is the Greater Cause. And the third triplet declares that he is the Posterity.

The confession is followed by the 'ampe' dance by the characters. The dance in the African context is supposed to bring about a spiritual realisation and give a new birth as it were to them. Out of darkness and wilderness, there is expected an emergence of light and order. They learn the lesson of sacrifice and expiation and wish to know the future. But the future is not clear to them. Wole Soyinka seems to suggest through the ritual sacrifice and expiation supervised by the Forest Head that although the Africans have a rich religion, mythology and a pantheon of gods, they have to rely upon themselves for their actions. Similarly he seems to suggest that the ancients have become dysfunctional and even disrespectable in the present although they happened to be ideal and integrated people in the past. Soyinka is very ambiguous about the future of the country, because of the corruption in bureaucracy, exploitation of the countless anonymous citizens, selfishness etc. Soyinka laments the spiritual stagnation in Africa. As Eldred Jones explains, "Here there is little real progress in man's spiritual achievement. In other areas to, man seems to reproduce the old types with the changes only in the cultural context in which they operate."[24]

The only way to improve the future of the country is through the spiritual awakening and expiation of their sins and crimes. As Mary T. David has rightly summed up, "A relentless criticism of the nation, not only of the present, but of the venerated past could have been given only by a writer whose love for his country is deep and who has exorcised the fascination of the past. It is the work of a playwright who passionately believes in the need for a spiritual awakening of his countrymen. The criticism is sharp and unsparing but Soyinka also gives the remedy or at least points out the path the nation should follow in order to avoid a catastrophic course. This path is the path of regeneration through atonement."[25]

REFERENCES

1. Wole Soyinka, *A Dance of the Forests, Collected Plays*, and Vol. I (London: Oxford University Press, 1973), 7.
2. *Ibid.*, 8.
3. *Ibid.*, 9.
4. *Ibid.*, 29.
5. *Ibid.*, 47.
6. *Ibid.*, 55.
7. *Ibid.*, 48.
8. *Ibid.*
9. *Ibid.*, 54.
10. *Ibid.*, 56.
11. *Ibid.*, 56-57.
12. *Ibid.*, p. 57.
13. *Ibid.*
14. Oyin Ogunba, "Modern Drama in West Africa." *Perspectives on African Literature*, ed. Christopher Haywood (London: Heinemann, 1979), 104.
15. Wole Soyinka, *A Dance of the Forests*, 16.
16. *Ibid.*, 18.
17. *Ibid.*, 24.
18. *Ibid.*, 9.
19. Eldred Jones, "Progress and Civilization in the Work of Wole Soyinka," *Perspectives on African Literature*, 135.
20. Wole Soyinka, *A Dance of the Forests*, 30.
21. *Ibid.*, 31.
22. *Ibid.*
23. *Ibid.*, 43.
24. Eldred Jones, "Progress and Civilization in the Work of Wole Soyinka," *Perspectives on African Literature*, 136.
25. Mary T. David, *Wole Soyinka: A Quest for Renewal* (Madras: B.I. Publications Pvt. Ltd., 1995), 64.

14

"Only Connect": *Anthills of the Savannah* and Achebe's *The Trouble with Nigeria*

Neil ten Kortenaar

The work of Chinua Achebe is a valuabled locus for studying the interplay of village, ethnic unit, nation-state, and race in the configuration of identity in Africa. Achebe is himself the chief of his village, Ogidi, and at one time he supported Biafran independence from Nigeria. The founder of a journal dedicated to Igbo culture, he is so identified with "Igboness" that his style has been called an Igbo style in contrast to the Yoruba style of Wole Soyinka. More recently, however, he has written *The Trouble with Nigeria*, a brief tract that presumes a stake in the nation-state. Achebe has also, of course, assumed the mantle of spokesman for Africa as a whole, a mantle cast on every writer from Africa and perhaps falling especially heavily on the shoulders of the editor of the Heinemann African Writers Series. That there are tensions between these different identities is, I believe, borne out by the long literary silence that Achebe maintained after the defeat of Biafra and by the novel that finally broke that silence, *Anthills of the Savannah*.

The tensions between these identities are not always acknowledged, and the identities themselves are often conflated. "African nationalism," for instance, does not usually mean the process of nation formation among African states, but the assertion of a black African identity as a means of resisting imperialist European nations of the universal. The identity of Ghana, the first African state to win its independence in modern times, was inextricably linked to Kwame Nkrumah's Panafrican vision. In Simon Gikandi's definitive study of Achebe, the first chapter, entitled "Nation Formation and the Novel," is not about Nigeria but about Achebe's appropriation of a European genre to negotiate an African problematic: vindicating Nigeria and Igbo culture is a part of this larger strategy. Gikandi's conflation of race, nation-state, and ethnic grouping has validity because it is Achebe's own. A grain of hope for the future of Africa is held out by *Anthills of the Savannah*, and it is based on the redemption of an African nation-state.

Nationality, ethnicity, and race are not always conflated in this way. Christopher Miller has forcefully made the case for the centrality of ethnicity to an understanding of African literature. According to him, the nation-states into which Africa is divided can be dismissed as arbitrary divisions that were imposed by the colonizers and that have little impact on the identity of the colonized (48). Kwame Anthony Appiah shares Miller's opinion on Africa's nation-states: he argues that a second wave of African fiction has abandoned realism, as well as the nationalist legitimation association with realism, because nation-states have been hopelessly compromised by the African bourgeoisie. Novelists now are Pan-African in their vision, he concludes, and they open their texts to the suffering of the continent. My essay assumes that the nation-state, the ethnic culture, and the continent are configured differently in the imagination and that Achebe's conflation of them is a utopian strategy.

Anthills of the Savannah is a fictional working out of Achebe's concerns in *The Trouble with Nigeria*: Nigeria's leaders have placed their own interests before those of the nation. The novel is set in the fictional West African country of Kangan and focuses on a circle of three friends who have known each other since their early years and who since then have risen to hold some of the most powerful positions in the country, including that of head of state. They are intelligent, articulate, and committed—"the cream of our society and the hope of the black race" (2). But power corrupts. Sam, the military commander who has assumed the presidency in a coup, brooks no opposition, and he is starving a dissident province into submission to the central authority. The three friends must learn that "this world belongs to the people of the world not to any little caucus, no matter how talented..." (232).

Kangan, like other independent African states, has been defined in terms of colonial borders that were originally drawn by the British. Authority within the territory has been usurped by Sam, whose thirst for power has been fostered at English schools.[1] "Lerat c'est moi," Sam might say with sincerity. If Sam is concerned only with the power wielded by the institutions of state and not with the nation, the people he rules over, others regard the state itself as a foreign imposition. The Abazonians, metonymical representatives of traditional Africa, suffer the most under Sam's rule, and they constitute a homogeneous ethnic group, what Ali Mazrui and Michael Tidy would call a "cultural nation" defined by a common culture, as opposed to a "political nation" defined by territorial borders (85).

The educated elite living in the capital, among whom are Chris, Ikem, and Beatrice, cannot accept the distinction between state and nation—a distinction that Sam and the Abazonians both assume. They are nationalists who believe in the nationstate, in the identification of state and nation. The ruler of the state must be from among the people of the nation, and what is more, he must identify with the people. The people would then identify with the state.

Ikem is editor of the national newspaper, and his job (as conceived by Sam) involves broadcasting the President's messages to the people, a dissemination of information from the center to the periphery mirroring Sam's conception of his own power. Ikem, however, believes in the independence of the press and wants to close the circle of communication between the people and the institutions of state. He himself "had always felt a yearning without very clear definition, to connect his essence with earth and earth's people" (140-41). Kangan's problems, Ikem believes, can be traced to "the failure of our rulers to re-establish vital links with the poor and dispossessed of this country, with the bruised heart that throbs painfully at the core of the nation's being" (141).

The circle of communication between leaders and led was closed in the tribal society that predated colonization. (I use "tribal," as Nsame Mbongo does [31], to refer to a specific kind of social organization, pre-capitalist and without a centralized state or a division into economic classes, not as a comment on a culture's capacity to sustain a nation-state.) All that we readers ever see of drought-stricken Abazon are the six representatives who come to the capital to beg an audience with His Excellency, but we understood that their appearance is enough: when they speak, Abazon speaks. Information in the tribal model does not come from the top down; nor does it travel from the bottom up to the leaders. Instead, the leadership embodies the will of its citizens, and information is always shared because it is never divided.

At times in *Anthills of the Savannah* Abazon expands to include all the hinterland outside the capital, and at times it contracts to become a mere village, like Umuofia in Achebe's *Things Fall Apart* or Umuaro in *Arrow of God*. The Abazonians have a legend of their origins. In flight from a terrible drought that occurred in the distant past, the Abazonians descended from the North and dispossessed those whom they found living in "the tiny village of Ose" (33). Chris, when speaking of Abazon to the long-time Kangan resident, the Mad Medico, reminds him, as if he might have forgotten, "you know the drought place" (57). Depending upon the context, Abazon is either one of four regions into which the country is divided or merely a remote village that someone might not have heard of. This contraction of the province into a village is explicable if one recalls the portrait of pre-colonization Igboland in *Things Fall Apart*: as depicted in that novel the community with which Igbos identified prior to colonization was not the ethnic group but the village or clan.[2] Abazon is a community in which everyone knows everyone else, if only potentially or as the son or wife of someone who is known. Abazon exists in the imagination of its members; it is not, however, what Benedict Anderson would call an "imagined community." A nationstate, unlike the village, must be imagined. Because no member can ever know more than a small fraction of his fellow members, the nation-state can never be seen whole except in the imagination.

In an essay on African art, Achebe contrasts the "rather small, reasonably stable and self-contained societies" of precolonial Africa to the "very different, wide-open, multicultural and highly volatile condition known as modern Nigeria," where it is not clear how a writer can "even begin to know who his community is let alone devise strategies for relating to it" (*Hopes and Impediments* 40). The task of closing the circle of communication in a modern nation-state is not just greater than the completion of the circle in Abazon; it is a different task.

Chris, the Commissioner of Information in Sam's administration and Ikem's immediate boss, thinks it possible to create the nation-state from the top down, by starting with the idea of the state. Drawing upon "his incredibly wide reading and fluency," he explains that Sam's rule is not based on the model of contemporary European nation-states, but on the ancient empires of Moghul India and precolonial Africa:

> Nations, he said, were fostered as much by structures as by laws and revolutions. These structures where they exist now are the pride of their nations. But everyone forgets that they were not erected by democratically-elected Prime Ministers but very frequently by rather unattractive, bloodthirsty medieval tyrants. The cathedrals of Europe, the Taj Mahal of India, the pyramids of Egypt and the stone towers of Zimbabwe were all raised on the backs of serfs, starving peasants and slaves. (74)

Chris's argument is that, although Sam does not behave like the president of a modern nation-state (as defined by Europe), his empire-building might still result in the creation of a nation. After all, the original European nation-states, the models for all other would-be nation-states, were not originally democratic expressions of a people's sovereign will, as they now claim to be. They were created according to Sam's model of the nation, from the top down and from the center outward, and they illustrate Ernest Renan's principle that nations must suffer from amnesia if they are to bring together the descendants of conquerors and conquered alike.

Although Chris's of *realpolitik* enables him to present an accurate description of the way in which the first nation-states were created, it cannot serve to justify the exercise of absolute power in the late twentieth century, as Sam discovers. Sam is not in the position of an Egyptian pharaoh or a Moghul emperor, his authority must be ratified by an appeal to nationalism. Indeed, his legitimacy is in question because he came to power in a coup that overthrew a civilian government. As a result he feels that he must have this legitimacy confirmed in a referendum. This situation reveals the paradox of Sam's power: it is his, and it belongs only to him, but it must be confirmed after the fact to demonstrate that it actually emanated from the people. The electorate is asked to vote on whether or not Sam's presidency should be extended for life, a question that implies a prior consensus on his right to hold the presidency for a shorter term.

Ikem had originally come home from London in order to join Chris and Sam in "nation-building," but he eventually rejects that project as so much "crap" (91). He now believes that the true nation-state is not built but rather grows from below, starting from the nation and not from the state. Ikem finds a nation-in-itself already in existence, not in Abazon, but in the community that includes his woman friend Elewa (the daughter of a market woman) and the taxi drivers that he meets on the street. He envies the "artless integrity, a stubborn sense of community which can enable Elewa to establish so spontaneously with the driver a teasing affectionateness beyond the powers of Ikem" (142). Ikem's search is for a way in which he too can "partake of this source of stability and social meaning" (142).

The novel calls for a radical decentering of the nation, but it remains itself centered on Chris, Ikem, and Beatrice. The overt message is that Chris and Ikem must learn the importance of ordinary citizens, but the novel itself focuses more upon the manner in which they learn this lesson than upon the people they must learn about. The school friends learn that they are not significant in themselves, but the novel is predicated on their significance. They are not just anyone: their stories are the story of the nation, their quarrels are a national crisis, their deaths a national disaster. Achebe has admitted that the novel is addressed to Nigeria's leaders (Moyers 340).

The contradiction in the novel is a contradiction that lies at the heart of nationalism. As Ernest Gellner points out, nationalism "claims to defend folk culture while in fact it is forging a high culture; it claims to protect an old folk society while in fact helping to build up an anonymous mass society" (124). What is true of nationalism is particularly true of third-world nationalism, which Partha Chatterjee sees as concerned with re-equipping the colony and transforming it into a nationstate according to European standards, even as it turns toward the "folk" and pretends to validate culture, languages, and traditions that Europe had denigrated: "the philosopher-kings of the Third World all act as westernizers and talk like narodniks" (4).

Gellner, Eric Hobsbawm, and Benedict Anderson all assume that nations do not pre-exist but are created by states and by nationalists. Ikem and his friends create the nation, but for the nation to have legitimacy, it must be supposed already to exist. So it is that Ikem discovers a nation among the taxi drivers and market women. The "stubborn sense of identity" that Elewa and the taxi drivers share might also be interpreted as class consciousness, but Ikem sees it as an embryonic national identity because that is what he wants to find. The heart of Kangan cannot be located in traditional Abazon either. The shared language, ethnicity, and religion that hold Abazon together are at best "proto-national forces" (Hobsbawm 73) that must be appropriated by a nationalist movement if they are to become the raw materials of nation-building and not obstacles to national identity.

Gellner shows how the modern nation-state (in which old hierarchies were dismantled in the name of universality and social mobility) could claim to be the most efficient and rational organization of modern industrialized society (57). Ikem's nation-state is centered on an industrialized economy, based on the exchange of commodities (the market women), social and physical mobility (the taxi drivers), and the interchangeable, anonymous individuals who comprise the masses. This nationstate presumes the mingling of social classes and ignores ethnocultural distinctions. Ikem stresses the importance of workers and students to the nation-state in an address to the students at the University of Bassa that was "so well crafted and so powerfully spoken it took on the nature and scope of an epic prose-poem" (153). According to his "epic" statement of national purpose, peasants cannot be expected to lead the nation; Ikem points to their absence from the audience as proof that they are uninvolved in the national discussion. Instead, he summons workers to build the nation, but first, he argues, they must reform themselves, become more productive and more disciplined so that they can extend "the villages" (159). As conceived by Ikem (and no doubt by Achebe who gives such fulsome praise to Ikem's speech), the nation presupposes a modern industrialized economy based on efficiency and competitiveness. Workers and students are essential, for if they accept responsibility and discipline, they can put the nation "finally on the road to self-redemption" (160).

Ikem and his university audience live in a mobile society; the range of tasks the students will perform is more varied and less stable than the range of tasks assumed by people in tribal society. But there are limits to their employability, limits that coincide with the political boundaries of the former British colony in which they live. At every stage in their careers these educated Africans encounter others whose careers are circumscribed in the same ways. For instance, the students to whom Ikem addresses his speech will be obliged to perform some form of National Service after graduation (like Nigerian students). In this way, members of the educated middle class become aware of the fact that they constitute a nation.

This nation is what Chris discovers at the climax of the book during his journey north from the capital toward drought-stricken Abazon. He had chosen Abazon as a refuge because it is Ikem's native province—"the distance sustainer of all his best inspirations" (195)—and Ikem had just been abducted and murdered. Chris comes to realize that the capital is not the nation: "the ensuing knowledge seeped through every pore in his skin into the core of his being continuing the transformation, already in process, of the man he was" (204). But Chris's discovery of the nation occurs as he contemplates the changes in the landscape from the window of the bus in which he is riding. Although this nation is said to exist already, is it not a product of looking at the territory through nationalist lenses? Chris's flight to the hinterland merely stands on its head the "pilgrimage" from province to capital that Anderson describes as the career trajectory of the colonial civil servant, the pilgrimage that first allows a social class to define itself as a nation (56). The ambitious, educated middle-class elite on different sides of a border undertake pilgrimages to different centers, and these pilgrimages define different nations. Chris himself is amazed to discover that "provincial boundaries drawn by all accounts quite arbitrarily by the British fifty years ago and more sometimes coincided... completely with reality" (208). The provincial border of Abazon corresponds to a natural border—the rainforests of the south give way to the savannah—but, more importantly, Chris's identity has been defined by the borders established by the British. As Benyamin Neuberger points out, in Africa it is always the colonial self—the self as defined by colonial borders (as opposed to the ethnocultural, the geographic or the historical self)—that seeks national self-determination (30).[3]

Nation-states are artificial constructs (and not just in Africa); they can, however, release great energies. As Anderson points out, people have been willing to die for their nations, but have rarely been willing to die for the sake of class solidarity. The important question is whether nation-states can serve the ends of liberation. Frantz Fanon thought they could. In *The Wretched of the Earth*, he argues that liberation can only occur within national structures and that an authentic national consciousness must precede an international consciousness. He looked forward to the day when there would be no more Africans, only Nigerians, Kenyans, and Senegalese. Fredric Jameson also sees third-world nationalism as a mode of resistance in the era of multinational capital.

The UNESCO-sponsored New World Information and Communication Order was a project to promote national resistance to cultural imperialism. Those opposed to NWICO argued that the project would only put more power into the hands of states, with dangerous consequences where these were ruled by tyrants. Christopher Miller argues that a similar danger was implicit in Fanon's political philosophy (45-67). The disjunction of nation and state in the third world makes nationalism an ambivalent programme.

Anthills of the Savannah is an attempt to resolve this potentially disastrous discrepancy between state and nation. It is Achebe's response to the challenge he described in a 1975 interview:

> ...if you create out of a number of what you call tribes another unit which you might call state or nation, then what you should do is to think about what you should put into it so that all these people that you have drawn into the new unit will have a stake in it...[something] must be done, to make people feel they want to sacrifice their lives if necessary for this other unit, because it is so exciting, so powerful, so strong. (Morell 52)

Achebe clearly believes that, although the nation-state might be artificial, it is essential. He readily acknowledges the fictional nature of communal identities. In *Arrow of God*, the villagers of Umuaro never forget that they have themselves invented Ulu, the village's patron deity. Whether based on ethnicity, nationality, or race, identity must be invented and reinvented.[4] It is the potential power of an identity based on the state that attracts Achebe.

Benedict Anderson argues that a national consciousness is fostered by print literacy and associated with newspapers and the novel as a genre. Like the members of a nation, the characters in a realistic novel share a world of specific landmarks that are circumscribed by common horizons. Readers recognize their own world in the people, places, and things represented within a fictional space by novelists who adopt the realistic mode. Achebe's earliest novels established just such a community among readers. In *Anthills of the Savannah*, Beatrice tells Chris that she sometimes feels like "Chielo in the novel, the priestess and prophetess of the Hills and the Caves" (114). She and Achebe assume that Chris and the reader realize that she is referring to *Things Fall Apart*, that classic of African literature. The university students that Ikem addresses as citizens of a former British West African colony, might well have had to write school-leaving examination on *Things Fall Apart*.

But if the nation to which middle-class readers are conscious of belonging is to achieve legitimacy, other classes must be convinced that they too belong to it; a tradition must be invented. In *The Invention of Tradition*, Eric Hobsbawm and Terence Ranger argue that nationalism and colonialism at the end of the nineteenth century both successfully invented traditions. Achebe's invention of the nation requires that he close two circles: the circle joining the national elite and the masses, and another that joins the traditional participatory community of Abazon with the mass society of Kangan.

To close these two circles Achebe runs together two different conceptions of the nation—the nationalist and the revolutionary-democratic (Hobsbawm, *Nations and Nationalism* 22). Nationalists believe that the creation of the state depends on the prior existence of an ethnic community that is distinguished from "foreigners" by virtue of language and culture. For the revolutionary democrat, the nation must express the sovereign will of its citizens: people are French, for example, if they accept the conditions of French citizenship. This distinction between nationalists and revolutionary-democrats corresponds to the differences between Werner Sollors's concepts of descent and consent, two metaphors for the ties that bind individuals to a community. Those who emphasize descent value ancestors, memories, birth, and blood. It is the metaphor invoked when ethnicity and race are used to fashion an identity that is regarded as natural and ineluctable. The notion of consent, on the other hand, corresponds to Ernest Renan's definition of the nation as a daily plebiscite, and it is just as much a metaphor as the notion of descent. Achebe adopts the trope of consent to suggest how the rulers and the ruled may be brought together, and the trope of descent to join the nation-state and the tribal society.

Descent and consent are the governing tropes of two different narratives. In *Anthills of Savannah*, the white-bearded elder who heads the Abazonian delegation declares that storytellers are greater than warriors because warriors only fight wars, whereas storytellers can recreate the war and make people remember it. The stories they tell are what distinguish a people; stories are "the mark on the face that sets one people apart from their neighbours" (124). The Abazonian assumes a world in which people are defined according to physical features and shared memories—a world that is configured by descent. When Ikem speaks at the university, he argues something quite different. He argues that storytellers should be a threat; "they frighten usurpers of the right-to-freedom of the human spirit—in state, in church or mosque, in party congress, in the university of wherever" (153). According to him, the writer's task is to promote self-examination among his or her readers. The trope of consent holds together Ikem's community of strangers whose careers share a common horizon: they accept the assumption that the problems of the nation are *their* problems.

A national identity is the product of literacy and of a standardized modern education. Yet nationalism longs for an older model of communication that cements community with shared memories. Speaking to Bill Moyers, Achebe claims that the novelist should be *both* a social critic (in Ikem's terms) and the guardian of collective memory (the role suggested by the Abazonian elder). During the interview, Achebe makes the same distinction between the warrior who fights and the storyteller who keeps alive the memory of the struggle (337).

Kangan's legitimacy is ratified by appropriating the means according to which the cohesiveness of the traditional tribal community was established: genealogy and ritual. At the end of the novel, a "born-again" nation is ratified by the blood of two sacrifices: that of Ikem (a victim of Sam's political repression) and that of Chris (killed as he tries to prevent a rape). The two deaths bring together the friends of the slain, who come from different classes and speak different African languages. The two men's sacrifices are then commemorated in communion rites that involve the breaking and sharing of a kolanut. Hope literally assumes the form of a new birth, for the occasion of the gathering is the christening of Ikem's posthumous daughter, in whom the blood of an intellectual and that of a market woman are mingled. Chris's death also creates a legacy that can be passed on. Emmanuel, the student leader who accompanies him on his journey, adopts Chris as a father. Emmanuel's own father had died disgracefully, and Chris had taught him how one can die with dignity (231). Thus, consent and descent reinforce each other as the nation-to-be acquires a myth of origin that is based on blood in the dual sense of paternity and sacrifice.

The Christian echoes at the end are not the only romance elements on which the novel relies. The young nationalists attribute Sam's fall (he is killed in a coup) to his failure to embrace the nation. The idea of the embrace is quite literally represented when Beatrice receives an invitation to the Presidential Guest House. Chris, her lover, tells her to keep her options open, for Sam "knows things are now pretty hopeless and may see in you a last hope to extricate himself" (69). Making love to Beatrice is thus presented as somehow holding out the possibility for Sam to solve his political difficulties. After obeying the presidential summons, Beatrice discovers that "the sacred symbol of my nation's pride, such as it was" (80) is accompanied by a white American journalist, in whom Beatrice recognizes a rival. Ever since the skillful fellatio of a white woman in London had made Sam aware of sexual resources he had not thought he had possessed (69), he has been vulnerable to white women and their seductive tongues. The woman with whom the Head of State sleeps is metonymically linked to the people he serves, be it the people of Kangan or the Americans. For the good of the nation, Beatrice determines to seduce Sam, throwing herself at him "like a loyal batman covering his endangered commander with his own body and receiving the mortal bullet in his place" (80-81). Unfortunately, she is not successful: when she tells him not to trust American temptresses, he pushes her away in a range. The novel thus makes sexual desire a metonymy for the love of one's country: a genuine national leader must be wedded to African womanhood and to the land itself. Because the "right" woman fails to seduce him, Sam is doomed to fall. On the morning after her defeat, Beatrice thinks to herself, "the king's treasury was broken into last night and all his property carried away—his crown, his scepter, and all" (108). Sam's fall is not immediate, but it is now inevitable.

The communion at the end of the novel represents a fulfillment of romantic love, in contrast to the false unions suggested by the American journalist's seduction of Sam and by the rape that Chris dies in attempting to prevent. The pairing of Ikem (the intellectual) with Elewa (the daughter of a market woman) symbolizes a conjunction that must be made on a larger basis throughout the nation. Chris and Beatrice also had a successful union, representing the wholeness to which the young intellectuals and the nation itself aspire. To borrow a phrase from Doris Sommer, Ikem's goal of increased productivity implies reproductivity (86).

The group of like-minded individuals who gather to commemorate Ikem and Chris and to see the christening of Ikem's baby are brought together by chance. The taxi driver, the woman rescued from rape, and the student leader had contingent and random encounters with the two slain friends, but this is precisely the point of their gathering: they constitute a community of consent that transcends the boundaries of the ethnic communities from which they come. But are they brought together merely by chance? Beatrice is depicted as an unwitting instrument of Idemili, the Igbo goddess who links the sky and the earth. The community that gathers around Beatrice thus expresses a divine intention and is based on more than consent. By introducing a mythic dimension at this point, Achebe is trying to evade the nationalist conundrum: the nation must be created, but it is envisaged as having always existed in the eye of God. The meaning of the novel depends on the fact that the friends who gather in communion actually choose to join in a new community, one based on a vision of just power relations. At the same time, once they come together, their new community must have a greater degree of legitimacy than can be claimed by a group of strangers; it must be shown to have divine sanction. Beatrice both is and is not the vehicle of this message. Legitimacy and credibility require that the new community be consensual; ideology and narrative exigency require that it have a transcendental underpinning.

The anthills in the title allude to the admonition that people must remember those who have gone before, just as the anthills remember the fire that cleared the grasslands the previous year and as the survivors gather to remember Chris and Ikem. However, the fire is as necessary as the anthills; amnesia is as important as memory. The internal frontier between the capital Bassa and the province of Abazon is never crossed in the novel (Chris is killed just as he is about to cross it). The novel itself is as unable to enter Abazon as Chris is, and the only images of it that are communicated to readers are those that lie behind the Abazonian elder's utterances. Ironically, the elder (whose imprisonment by Sam precipitates Ikem's incendiary speech and leads to his abduction and death) is forgotten at the end when Chris and Ikem are remembered. The memory that would create a communal identity must be selective. Not memory but invented memory is necessary for the nation.

Memory might well be a fiction,[5] but if the fiction is to hold together an imagined community, it must be shared, not just among the characters but with readers as well. In *Anthills of the Savannah*, a metaphorical circle links the elite and the masses by consent; another circle links past and present by descent; however, these two circles are not concentric with the hermeneutical circle that links the text and its reader. In *Arrow of God*, it is suggested that Ulu, the patron deity of Umuaro, is but a convenient fiction; nevertheless, Igboland is successfully imagined for Igbo readers, and traditional Africa is imagined for Nigerian and other African readers. Igboland in that earlier novel is metonymically related to Africa, a part that is both self-sufficient and related to the whole. But Kangan in *Anthills of the Savannah* is an allegory of Africa, a part that is coterminous with the whole and that advertises its own fictionality. *Anthills of the Savannah* is a paean to memory, but does not actually remember anything itself: it creates a viable national myth for a community that is so imaginary that it exists nowhere outside the novel.

Achebe's novel is not the fictional reconstruction of a history-making resistance movement, like Sembene Ousmane's *God's Bits of Wood* (or Ikem's own play about the Women's War); not is it an injunction to remember a historical figure, like Mongo Beti's *Remember Ruben*. Ikem apostrophizes 1960, the year Nigeria received its independence, as "the year of wonders in which Africa broke out so spectacularly in a rash of independent nation states" (139). If we assume Kangan achieved independence in 1960 and then experienced nine years of civilian administration and three years of military rule (146), the novel would be set in 1972, but it is not, for there is a specific reference to the Entebbe raid by Israeli commandos in 1976. We know also that the events of the novel take place after Kangan's oil boom, which is likely to have coincided with Nigeria's during the late seventies after the OPEC states had started raising the price of oil. The tentative hope with which the novel ends is enacted in an imaginary land and at no time in particular.

What do we as readers do when presented with a fictional African nation? African readers and non-Africans who know something about Africa are likely to read "Nigeria" wherever "Kangan" appears in the text, allowing what they know about Nigeria to fill in what Achebe does not tell them about Kangan. Much of Kangan is recognizably Nigerian. It is located in West Africa on the Niger River. The characters' names—Reginald Okong, Beatrice Okoh, Joe Ibe, Ahmed Lango—are plausibly Nigerian and not, for example, Ghanaian. There are references to the National Electric Power Authority (NEPA), to Lord Lugard College (Lugard was the British founder of Nigeria), and to an oil boom.

If Kangan represents Nigeria, the dissident province Abazon corresponds to Igboland (Eastern Nigeria), the one province out of four that does not go along with the President's wishes in a national referendum, much as Eastern Nigeria sought to separate from the other three regions of Nigeria in 1967. The people from Abazon have names like Okeke, Mgbafo, and Ikem Osodi—good Igbo names. They speak Igbo as well: Ikem writes that the ancestory used to say Nneka, Igbo for "Mother is supreme" (98). The Abazonians speak of Agwa, the Igbo *arusi* or spirit of divination, and refer to a man's *chi* or personal god, a concept familiar to readers of *Things Fall Apart*. The play that Ikem writes about "the Women's War of 1929 which stopped the British administration cold in its tracks" (91) corresponds to historical events in Aba (see Isichei 151).

However, if such allusions recall Igboland, other things do not fit. Abazon is located in the Northwest (57), not the Southeast. The drought and subsequent starvation recall the crisis in the Sahel during the early 1980s and not the blockade of Biafra. The landscape is what one would expect of a northern landscape in West Africa: open savannah dotted by anthills and not the rainforest of Southeastern Nigeria. The Abazonian woman whom Chris saves from rape, Aina, is a Muslim, a detail that would fit a Northern Nigerian state but accords poorly with Igboland.

If Abazon both is and is not Igboland, the same might be said of Kangan as a whole. If, as we have seen, Abazon can contract to a mere village, the land where Igbo is spoken can expand to fill all of Kangan. It is clear that several African languages are spoken in Kangan. A character named Abdul, for instance, needs to have Elewa's uncle's words translated for him (225). Chris Oriko and his political ally Emmanuel Obete compare the proverbs that their people use (189). There are ethnic divisions in Kangan, and at the end of the novel the small group of like-minded people who gather to mourn the deaths of Ikem and Chris is calculated to suggest these divisions and to show how they can be transcended. Christians and Muslims, educated and uneducated, southerners and northerners, men and women are united by the communion rite that celebrates the christening of Ikem's child. Yet the novel as a whole seeks to negate or obscure difference. Whenever an African language is spoken in the text, it is Igbo. Elewa's child is called Amaechina, Igbo for "May-the-path-never-close" (222). Elewa's uncle performs the christening with the kolanut ritual of Igboland. Abdul is the only one who needs a translation and he gets one from Emmanuel, who does not belong to the same ethnic group as understand Igbo. In the traditional dialect of the capital, *Ife onye metalu* is said to mean "What a man commits" (202): the traditional dialect of Bassa is therefore Igbo, the same language that is spoken in Abazon! Similarly, Braimoh, whose name suggests a Northern Nigerian, uses the Igbo word *inyanga* to mean "showing off" (223).

Beatrice is not from Ikem's Abazon, yet her name is Nweanyibuife, Igbo for "a female is also something" (87). She is from the country between Omambala and Iguedo (103), where the goddess Idemili has a stream flowing from her lake to Orimili, "the great river which in generations to come strange foreigners would search out and rename the Niger" (103). Orimili is the Igbo name for the Niger. Among Beatrice's people, as among the Igbo, the hierarchy is called *ozo* (103), the python or *Eke-Idemili* is sacred (105), and the markets are held every four days (217).

That Igboland expands to fill the nation does not reflect a hegemonic intention on Achebe's part. If everyone in the novel is Igbo, then no one is Igbo, for "Igboness" ceases to matter and is absorbed in a Kangan identity. In Africa, descent and consent are usually conceived as opposing tendencies: the ethnic group into which a person is born and the state of which a person is a citizen are rival identities. Nsame Mbongo explains that communities of descent retain their hold over Africans partly as a result of the oppression which they suffer: "In effect, absolutism engenders the conviction that anything can happen to you, even the most unjust and fatal of occurrences, while material misery existing alongside opulence creates the impression that the social organization is totally absurd, two sentiments that push you on the most elemental level to cling to the ethnic group as a last hope" (50). The cruel absurdity of life in Kangan under Sam's rule could conceivably engender ethnic rivalries such as those that have, in the past, torn Nigeria apart. By transforming everyone within the nation-state into an Igbo, Achebe eliminates the disruptive potential of ethnic loyalties. The Igbo language in this novel is thus not a marker of communal identity but a sign for the language that has been learned at one's mother's knee, the language that remains heavily dependent on context and is shared by a tribal community which does not have to be imagined because everyone knows each other. In

Kangan, English is not needed to perform the trans-ethnic functions that it does in Nigeria; it merely signals the context-free language that makes possible communication between strangers in a modern mass society.

Having the characters share an Igbo identity allows was the focus of *Anthills of the Savannah* to pass unobstructed from the ethnic group to the nation-state. But the fictional setting of the novel causes the focus to slide from the nation to the continent. Something similar happens in Nadine Gordimer's *A Guest of Honour*, set in an anonymous Central African republic. James Bray, a one-time district officer with socialist convictions who has returned to help the newly independent republic, dies a violent and gratuitous death at the end of the novel. As with Chris's death at the end of Achebe's novel, the point is that the individual must accept his personal insignificance and recognize that meaning is located in larger historical processes of liberation. *A Guest of Honour* is not interested in the particular nationstate but in Africa: it assumes that all nation-states are the same and that eventually the state will even wither away. Gordimer's novel is concerned only with consent and the revolutionary-democratic definition of the nation (how the state can be wrested from those who control it in order to implement socialist principles); she is not concerned with descent, whether constitutive of ethnic or national identity.

Insofar as the lesson explicitly drawn is the insignificance of any one individual, Chris's death resembles Bray's. But Achebe has given Chris's death particular significance: Chris's death is heroic and will be remembered as part of the myth that will create a new nation. Gordimer, of course, is writing about a nation not her own and her protagonist is a foreigner there; the setting can remain anonymous. The pseudonymity of Kangan is harder to reconcile with the fact that Achebe is writing about a nation like his own and apparently desires to show how a national memory might be forged.

Achebe's 1966 novel *A Man of the People* is set in an anonymous country whose capital is called Bori; in this case the country's anonymity corresponds to the level of national consciousness among its citizens. No one feels any "ownership" of the state. *Anthills of the Savannah* appears to be about how a sense of national ownership can be fostered. Yet in the fictionality of its setting it resembles the novels of Appiah's second generation of African novelists—novelists for whom African nation-states are interchangeable because they have been thoroughly discredited. Kangan seems no different from Ouologuem's Nakem-Ziuko. None of these pseudonymous nations is "on the road to self-redemption," and the novels in which they appear can only be described as post-national or, in Abrahams's case, praeter-national.[6]

In *Anthills of the Savannah*, Achebe longs for consent and descent to reinforce and legitimize each other, as they do in the identities of European nations, where being a native and being a citizen are often conflated. Nations everywhere are artificial, but in Europe the tropes of consent and descent have been naturalized; in Africa, their artificiality cannot be designed. Sam's attempt to have his own desire confirmed as the will of the people is doomed because he is a tyrant in an age of nationstates; similarly, Achebe's desire in the novel to redeem the nation is inevitably compromised in the postmodern, postnational moment in which he is writing. Indeed, Achebe is not writing for Nigerians in the same focused way that Balzac, for instance, wrote for French readers. *Anthills of the Savannah* does not offer a solution to Nigeria's woes, but says, "Here's what a solution would look like if one could be imagined." Although Achebe argues in the novel that a national identity must be imagined, he himself does not imagine a Nigerian identity. Is he perhaps admitting that a Nigerian identity cannot be imagined?

NOTES

1. Ali Mazrui and Michael Tidy argue that the British were more successful at establishing statehood, a level of authority, than nationhood, a level of identity, in their African colonies. The French, on the other hand, forged nations but not true sovereign states (384).
2. In *Arrow of God* the Umuaro people are conscious of being Igbos as opposed to the Olu or riverine people. But *Arrow of God* is set twenty or so years later than *Things Fall Apart*. It is also important to remember that elsewhere in Africa identity was, of course, configured differently than in Igboland.
3. Biafra claimed to be the first African state to seek self-determination for an ethno-cultural rather than a colonial self. Yet, at the same time, it defined itself in reference to the colonial borders of Eastern Nigeria. Whatever the principles at stake, that tragic war was also a struggle for the oil fields that fell within the borders of rival "selves" with competing claims.
4. The notion that ethnic identity in Africa is an invention can be found in the essays collected by Jean-Loup Amselle and Elikia M'bokolo in *Au Coeur de I'Ethnie*. For the argument that Africa and the African race are inventions needing reinvention, see V.Y. Mudimbe's *The Invention of Africa* and the essays collected by Henry Louis Gates in *"Race," Writing, and Difference.*

5. Even to speak of invented memory may be misleading because to do so suggests that there can be a memory that is not invented: Wright Morris argues that "anything processed by memory is fiction" (qtd. In Fussell 205).
6. One novel that resembles Achebe's in positing the redemption of a fictional nation is Wole Soyinka's *Season of Anomy*. The novel is an unabashed romance: Ofeyi descends into Hell to rescue the beautiful Iriyise, the living symbol of the unnamed nation. Yet the novel maintains a critical distance from the nation it redeems. It is made clear that the identification of the nation with Iriyise is the result of a manipulative commercial advertising campaign. The guerrilla leader known as the Dentist explicitly hopes to make use of Iriyise as a symbol for the masses who only respond to such symbols.

WORKS CITED

Abrahams, Peter. *A Wreath for Udomo*. London: Faber, 1965.

Achebe, Chinua. *Anthills of the Savannah*. London: Heinemann, 1987.

— *Arrow of God*. London: Heinemann, 1974.

— *Hopes and Impediments: Selected Essays 1965-1987*. London: Heinemann, 1988.

— *A Man of the People*. London: Heinemann, 1966.

— *Things Fall Apart*. 1958; London: Heinemann, 1962.

— *The Trouble With Nigeria*. London: Heinemann, 1983.

Amselle, Jean-Loup and Elikia M'bokolo, eds. *Au Coeur de l'Ethnic: ethnies, tribalisme et etat en Afrique*. Paris: Editions de la Decourverte, 1985.

Anderson, Benedict R. O'G. *Imagined Communities*. London: Verso, 1983.

Appiah, Kwame Anthony. "Is the Post-in Postmodernism the Post-in Postcolonial?" *Critical Inquiry* 172 (1991): 336-57.

Chatterjee, Partha. *Nationalist Thought and the Colonial World—A Derivative Discourse*? London: Zed Books, 1986.

Fanon, Frantz. *The Wretched of the Earth*. Trans. Constance Farrington. Harmondsworth: Penguin, 1967.

Fussell, Paul. *The Great War and Modern Memory*. Oxford: Oxford University Press, 1975.

Gates, Henry Louis, Jr., ed. *"Race," Writing, and Difference*. Chicago: University of Chicago Press, 1986.

Gellner, Ernest. *Nations and Nationalism*. Ithaca: Cornell University Press, 1983.

Gikandi, Simon. *Reading Chinua Achebe*. Postmouth, N.H.: Heinemann, 1991.

Hobsbawm, Eric J. *Nations and Nationalism Since 1780: programme, myth, reality*. Cambridge: Cambridge University Press, 1990.

—and Terence Ranger, eds. *The Invention of Tradition*. Cambridge: Cambridge University Press, 1983.

Isichei, Elizabeth. *A History of the Igbo People*. London: Macmillan, 1976.

Jameson, Fredric. "Third-World Literature in the Era of Multi-National Capitalism." *Social Text 15* (1986): 65-88.

Kouroma, Ahmadou. *Les Soleils des lndependances*. Paris: Seuil, 1970.

Mazrui, Ali and Michael Tidy. *Nationalism and New States in Africa*. London: Heinemann, 1984.

Mbongo, Nsame. "Problems theoriques de la question nationale en Afrique." *Presence Africane* 136 (1985): 31-67.

Miller, Christopher. *Theories of Africans: Francophone Literature and Anthropology in Africa*. Chicago: University of Chicago Press, 1990.

Morell, Karen L., ed. *In Person: Achebe, Awoonor, Soyinka*. Seattle: University of Washington, African Studies Program, 1975.

Moyers, Bill. "Chinua Achebe." *Bill Moyers: A World of Ideas*. Ed. Betty Sue Flowers. New York: Doubleday, 1989, 333-44.

Mudimbe, V.Y. *The Invention of Africa*. Bloomington: Indiana University Press, 1988.

Neuberger, Benyamin. *National Self-Determination in Post-Colonial Africa*. Boulder, Colorado: Lynne Rienner, 1986.

Ouologuem, Yambo. *Le Devoir de Violence*. Paris: Seuil, 1968.

Renan, Ernest. "What is a Nation?" Trans. Martin Thom. *Nation and Narration*. Ed. Homi K. Bhabha, London: Routledge, 1990, 8-22.

Sollors, Wernet. *Beyond Ethnicity: Consent and Descent in American Culture*. New York: Oxford University Press, 1986.

Sommer, Doris. "Irresistable romance: the foundational fictions of Latin America." *Nation and Narration*. Ed. Homi K. Bhabha, London: Routledge, 1990, 71-98.

Soyinka, Wole. *Season of Anomy*. 1973. London: Arrow, 1988.

15

The White Man's Power and Magic

P. Suneetha

Colonization is generally taken as a political process perhaps because of the etymological associations with the word 'colony.' The word 'colony' in the sixteenth century was used to mean 'farm,' 'settlement,' and 'landed estate.' The word acquires the derivational farm colonized during the seventeenth century and with the European colonies all over the world, expands into colonized, colonial, colonist, and colonization. The term 'colonialism' connotes a practice by which a powerful country controls less powerful countries and uses their resources in order to further its own interest, wealth and power. There are many aspects of colonialism like Economic colonialism, Cultural colonialism, Linguistic colonialism. Exploitation and power politics are innate human tendencies that represent the different manifestations of power dynamics.

Many European countries established their colonies in Africa in the nineteenth century. The British settled down in Africa and established their rule. But the native East African leaders never appreciated the British settlement in their country. They waged an independent war called Mau Mau in 1963 and won independence. The leaders who participated in the Mau Mau revolution suffered the pangs of poverty but boldly opposed the settlers' dominance on them. Ngugi in his writings never hesitated to oppose the British influence on Eastern Africa. He believed in African ethos, values, and moral fervour. He became vociferous in recording the exploitation meted out by the Africans at the hands of the Europeans. In his own words,

> I believe that African intellectuals align themselves with the struggle of African message for a meaningful national ideal...the African writers can help in articulating the feelings behind the struggle.[1]

This passage tells us about Ngugi's commitment for his society.

Ngugi's fictional works vividly record his commitment to the Africans and his strong voice against the whites who indulged in the exploitation of the Africans. He clearly identifies three facets of encounter of the Africans with the Europeans imperialists...slavery, colonialism and Neo-colonialism. His first three novels, *Weep Not, Child, The River Between*, and *A Grain of Wheat*, deal with the period of a slavery and colonialism.

The River Between grippingly discusses how the Africans were exploited by the Britishers. The novel tells upon the impenetrable Kenya in all its beauty. At first, the Kenyans have had a happy peaceful and united life with their traditions and customs which bound them together to their land. They believed that the land on which they lived was their God, Murunga's gift to their first parents...Gikuyu and Mumbi. Murunga showed them the vast portion of land and told them....

> This land I give to you, Oh men and women it is yours to rule and till, you and your posterity.[2]

The River Between powerfully examines the consequences of alienation of the people from their land. Mugo wa Kibiro, a great Gikuyu sage, prophesied the invasion of the country by the white man. In his own words:

> There shall come a people with clothes like butterfly. (*RB*, 2)

Mugo was ignored by his people in his own day. As his later day heir, Chege, a respectable man of the ridges and descendant of Mugo was chosen. He warned the people of ridges of the arrival of the Europeans. The whites had already set up their houses and took their land in the place of Murungu, Nyeri and Kiambo. But the people never gave credentials to the words of Chege. Though the railway line laid by the whites was running across the country, the people, did not know much about it.

> The white man cannot speak the languages of hills. And knows not the ways of the land.

The Africans, due to their ignorance and deep belief in their impenetrable nature of the hills, could not forestall the invaders from setting down at Siriana, a place situated at the outskirts of Makuyu and Kameno ridges. The novelist rightly:

> Succeeds in evoking the atmosphere of ridges chronicling the traditions and customs they embrance.[3]

The whites occupied the surrounding land and with their religious preachers they were able to covert to their faith quite a few natives like Joshua and Kabonyi. The act of conversation is the first step of colonialism.

Livingston, a leading missionary, visited the hills with a view to giving new life and energy to his followers there Joshua his agent, carried on his main work of preaching to the Africans about the existence of one god... Jesus. Through Joshua, Livingstone was able to convert many Africans to take to the new faith shedding their faith with the native religion. Because of the new faith, the old conformity of the African society was broken. This is brought out symbolically by Ngugi through Joshua's building.

> The round thatched huts standing in groups of three or four convey a picture of conformity broken only by Joshua's house which has a tin roof and is rectangular. The very presence of the house is an indication that the old isolation of Makuyu from the rest of the world was being broken down. (*RB, 28*)

The preaching of new values of life through a new religion had a drastically adverse effect on the old beliefs.

The clash between the two antagonistic ways of life was indeed most catastrophic and tragic. As a committed writer, Ngugi portrays remarkably in *The River Between* the tragic predicament of the Kenyans torn by lacerating conflict, the loss of cultural heritage and identity in the exploitative colonial context at both the individual and societal levels. In the words of Arthur Ravenscraft,

> The disinheritance of the Gikuyu religion and tribal culture by white colonialism figures in the novel.[4]

The whites began to pour into the interior in greater and greater numbers. The newly built railway lines, the settled land of the whites around Siriana Missionary and ever increasing number of converts caused their way to spread farther and farther.

The impenetrable thick line that distinguished the outsider from the insider became penetrable. The white people as well as the Indians started business on the Kenya Land. The white government operated from Siriana. The Government administrators were not seen directly but were heard through the missionaries. This was announced to the Makuyu ridges that Government post was soon going to be established there and that the people would be ruled from there. Missionary people also spoke of the taxes the natives had to pay to the white Government in Nairobi. The lands were intact for them. So, the native people did not take serious notice of the ways of the whites or of the taxes being imposed by them.

Siriana Missionary centre started a school. Chege, *an embodiment of tribal ideology*[5] believed in the ancient prophecy of Mugo that the salvation came from the blood that flowed in him. He thought of imparting his knowledge to his son Waiyaki, whom he named after the greater Gikuyu warrior. He told them:

> Arise, Hear the prophecy. Go to Mission place, learn all the wisdom and all the secrets of the white man. But do not follow his vices. Be true to your people and ancient rituals. (*RB, 20*)

Chege's speech almost becomes the record of novelist's opposition to the colonizer. Like the novelist, Chege believes in the dictum that the colonized would learn the tricks of the aggressor and use them against the aggressor himself. Like the novelist, Chege is able to realise the kind of education that was imparted as Siriana Missionary cenre.

> The learning and wisdom that the people's hope require has such potential to destroy the old ways as to preserve them by fighting the white man with his own weapons.[6]

Ngugi reveals his commitment to the colonized by drawing our attention to the exploitative steps in the field of education followed by the colonizers.

The education imparted to the students in the Siriana Missionary School was mainly directed to advance the interests of the British Empire. The colonizer very much wanted to convert the Africans into their faith and thus assist them to spread their religion. They also wanted the students to help them in the rule of the natives.

Thus, Livingstone pinned his hopes on Waiyaki and saw in him a possible supremacy of their religion and began to condemn the native rituals, customs and traditions. As a committed writer, Ngugi becomes critical of the English education. In his own words:

> A is sitting on B...what kind of education will A want to B to set? In other words, 'A' will want 'B' to believe that he, B has no culture or his culture is inferior. 'A' will want to 'B' to imbibe a culture, inculcate in his values of self doubt and self denigration, in a word a slave consciousness. He will now look up to A, a superior culture.[7]

This passage reveals to us the inherent potentiality that has gone into human psychology. Ngugi also was opposed to the Britishers who considered traditional customs as satanic works. They called Gikuyu god 'the Prince of Darkness.' At Siriana the preaching went on thus:

> Those who refuse him are the children of darkness:
> Those sons and daughters of evil one, will go to Hell;
> They will burn and burn forever more, world unending. (*RB, 29*)

These words frighten the converts like Joshua. It is said that Joshua's whole body shook to the very roots of his being. It is only when he was baptized that he felt at peace and stopped 'trembling.' The effect of such preaching was so much on Joshua that he represented all his life for having married circumcised Miriamu. He did not like his children to undergo such rituals. He felt that they would get contaminated if they listened to the limitation songs. Having got to believe in The Bible and to give up their traditions. By condemning the nativization in favour of the new faith and by becoming a preacher himself, he was at once, the exploited as well as the exploiter.

Chege witnessed the strength of strange forces of new faith, which influenced many Africans to get converted. He was disappointed for his inability to do any thing in his lifetime. He feared if his son Waiyaki too might begin to dislike the way of the ridges and its rituals. In fact, he had great expectations on his son to the effect that he would be the saviour of the ridge. Though Waiyaki did not condemn the rituals, the impact of missionary education was clearly seen on him on the day before circumcision. At first, he stood as an outsider though he liked to be involved like the other boys of his age. He grew uneasy to listen to the songs of circumcision sung by the young Kenyan boys and girls. Later, when he was pushed into the circle, dancing around the fire his body mechanically moved rhythmically according to the music of the whistles and horns but the voice of white man's education made him guilty and could not put his soul on it. In fact, he remembered Livingstone and his reaction to it. Ngugi's commitment is revealed in his vehement comments on the disruptive influence of Christianity on the African life.

> Christianity as an organized religion is corrupt and hypocritical: besides acting as an agent of imperialism, it exercised a highly disruptive influence on the African life and was the chief villain in alienating the African from his own culture. (*HC*, 31)

This passage clearly reflects Ngugi's commitment to African tradition and African culture.

Waiyaki was unable to choose between the two competing faiths in the community. Despite being well versed in every ritual of the tribes, Waiyaki was subjected to the influence of the missionary people and white man's education. Muthoni, the younger daughter of Joshua, was completely carried away by her father's principles which condemned the rituals of the tribe. Like Waiyaki, she too believed that the rituals of circumcision were important to the people who lived there. But unlike him, she was able to participate fully in the celebrations of circumcision.

At the same time she believed in the foreign faith her parents had embraced. Waiyaki was surprised to know the Muthoni revolted against her father's will to get circumcised. He could not think of being a rebel placing himself in Muthoni's place. With his subjugated mind he was unable to make a clear choice and hence the chances of his becoming a successful saviour became less. In fact, he always felt like a stranger in his land and behaved detachedly from the politics of the land.

As a committed artist, Ngugi grippingly describes the cultural exploitation of the Africans by the whites. In his narration of the ceremony of circumcision, he draws a number of elements loosely held together. In chapters 3 and 4, he describes at length, the importance of the circumcision to the people of Africa. He makes it clear that the act of circumcision is the most central in the Gikuyu way that kept the people together.

> It was the core of the social structure and something that gave meaning to a man's life. End the custom and spiritual bias of the tribe's cohesion and integration would be no more. (*RB*, 79)

Obsessed with the foreign faith, Joshua forgot fatherly love towards his daughter Muthoni, when she got infected after cleriodectomy and disowned her for following traditional faith of the land. Even when his health deteriorated he did not move out of his place. Instead, he wanted to plant a curse on her and finally when she died he thought that she deserved it for following satanic ritual. He thought that this would teach a lesson to the Africans who followed it. The early converts had to prove 'how Christian he was through rejection of his past roots...so that in Kenya...the missionary robbed people of their soul.' The death of Muthoni had far-reaching circumstances. Livingstone earlier believed in gradual eradication of the traditional customs of the Africans. Inspite of the pressures by his authorities at home and in Kenya he repulsed to adopt rash and desperate measures. But he realised, after his twenty-five years of stay in Kenya, that he was not making such progress. Now Muthoni's death forever, confirmed the barbarity of Gikuyu customs. He thought...

> Circumcision had to be rooted out if there was to be any hope of salvation for these people...it was Christ who would be fighting the Princess of Darkness through him. (*RB*, 56)

He began to adopt vigorous methods to suppress the Gikuyu customs and decreed a law that circumcised Africans are not allowed to missionary schools. He called him African agents... Joshua and Kabonyi...to help him in the war. Thus, *The River Between* reveals to us,

> the Blackman's sense of insecurity, his sense of threat to his environs to his method of life.[8]

Joshua becomes more jealous and adamant in preaching Christian doctrines. Unable to follow completely the new faith, many converts alienated themselves from Livingstone and Joshua, the pro-Christian leaders. A new political organisation, 'Kiama' was raised to safeguard the traditions. Just as Joshua condemned everything traditional, Kiama attacked everything that belonged to the white man. The people of Kameno and those of Makuyu ridges, who followed different faiths moved away from each other. Thus, conflicts and splits occurred not only in the psyche of individuals but also in the society. Here, one may recall Achebe's account of African religion in his novel *Things Fall Apart*:

> How can he when he does not even speak our tongue? But he says that our customs are bad; and our brothers. He came quietly and peacefully with his religion. We were amused at his foolishness and allowed him to stay. Now he has won our brothers, and out clan can no longer be like one. He has put a knife on the things that held together and we have fallen apart.[9]

The people of the ridges ceased to talk to one other. The clear edges of life had completely disappeared under the impact of white man's religious attitude towards the natives.

The problem with the circumcised Africans is that they are not allowed to pursue their studies in the missionary schools run by the West. Waiyaki, a circumcised person, could now carry on his studies as per the missionary laws. So he started a new school—the first one in the foreign faith. Both were the victims to white man's twin tools—religion and education. Waiyaki shunned all forms of politics and repulsed even to suppress the Kiama activity inspite of his earlier oath, for they might come on his way to education the people.

> Perhaps the preaching Livingstone, that education was valued and his boys should not concern themselves with that the Government was doing of politics, had found a place in Waiyaki's heart. (*RB, 65*)

As a victim to the British Educational system, Waiyaki was unable to understand the politics of the time. In the process to educate the people to the ridges, he had not even been able to see the increasing influence of 'Kiama' to fall on him. In fact, white man's education acted as a hidden world for him.

Waiyaki tried to reconcile to the Christian faith with the traditional faith of the land. The essence of education was to him a clarion call to unite all the people and to drive out the white settlers. He recalled the nature of work his father has assigned to him in the journey after circumcision. But preoccupied with his education, he lost the track of his goal of ensuing unity in his community. Waiyaki appeared to be in a state of confusion created by the Europeans with their religion.

In this powerful novel, one perceives conflict between tradition and modernity. This is evident from the tragic story of love between the circumcised elder daughter of pro-Christian Joshua and the circumcised educated son of traditional Chege. After the death of his younger daughter, Joshua was preoccupied with preaching Christian principles vigorously to the people and he did not notice the change in his elder daughter who grew vexed with his new faith that had no humanity. In her own words,

> If the faith of Joshua and Livingstone came to separate; why, it was not good. If it came to stand between a father and his daughter so that her death does not move him, then it was inhuman. She wanted the other. (*RB*, 134)

Here, the expression 'the other' connotes her love for 'Waiyaki.' Thus, white man's religion has blinded the early converts like Joshua. His family was completely disintegrated when Nyambura walked out with Waiyaki proclaiming openly her love for him in the presence of the people who came to listen to Joshua's Christian preaching. It was a lapse on the part of Joshua who as a parent and preacher, was not able to bring up his children in the light of his new faith. He always wanted to show to the people that his was an ideal family and that he would set an example to others.

The conflict between tradition and modernity persists in the institution of marriage. According to the tradition, an uncircumcised man or woman was not eligible to marry within the tribe. The leaders of Kiama wanted the people to punish Waiyaki for violating the oath of Kiama so as to enable other people not to commit similar sacrilege. Waiyaki saw in the union of the two sides a reconciliation of the two faiths. But the people were not ready to judge it that way. They were confused about the religious conflict that arose because of the new faith. The novelist presents graphically the confused state when the two lovers were placed for the judgement before Kiama.

> The crowd rolled back 'Yes' as if the burden of judging their teacher were removed from them. They went away quickly glad

> that he was hidden by the darkness for they did not want to look at the teacher and they did not want to read the guilt of one another faces. (*RB*, 132)

The dilemma of the masses to make a choice between traditionalism and the new faith leads to utter confusion and as a result tragedies occurred. In this context, Werner Glinga who conducted research on Ngugi observes:

> The confusion as the key to understand Kenyan history from the beginning of European instruction and sets out to explore with the benefit of hind-eight, how the people of the early vital interest. Ngugi's idea of African hero of colonial occupation originated in the pre-independence pro-literary tradition in Kenya.[10]

This passage shows the harm done by the whites to the African culture. The novelist presents the picture of Gikuyu who stands as a weak willed person. He also expresses his commitment to the Africans and African society. His commitment is overtly clear and he easily becomes

> a spokesman for a people whose sacred bond with soil caused them to undertake a bloody uprising against the colonial power.[11]

This theme of commitment to the colonized recurs in *Weep Not, Child,* his another powerful novel. In this novel, the weeping child is at the centre of the novel for he has the fear of being exploited at the hands of others. Here, the child Njoroge has *the sympathy of the others for him.*[12]

Ngugi comments on the plight of an African thus:

> He is like Blitzer, the boy in *Hard Times* only to know a horse in words as a mental abstraction.... His education has been used to mystify and obscure reality.[13]

The novelist expresses through Njoroge, his commitment to the young Kenyan children who were to grow into responsible Kenyan citizens. He exemplified Waiyaki's realization at the end of the novel *Weep Not, Child* that education for the oppressed people is not education all.

In *Petals of Blood* Ngugi as a committed writer,

> makes an attempt to think alone about the problems of modern Kenya...the sharp contrast between the ill-gotten wealth of the new African middle class and worsening plight of the unemployed workers and the peasants.[14]

Munira in this novel, becomes a victim to the imposed foreign faith. He as the son of brother Ezekiel wa Weru, felt that the new faith has no relevance to the situation in which he was living. When he was young he attended circumcision ritual without the knowledge of his father. There he met Wanziru singing and dancing in one of the circumcision dances. He fell in love with her and married her. But after the marriage she changed over to a Christian name Julia, under the influence of Munira's father and became a good Christian daughter-in-law. Munira did not like her praying in the Christian fashion even when she was in bed with him. So he had the feeling of emptiness in him. He ran away to Illmorog in search of something to fill the emptiness. In the words of the novelist,

> he was still a prisoner of his own upbringing and Siriana missionary education. It was not that he did not enjoy the experience. On the contrary despite that upbringing he knew that there was nothing so great, nothing so joyous as those few seconds of expectation before entry into a woman unknown. (*PB*, 72)

This passage tells us about Munira becoming a victim to the colonial religion and education.

As a committed novelist Ngugi continues to exhibit and also record the oppressed feelings of the Africans. The Siriana school produced corrupt officials like Chui, Nderiwa, Kimaria who exploited their fellow Africans. Munira blamed Cambridge Fraudsham, the headmaster of the Siriana school. Fraudsham wanted to mould the people to be sincere subjects of the British Empire to subserve its interests. He played with African students, made them salute the British flag everyday and pray in choral voice.

In his capacity as the head of Siriana school, Fraudsham worked towards the perpetuation of the white domination while the Kenyans associated education with advancement of political freedom and even with economic freedom. The colonial education was meant to obscure many forms of oppression. The purpose of imperialist education was thoroughly scrutinized and its relevance to the African situation was questioned throughout the novel.

The evil effects of the colonial education are grippingly described in *Petals of Blood*. The effect of colonialism is such that the Christian converts in Kenya are always unsympathetic towards other Kenyans. Ngugi, as a committed writer, cannot understand why the converted Christians behave as the white man's lackeys. For example, in his *Petals of Blood* Jerrod Brown, the pastor of the 'All Saints Church' in New Illmorog, turned away the hungry famished and ailing village from palatial home in the most unchristian fashion. Instead of providing the crowds with food, he discusses at length, spiritual illness. He finds fault with the Kenyans for their spiritual lameness. He says:

> The Bible is then clearly against the life of idealness and begging. This is that is wrong with the country. (*PB*,148)

Colonial education taught the Africans about the Western conquerors, inventors, creative writers and many religious leaders. It bore an evil influence on the Africans. It always wanted the Africans to look up to Livingstone as their saviour and Mau Mau patriots as traitors and terrorists. When Karega in *Petals of Blood* went through the history of Africa, he only found the description of the Africans as wanderers who had no civilization. They were considered as primitives and barbarians. But they covered up their equal treatment. Karega said that the writers of history were obedient to the imperialistic masters. He also lamented that their past had a broken civilization because of the white's cultural exploitation.

Gatuiria in *Devil on the Cross* reiterated the same idea as Karega did in *Petals of Blood.* As an African research student in culture, he was sorry that the wisdom and philosophy of their ancestors had to take a back seat in the foreigner's eyes. The natives were not even able to find books in their national languages. Their native songs, riddles, stories, customs, traditions, and everything about the African heritage had been lost to them. Gatuiria rightly observes:

> They cannot go anywhere to know the history of their country. They are left like a child without present to counsel them.[15]

We may tune with David Cook and say:

> Ngugi in his *Devil on the Cross* seems at all times to sort out the ultimate goal of any committed writer...to harness the laws of heart to the dictates of his own consciousness.[16]

The Africans not only suffered the loss of culture, but also lost their lands to the Europeans during the colonial times. The novelist becomes critical of the political and economic exploitation of the Africans by the Europeans. For example, in his *Weep Not, Child* he discusses the colonists who exploited the natives by depriving them of the ownership of their lands and reducing them to the miserable state of workers at their behest, on these lands. Waiyaki says:

> The shame of people's land being taken away, the shame of being forced to work on those same lands, the humiliation of paying taxes to a government that you know nothing about. (RB, 164)

These lines which are mentioned casually occupy the centre of stage in *Weep Not, Child.*

As the novel opens we see many natives working in settled areas and in foreign shops to make their living. There is a clear demonstration of fertile lands occupied by the whites allotted for the Blacks. The novelist depicts the confirmation between whites and blacks and the alienation of the lands.

> You could till the land of Black people because it was red, rough and tickly, while the land of the white settlers was green and was not lacerated into small strips. (*WNC*, 8)

In Kenya a person with land was considered to be richer than a person with a lot of other material wealth. It was because most of the people live as peasants. The Kenyans had a deep attachment to the land which satiates them both materially and spiritually. According to Jomo Kenyatta,

> The Gikuyu consider the earth as the mother of tribe.... It is the soil that nurses the spirit of the dead or eternity. Thus, the earth is the most sacred than above all that dwell in or on it. Among the Gikuyu the soil is especially honoured and an everlasting oath is to swear by the earth.[17]

Naturally any loss of land constituted the greatest disparity and suffering to Kenyans.

Ngugi's main concern in his novels is the dispossession of the Kenyans of their land. Kamau in *Weep Not, Child* says:

> Yes, Black people have their land in the country of black people, White men have their land in their own country. It is simple. I think it was God's plan. (*WNC*, 49)

In his interview Ngugi says:

> I believe that no Kenyan should be able to sleep with any peace of mind for as long as he knows that what he is feeding upon had been taken from the mouths of thirsty and hungry in Kenya. I also believe that no Kenyan should be able to sleep peacefully for as long. As he knows that the wealth of the country is still controlled by foreign merchants.[18]

The whites did not conquer the whole of Kenyan land. They dispossessed the Kenyans of their lands during the two great wars. Ngotho narrated to the barber how he had become a 'Muhoi' on his own lands.

> It was the first big war.... All of us were taken by force. We made roots...the war ended.... My father and many others had been moved from our ancestor's lands. He died lonely poor man waiting for the white man to go. The white did not go and he died a 'Muhoi' on his own land. (*WNC*, 29)

Ngugi easily becomes critical of the colonizers who exploited the Africans during the war. The colonists promised that after coming back from the war they would give back to the Africans the land they occupied. On the contrary, they had occupied even more land by the time the Africans returned from the war. They did not fulfill their promise to the natives even after the second world war. How lands did not appreciate Ngotho's attachment to his lands, made his work on low wages and made good profit. The novelist records his views on the double exploitation of the Blacks by the Whites thus:

> Black people have been victims of double exploitation. They have been exploited on the level of the working class and the labouring masses. They have also been exploited on the dimension of race because of the whole colonial context in which Black and White people have met.[19]

In *Weep Not, Child*, Boro, the son of Ngotho, exhibits his anger against exploitative settlers and Government thus:

> The land has been taken away, through the Bible and sword... the Bible paved the way for the sword...their forefathers pitied the stranger and welcomed him with open arms into their fold. (*WNC*, 65)

Boro and his brothers were not left with land to live on it. Ngotho's sons were scattered to make their living. Ngotho is aware of the fact that Howlands is responsible for his poor economical conditions. Howlands's exploitative and oppressive attitude is brought clearly during the emergency. When Ngotho joined the strike to get back his occupied lands back, Howlands wanted

> to bring Ngotho to submissive humiliation...this would be the crowning glory to his career. (*WNC*, 111)

Howlands's economic condition was not good before Ngotho joined as a worker in his fields. It was only with his labour that Howlands grew rich. Instead of giving him reasonable wages, Howlands became aggressive and thought of cutting him to size. In this context, David Cook observes:

> For Ngotho, his white employer, is the ever present perpetrator of the loss he has suffered.[20]

Howlands raises his African agent Jacobo, to a chief's position to arrest Ngotho and his sons even on false allegations. Before Ngotho's very eyes he got arrested Ngotho's wives and children. To Howlands, Ngotho became a symbol of evil stood on his way in his possession of Ngotho's land.

As was the usual practice with Government agents, Howlands took the law into his hands and harassed and illustrated Ngotho to forcibly extract information from him about Jacobo's death. He treated Ngotho so cruelly that even the homeguards who worked with him got scared to be in the place where Howlands was harassing Ngotho. Finally Howlands drove Ngotho to death after making him suffer both physically and mentally.

Howland's selfish and exploitative nature was clearly exposed when he just utilized the services of Jacobo and did not care to protect him when his life was in danger. In fact, he set the Africans against their fellow Africans. Look at his exploitative nature.

> He would use them. The very ability to set these people fighting among themselves instead of fighting with the white men give him an amused satisfaction. (*WNC*, 88)

Howlands was so mean that he got Ngotho's family members arrested by Jacobo. His wife also indulges in the exploitation of the African workers. Whenever Howlands was busy and neglected her, she abused the African farm workers and removed them from work. She and her husband were never conscious that they were usurpers of Ngotho's land.

The white people arrested Jomo Kenyatta, the leader of the strike, and the people were deprived of leadership for organizing the strike. The Government declared an emergency. Fear gripped the Gikuyu land in the form of curfews, arrests, repressive measures and deaths. Njeri interestingly discusses the Draconial laws of the Whites.

> The white man makes a law or rule. Through that law or what you call it, he takes away the land and then imposes many laws on the people concerning that land and many other things all without people agreeing the old days of tribe. Now a man rises...who can win even if the angel of God were his lawyer. (*WNC*, 84-85)

Even in *A Grain of Wheat*, the novelist describes the exploitation of the Europeans during emergency period. Howlands and Livingstone were the only prominent people in *Weep Not, Child* and *The River Between* respectively. In *A Grain of Wheat* the number of Europeans increased and with them the intensity of exploitation of the natives also increased. Mr. Rogers, an agriculture officer, wanted to set up a Forest Research Station in the dark Africa but a train at Githima crushed him. Thompson, a white representative, is a typical colonial reader. Lme Lkeidden calls him,

> 'A firm grip of the European colonial time.'

According to G.D. Killam,

> In *A Grain of Wheat* there is a larger community of whites, British for the most part...and we see the forces of the belief in the civilizing mission with its emphasis as a benevolent paternalism. This theme is consolidated in John Thompson.[21]

Thompson becomes an exponent of the ethics of imperial colonialism. According to Lkeidden,

> he embodies for Ngugi that most odious form of political authority, colonialism, so of all his characters it is on Thompson that he pours most scron.[22]

For Thompson, Colonization is process of civilizing the savages of the African continent. He considered it as white man's burden. He was of the opinion that the darkness and the mystery of the forest led the primitive man to magic and rituals and condemned them on like Livingstone in *Weep Not, Child*. He firmly believed that it was with the effort of the Europeans, the wild bushes were turned into modern cities. The nationality, inconsistency and superstition of the Africans yielded place to the western principles of reason, order and measure. He planned to motivate the African people towards the British way of living by altering their social and cultural environment. He held a high opinion about the British and their way of living. His administration for the British is such that he writes down a few lines from Dr. Albert Scheweitzer. 'The Negro is a child, and with children nothing can be done without the use of authority.'

Thompson, a colonial administrator, became a symbol of unmovable white power in Kenya. He considered the Mau Mau movement as the evil one that stood between him and his morals. He considered himself as Prospero in Africa. So he made attempts to suppress Africa brutally. Those who did not co-operate with the white Government were considered as Mau Mau terrorists and were detained. It is pertinent to recall the observation mady by David Cook.

> Thompson's hypocritical visions are exposed a sham and together with them he is shattered and broken. At the same time he is cuckolded and despised by a forlorn and unfulfilled wife who has grown tired or playing a secondary role to his hollow ambitions.[23]

In *A Grain of Wheat* the white man's underlying energy caught in senseless mass cruelty is portrayed in detail. There were several detention camps spreading from the Manda islands in the Indian Ocean to Magata

Islands in Lake Victoria. Manda camp housed 18,000 people at a time. The suspected as well as the young men were caught and were sent to the detention camps. Their legs and hands were chained. The sanitary conditions were poor. Mugo said that at Rira camp they were given 8.03 grams of meat per week and 7.03 grams of flour per day. Those who were attacked by typhoid were not given any treatment.

John Thompson who already became popular while working at Yala camp on behalf of white Government was posted to Rira camp. He represented change in the attitude of the white Government just before Uhuru. He changed the way of extracting secrets from the detainees. He spoke with their detainees individually about homes and family members before trying to extract oaths from them. In his attempt to extract information from the detainees at Rira camp, he even began to give treatment to those who were suffering from Typhoid. When he was not able to make Mugo confess, he resorted to whipping him hard. The novelist avoids excessive details in the description of such oppressive physical torture or pains infected on detainees and consequences of the atrocities. Mugo said:

> I saw men crawl on the ground.... Their hands and feet were chained with iron all the time. Now he spoke in a subjugated voice like a child. Once bottled necks were hammered into people's back side and the men whimpered like caged animals, that lost was at Rira. (AGW, 208)

The novelist, besides delineating the untold physical and mental sufferings of the people in detention camps, describes the agonies of the people outside the camp. They are not allowed to give refuge to Mau Mau revolutionaries. The remaining members of the family were forced to work in the fields of the white settlers and some to dig trenches. Those who did not work properly were beaten. Look at the sufferings of the natives.

> The children of Israel;
> When they were in misery
> Were made to do work
> Harder than done by cow and donkeys. (*AGW*, 164)

These lines exhibit '*the resurgence of new socialist awakening*.' The novelist also describes the unrest that came into existence during the Mau Mau rebellion. Everyone is under the grip of fear. The individual betrayals are also recorded. Mugo leaves Kihika, a Mau Mau patriot, with the white Government but Kihika wants him join the rebellion. But Mugo expresses his fear thus:

> If I work for him the Government will catch me. The white man has long arms and they will hang me. (*AGW*, 221)

The whites dragged a few young people like Mugo and Gikonyo and instilled fear in them to warm them not to act against the white Government. Thus, the fear induced by the whites had far-reaching effects on the Africans. At the detention camps Mugo and Gikonyo lived under constant insecurity and fear. They were physically and mentally stalled. At last they were back to their homes just before Uhuru. Because of the effect of such prolonged psychological stress, Gikonyo could not understand his wife in proper light. Similarly the feelings of insecurity haunted Mugo continuously.

Ngugi also dwells upon the harsh rule of the whites before giving independence. They confiscated the land of ever increasing number of detainees. Unfortunately, when the Africans went back from the detention camps they were left without anything to live by. They could not locate their houses for they burnt the whole of Thabai village which itself was shifted to another place. Thus, the white Government confiscated Mugo's land on which he pinned hopes. The confiscated lands were sold either to the white settlers or the Black people who were loyal to the white Government.

Ngugi records the group consciousness under exploitative conditions in his novels. In *A Grain of Wheat* he describes the trauma of the villagers of Thabai and in *Petals of Blood* he concentrates on Illmorog and the lives of its residents. In precolonial times Illmorog was a purely traditional society untouched by western groups. The peasants reckoned their wealth in land, goats and cows. With imperialistic intrusion, the decline of Illmorog began.

Settlers, colonists and petty Indian traders exploited it. After 'Uhuru' it was no more than a ravished, abandoned ghost of its formerself. After the Europeans had left, the African community was nothing but a tangle of disoriented isolated life. The economical exploitation of the Kenyans continued even after it attained independence because of the foreign investments, international corporations and the land occupations.

The novelist became critical of the white settlers who exploited the peasants by imposing taxes on land. So even the landowners suffer a lot at the hands of the whites. The yield from their land dwindled. They were now common grass fields as in the past because the settlers occupied most of fertile land. Ngunga's songs, unable to live on the limited lands they owned, most of them turned into workers in Europeans' farms. One of them became a cook in a European house. Ngunga felt sad that his grown up sons had to use his hands for cooking in the Settler's home.

The peasants after paying the taxes levied by the white rulers in the form of the cattle were reduced to a state of penury. The economical condition and the colonial exploitation of Illmorog had a devastating effect on the lives of the people who

> were unable to meet their demands. In the end, they joined the very labouring clan they were trying to avoid by the sale of their lands and property. (*PB*, 90)

The severe drought hit Illmorog and its surroundings. There was neither shade nor rain as the Europeans carried wood, charcoal from Illmorog forest to feed the machines and men. In the words of Munira:

> The railway line has eaten the forests; and after accomplishes their task to the two sails were removed and the ground became a road...a kind of road...that gave no evidence of its formal exploitation glory. (*PB*, 11)

The forest wealth of Kenya has been taken away by the whites. The trans-African road linking Nairobi and Illmorog had also connected many cities of the African continent. Every corner of the continent was now with the easy reach of international capitalists, robbery and exploitation. Through these roads, the whites made profits selling their products such as guns, tractors, blades, and diesel engines. This curbed the Iron-ore business in Africa. Ngugi focuses his attention on the economical exploitation of the Africans at the hands of the whites.

The economic exploitation of the Kenyans by the Europeans continued in the form of loans by their banks and in the form of international European companies owned by Europeans in neocolonial Kenya. This economic exploitation continued even after Kenya attained independence with the help of bourgeoisie Africans. In *A Grain of Wheat* Ngugi draws our attention

> not merely with the wickedness of the oppressors but with the weakness of indigenous people themselves.[24]

The commitment of the novelist to the fellow Africans who were exploited at the hands of their fellow countrymen is to be examined thoroughly by another researcher.

REFERENCES

1. Ngugi, *Home Coming* (London: Heinemann, 1972), 50.
2. Ngugi, *The River Between* (London: Heinemann, 1965), 2.
3. C.B. Robson, *Ngugi wa Thiongo* (London: Heinemann, 1989), 1.

4. Arthur Ravgenscraft, *Ngugi wa Thiongo Contemporary Novelist*, ed. Leslie Handerson (London: St. James Press, 1991), 165.
5. G.D. Killam, 22.
6. Robson, 7.
7. Ngugi wa Thiongo, *Education for a National Culture*, Ufahama, Vol. 12, No. 2, 1983, 24.
8. Jagadish Rai, The Wounded Psyche of Africa' as reflected in Achebe's *Arrow of God*, Palmer's *Turbottool* and Ngugi's *The River Between. Commonwealth Fiction*, Vol. 3 (New Delhi: Classical Publishing Company, 1988), 122.
9. Chinua Achebe, *Things Fall Apart* (London: Heinemann, 1950), 128.
10. Werner Glinga, 'The River Between and its Forerunners: A Contribution to the Theory of Kenyan Novel,' *World Literature Written in English*, Vol. 26, No. 2,1986, 213.
11. Adrian Rocoe, *Prose in his Uhuru's Fire African Literature East to South* (Cambridge: Cambridge University Press, 1977), 177-78.
12. T.N. Dhar, 'Private Dreams and Public Pleasures' Ngugi's *Weep Not, Child* and *The River Between, Commonwealth Fiction*, Vol. 13 (New Delhi: Classical Publishing Company, 1998), 235.
13. Ngugi on Education, 24.
14. *Contemporary Criticism*, Vol. 36, 313.
15. Ngugi wa Thiongo, *Devil on the Cross* (London: Heinemann, 1982), 58.
16. David Cook, 243.
17. Jomo Kenyatta, *Facing Mount Kenya* (London: Martin Sacker and Warberg, 1938), 21.
18. Magina Magina Interviews, Ngugi wa Thiongo, African Report, No. 10, February 1979, 30-31.
19. Bette J. Parker, B.B.C. Interviews Ngugi wa Thiongo, Black's Books Bulletin, Vol. VI, Spring 1978, 51.
20. David Cook, 72.
21. G.D. Killam, 56.
22. Ime Ikeidden, James Ngugi as a Novelist, *African Literature Today*, No. 2, 1969,10.
23. David Cook, 72.
24. Eustace Palmer, *An Introduction to the African Novel* (London: Heinemann, 1972), 26.

16

Naipaul's Second Childhood

Gunjan Chaturvedi

"I was eighteen when I came (to England) and in a way I have grown up here. I've had a second childhood, a second becoming aware of the world. I've grown out of one attitude and begun to understand the world from another point of view in my maturity." Thus, said V.S. Naipaul in the course of an interview in the year 1971. (Without a Place: Interview with Ian Hamilton: 1971: 39-40.) Many years later in 1987, in the novel 'The Enigma of Arrival,' he once again used the phrase 'the second childhood,' this time specifically for a magical decade spent by him at a manor house in Waldenshaw, Wiltshire. This retreat into the pastoral world from the exhaustion of his peripatetic life and weakness of a demanding vocation proved from him "something like a second life...a rebirth." (Naipaul: 'The Enigma of Arrival': India: Picador: 2002: 189. All the subsequent references are to this only.) In the benign land of Waldenshaw, at the advanced age of about forty, Naipaul, just like a child, learned the truths of life afresh and felt his personality grow bit by bit. There he recognized the fragmented aspects of his identity, came to understand what was necessary about his painful and awkward past and experienced a renewal which filled up the empty spaces in his own being and ultimately resulted in the acquisition of the desired maturity.

In 1690's John Locke, a physician and philosopher in his 'Essay Concerning Human Understanding and Some Thoughts Concerning Education' observed that a newborn child was like a clean slate or 'Tabularasa' upon which experience would write its story. Contact with adults and the outside world, he opined, would establish the character and mental ability that would remain the child's unique gift or curse throughout life. Sigmund Freud also asserted that what happens to an individual later in life is merely a ripple on the surface of a personality structure that is fashioned during the child's first six years (Freud: 1952). Poets and students of human nature have also been stating for a long time that the impressions of one's childhood days, though they, for the most part, remain buried in amnesia, leave indelible prints and incredible traces which can never be erased from one's psyche. Naipaul's experiences at Waldenshaw, however, evinced that a lucky individual like Naipaul himself, may find a second opportunity of enjoying childhood dreams and fantasies and also of developing visions and attitudes that may bring about a metamorphosis and enable the person to look at the world from a totally different perspective.

Indian by origin, Trinidadian by birth and Briton by citizenship, Naipaul was haunted by a sense of rootlessness. He had never felt at home in the land of his birth, was repelled by the fractured culture and society of the land of his origin and was disillusioned by the "less than perfect world" (EOA: 143) of the land of his vocation. As a result he regarded himself as a wanderer, a homeless being always on the run. His search for identity, he felt, was just like a piece of patterned cloth that one unweaves to trace the figures and that ends by being a heap of tangled threads. In 'The Enigma of Arrival' he has unravelled this stigma upon his being in the following words—"I had thought that because of my insecure past-peasant India, colonial Trinidad, my own family circumstances, the colonial smallness that didn't consort with the grandeur of my ambition, my coming to England with so little and the very little I still had to fall back on—I had thought that because of this I had been given an especially raw sense of an unaccommodating world" (EOA: 99). He had left Trinidad when still almost a child and had arrived in England expecting to find a "grand imperial land of continuous traditions awaiting him with open arms" (King: 1992:147). The actuality confined, small and surrounded by decay and ruin as it was, depressed and baffled him. As a result he "grew to feel that the grandeur belonged to the past; that...(he) had come to England at the wrong time; that...(he) had come too late to find the England, the heart of empire, which (like a provincial from a far corner of the empire)...(he) had created in...(his) fantasy" (EOA: 141).

The disturbance of his mind, together with the feeling of being a perpetual outsider, resulted in an extreme anguish. In such a situation even his writer's vocation "could never offer anything but momentary fulfillment" (EOA: 112). Through a book, which was the result of his research into the history of the West Indies from the time of the discovery of these lands in 1498 to the time of his writing of it, he felt that he had given himself "a past and a romance of the past. One of the loose ends in...(his) mind had vanished, a little chasm filled" (EOA: 179). He now visualized an opportunity of putting an end to his "time in England, shed weariness, not only the weariness of the writing, but also the weariness of being in England, the rawness of...(his) nerves as a foreigner, the weariness of...(his) insecurity, social, racial, financial; put an end to that journey which—in spite of the returns and other journeys in the interim—had remained the fracturing one..." (EOA: 172). The rejection of this book by the publishers broke his spirits completely. It was not only a financial strain but also a negation of his personality, task, goals and objectives. At such a moment of mental fatigue, suffering from terrifying nightmares, with a grief too deep for tears or rage and also with the dread of another failure, Naipaul arrived at Wiltshire where something like a miracle took place, where, says Naipaul, "I was like a child again. As though I had at last, after twenty years, travelled to the equivalent of the fantasy I had had in mind when I had left home" (EOA: 215). "In that unlikely setting," Naipaul reiterates, "in the ancient heart of England, a place where I was truly an alien, I found I was given a second chance, a new life, richer and fuller than any I had had anywhere else. And in that place, where at the beginning I had looked only for remoteness and a place to hide, I did some of my best work. I travelled; I wrote. I ventured out, brought back experiences to my cottage; and wrote. The years passed. I healed. The life around me changed I changed" (EOA: 111-12).

Waldenshaw turned out to be a place where Naipaul, for the first time in his life, found himself in tune with the landscape, where for the first time since he had left his moorings and geographical location, he came to learn "about the seasons... to link certain natural events, leaves on tress, flowers, the clarity of the river, to certain months" (EOA: 189), where he not only heard but also noticed, watched and listened to the larks for the first time in his life. In the beginning of his stay at the place Naipaul was unable to see where he was but then his cognition expanded and he learned not only to see where he was but also to understand and interpret it visually and verbally. It was as if, just like a child, he was "learning a language, after living among its sound" (EOA: 365). He felt a real curiosity about the different sounds and associations of the words of English language and experienced an almost childlike delight every time he learned a new usage. Naipaul very aptly calls the decade, "my second childhood of seeing and learning" (EOA: 93).

In the grounds of the manor, after a long phase of setbacks and self-doubts, Naipaul succeeded in making this discovery of his real self, the discovery of what really is the quintessence of one's presence in the midst of events. He came to realize that the process of creative growth has always to journey through experiences that are strange and impersonal. His engagement with the most pressing truths about existence enabled the expatriate writer to find his bearings. He came to understand that "his notions of and associations with his new home...(had) been wrongly influenced by his colonial influenced by his colonial education and readings in English literature. He must learn to see a new, to understand what he...(was) actually seeing rather than what he...(expected) to see" (King: 1992: 138).

In Wiltshire, Naipaul saw farming, gardening, dairy and farmyard activities and felt admiration for the people who had made a life for themselves on that chalky, flinty soil. He was specially impressed with Jack, a "fitting man fitting the landscape" (EOA: 14), a man "who had created his own life, his own world, almost his own continent, who "had created a garden on the edge of a swamp and a ruined farmyard; had responded to and found glory in the seasons" (EOA: 100), who lived in the middle of junk and there "amid the derelict buildings...had found fulfillment" (EOA: 31). The realization that despite not being rooted in the area Jack was able to make a home for himself, made Naipaul understand that it is the completeness of living in the moment that is more significant than anything else. He himself could get rid of the agony of rootlessness by accepting the present, by trying to plant his roots in the land of his residence and by making efforts to rebuild in accordance with his own image. If the deteriorating estate was a reminder of the "impermanence of men's doings" (EOA: 45), it lay very much within the capacities of human beings 'to do and do again' and ultimately to attain the desired goals. Perfection was not to be found in the past but to be realized in the present through hard work.

When Naipaul observed the Phillipses, the caretakers of the manor house, who always aspired for the pretensions of aristocracy, Pitton, the gardener, whose "intelligence and knowledge...had put his life in the hands of others," (EOA: 254-55) and Les and Brenda, who, despite being "proud and flaunting in one way" were "prepared in another corner of their hearts or souls or minds to go down several notches and be servants," (EOA: 70), he realized that even in the land of the masters people were not free. They were all struggling with varying degrees and indignities of servitude. Even Bray, the taxi-driver, who valued his freedom and was critical of those who were parasites on the state had "the variable fluid personality of the servant" (EOA: 270). All these persons gave the impression of being "safely installed above the currents of history which on a local or universal scale...(threatened) to dislodge and destroy others" (Barfoot: 2002: 109-10). In reality, however, all of them were "unanchored and floating," no more rooted that he himself was. If Naipaul was under pressure to succeed, the similar was the position of Les, who was also "under pressure. From his work on the farm and his uncertainty of what was going to happen with that very big venture.... From his obsession with Brenda, whose beauty so obviously tormented him. Possession of the woman not enough, constantly reminding him of what he might lose. And pressure, too, from his increasingly dependent relationship with the Phillipses" (EOA: 70-71). Naipaul's contact with these residents of Waldenshaw brought to him the comprehension of the underlying situation of all men and enabled him to feel at ease with the idea of the smallness of his colonial past in Trinidad, where the little Asiatic Indian Community, to which Naipaul belonged, was merely "a small world within small world" (EOA: 156).

The story of Alan, the writer, proved in effect to be a cautionary tale for Naipaul. This man who failed to have a true dialogue with his own self, who hid himself from experiences to the extent of falsifying things, imparts a warning to Naipaul of what could happen to an artist who refused to focus on his real identity and shied away from his real self. "Alan's tragedy," says Dooley, "is that he never manages, as Naipaul has managed, to discover himself, to enter the actual real world outside literature..." (Dooley: 162). Earlier, just like Alan, Naipaul also believed that literature was life. He had, therefore, been looking for the world described by Chaucer, Shakespeare, etc. in the real life of England. In the course of his stay at Waldenshaw Naipaul came to realize that literature was not life, on the other hand, life was to be made the true subject of literary compositions. The old English literary tradition, he understood, had decayed and become unsuitable for the expression of the sensibilities of modern man and now it was the duty of the people like Naipaul to guide it and give it proper shape in accordance with their own thoughts, images and needs. The house that Naipaul would later build in Wiltshire after radically redesigning two cottages of the past according to his own requirements, may be taken as symbolic of the declaration by a former colonial of the start of a new tradition in English literature.

Even as a child Naipaul had always seen the worst possibility of ruin at the moment of creation. This was, as he himself confessed, a part of his 'ancestral inheritance.' The beatitude and calm of the world surrounding him at Waldenshaw and the people residing in the area who had learnt to accept decay as a part of the recurring cycles of nature, made Naipaul learn a lesson of extremely high significance. He understood that decay and perfection are the constructions of one's own eye. What is perfection to one may be viewed as decay by someone else. He now started perceiving change as a perennial law of nature with decay as an essential corollary of creation. The place which in the beginning looked like a "perfect unchanging world," was actually not beyond change. It was a place where the present was "encroaching all the time on something more than the past, encroaching on antiquity, sacred ground" (EOA: 27). In this place also "People died; people grew old; people changed houses; houses came up for sale.... Everyone was ageing; everything was being renewed or discarded" (EOA: 32). Actually Naipaul's own presence in the valley was itself a proof of the change. It was a consequence of the decline of the English empire and the movement of the natives of former colonies to the metropolitan country—"the flotsam of Europe after the war," as Naipaul has called it (EOA: 157). During the period of ten years in Wiltshire, Naipaul came to accept that construction and destruction are different aspects of the same God. Here he learned to live, as he himself says, "not with the idea of decay... so much as with the idea of change...and learned profoundly not to grieve for it...to dismiss this easy cause of so much human grief" (EOA: 228-29). To maintain the world as it is, Naipaul realized, is actually to maim it. In his landlord's love of ivy, in his acedia, Naipaul perceived a corruption within the pastoral ideal of perfection and changelessness. In the wish of his landlord to keep the manor as it was, Naipaul saw a sign of inactivity. He came to believe that a man must always be a 'doer,' everyday of his life, no matter what happens. Herein lies the greatest glory of man, the secret behind his success in the world.

Naipaul felt that his life in Wiltshire was actually a compensatory gift of Nature to him "for being away from... (his) home; for that loss, for having no place of...(his) own..." (EOA: 95). Towards the end of the period, however, occurred Naipaul's serious respiratory illness which brought the fear of death in its trail and threatened to make him lose whatever he had gained during the miraculous decade of seeing and learning, of healing and encouragement, of calm and serenity. Coincidentally, the stay was followed by the death of his beloved sister Sati. This demise of someone very close to his heart paradoxically brought Naipaul back into touch with living. When the cremation of his beloved sister was going on in Trinidad he sat in England with his family photographs spread out on a coffee-table. He concentrated on his life and associations with Sati and the experience had a cathartic effect. It made him comprehend that it is possible to resist and overcome death and decay. By transforming an experience into art one can safeguard it from oblivion and extinction. He went to Trinidad to attend the ceremony of his sister's farewell where he came to realize that rituals are basically meant for healing a wound. He now became a celebrator of community besides being one of life and action. He comprehended that escape into the pastoral world is only a debilitating myth and started talking not about 'man' but about the religion of 'men'. To quote Timothy F. Weiss "the phrase "the religion of men"...should...be read...as an affirmation of community that his narrator and protagonist, a man for a long time in exile from other men, has put forward... it is the narrator as exile's affirmation of self and others. It is freedom as "escape to" rather than "escape from" to use Fromm's distinction" (Weiss: 1992: 208).

When Naipaul saw Sati's son performing the rites wearing jeans and jumper and not a traditional dress, in a suburban house and lawn rather than in a rural setting, he found that "the scared world of Indian villages of their (his and Sati's) childhood...(had) vanished and the island...(had) been transformed, remade in a late twentieth century industrial image" (Weiss: 1992: 201). The wish of Sati's family "for old rites, for things that were felt specifically to represent us and our past" (EOA: 384), despite the change that had come in their lifestyles and attitudes, made Naipaul understand that "Men need history; it helps them to have an idea of who they are. But history, like sanctity, can reside in the heart; it is enough that there is something there" (EOA: 386). He came to accept that "to have a past is valuable and necessary but...the past is not a simple static thing to be discovered but something to be 'remade' (Allen: 2002: 153). This realization converted him into a 'doer' once again and quickly he laid aside his "drafts and hesitations and began to write very fast about Jack and his garden" (EOA: 387).

Even without the external evidence given of it, it is safe to assume that the novel 'The Enigma of Arrival' is an account of Naipaul's own journey to maturity. According to his own testimony his dwelling at Waldenshaw was in reality "the second, happier childhood as it were, the second arrival...at a knowledge of natural things, together with the fulfilment of the child's dream of the safe house in the wood" (EOA: 95). The best thing about the life in Wiltshire was perhaps the fact that it was an experience of childhood delights and joys but the perception of the experience was that of an adult. The resultant effect of the whole was that the man who came out of the pastoral world of Waldenshaw, was no longer the man who had entered it. The one who had gone in was a bewildered, dejected and disillusioned being on the verge of wrecking nerves and the one who emerged was a developed, mature and sagacious person who had learnt to see and live life correctly during the magical decade of his "second childhood...so far away from... (his) first" (EOA: 93).

WORKS CITED

Allen Richard. 'The Enigma of Arrival and the Comfort of Influence,' 'V.S. Naipaul, An Anthology of Recent Criticism,' ed. Purabi Panwar. Reprinted with adaptations from Richard Allen, Harish Trivedi eds., *Literature and Nation: 1800-1990*, London: Routledge, 2000.

Barfoot, C.C. 'A Style of Mr. Biswas: Freedom, Fantasy and Romance in 'The Enigma of Arrival', 'V.S. Naipaul: Critical Essays,' Vol. 1, ed. Mohit K. Ray, New Delhi: Atlantic Publishers and Distributors (P) Ltd., 2002.

Dooley, Gillian. 'A Definition of the Writing Self: The Enigma of Arrival,' 'V.S. Naipaul: An Anthology of Recent Criticism,' ed. Purabi Panwar.

Freud, Sigmund. *An Autobiographical Study*, N.Y.: Norton, 1952.

Naipaul, V.S. 'Without a Place: Interview, Ian Hamilton,' 1971, reprinted in Savacou-9-10 (1974) and Critical Perspectives on V.S. Naipaul, ed. R.D. Hamner, Washington D.C., Three Continents Press, 1977.

King, Bruce, 'McMillan Modern Novelists: V.S. Naipaul,' London: Macmillan, 1992.

Weiss, Timothy F. 'Exile and Enigma of Arrival,' 'On the Margins: The Art of Exile in V.S. Naipaul,' University of Massachusetts Press, 1992.

17

"The Lunar and the Solar Alongside the Earthly" *Dream on Monkey Mountain*

G. Seetha Ramaiah

Most of Walcott's plays concern themselves with the Caribbean legends, life and the language. In his plays he is concerned with the quality of change than with mere change for its own sake. In a way, he is a revolutionary in that his play *Malcochon* dwells upon the exploits by the whites on the blacks and also the exploits among the Caribbeans themselves. This theme of oppression and exploitation that has been intensively brought out in *Malcochon* recurs in his highly acclaimed play *Dream on Monkey Mountain* that depicts "not only the Negro's righteous rebellion against the white master...it goes further to the heretic extent of having the protagonist reject the equally oppressive role imposed by the black racists."[1]

In the opening of the play, an old charcoal burner, Makak, brings his load down from the mountain to sell on Market Day. He spends Saturday night and Sunday morning in jail, having been arrested for appearing drunk and disorderly. Afterwards he returns to his hut, on the mountain. But, his behaviour is explained as the result either of a fit brought on by the full moon, (according to his friend, Moustique), or of his encounter with an apparition, "the moon, the muse, the white Goddess." The play, with six scenes framed by a prologue and an epilogue, constitutes an enormous, multi-faceted response to Lestrade's question 'what is your name?' (219).

"In an epic fashion set within a mock trial, Walcott equates man's search for identity, his dream, with a present desire for black brotherhood.

Following a Christian theme, the hero of the play who is betrayed, confesses that 'God dead,' and is condemned for attempting to escape from the prison of life. Materialized for his defence, even the best minds of the past cannot help him. He must personally destroy his God and his dream. But the argument and the conflict of the play are also only a dream as the action before the final curtain reverts to the opening scene of the simple man in his squalid life."[2]

Though Errol Hill pronounced *Dream on Monkey Mountain* to be "a tangled, incoherent piece,"[3] it has been well received by audiences and critics in general. Difficulties with the play are due to the multiplicity of interrelated themes, but the very form of presentation (dream framework) underscores its complexity. A production note, reminiscent of Strindberg's preface to the play warns of the play's "illogical, derivative, contradictory nature." Walcott suggests that the play's source is metaphor and it is best treated as a physical poem with all the subconscious and deliberate borrowings of poetry,[4] and that producers will need the kind of disciplined actors, dancers and singers who perform in Kabuki theatre.

In the beginning of the play we find Tigre and Souris, two felons in one cell, and Makak, a charbonnier, in the other. Corporal Lestrade, a mulatto, presides over those three. Makak, an old Black with a jute sack, is arrested for 'mashing up Felicien Alcindor's cafe' on Saturday evening, July 25th. Lestrade is the self-deluded representative of law and order, doing the 'white people work.' He condemns the Blacks as 'animals, beasts, savages, cannibals, niggers.' Those Blacks seem to turn that "place to a stinking zoo" for him (216). Makak's answers to Lestrade's questions reveal that Makak is nameless, and he belongs to a tired race and his religion is Roman Catholicism.

Both Tigre and Souris have sympathy for Makak, but they flatter Corporal Lestrade because, their need for sensationalism is to be satisfied. Lestrade yields to their flattery. He dons the garments of justice saying, "I can both accuse and defend this man" (220). Makak, in his first long speech, tells about his isolation and degradation:

> Is thirty years now I have look in no mirror,
> Not a pool of cold water, when I must drink,
> I stir my hands first, to break up my image.
> I will tell you my dream. (226)

This speech indicates that Makak refuses to confront the nature of his human image, not only because he is Black and thinks himself ugly, but also "because he cannot confront what he really is—fragmented and eclipsed. Paradoxically, he is true to himself and true to the fragmentation, the breaking up of a human image."[5]

Describing Makak Walcott observed:

> ...Makak comes from my own childhood.... I can see him for what he is now, a brawling, ruddy drunk who would come down the street on a Saturday when he got paid and let out an immense roar that would terrify all the children.... This was a degraded man, but he had some elemental force in him that is still terrifying; in another society he would have been a warrior.[6]

Scene One of the play takes to the Monkey Mountain. The 'practical realist' Moustique is introduced to us. He is a friend to Makak and he offers a balance to the latter's fantasy. Though Moustique is parasitic ('mosquito' or 'flea'), he helps keep Makak grounded in the practical world. But, Mosquito's tendency to extreme materialism is a dangerous one.

Makak : I going mad, Moustique.

Moustique : Going mad? Go mad tomorrow,
today is market day. We have three
bags at three-and-six a bag, making
ten shillings and sixpence for the
week and you going mad?... (232)

Moustique is described as 'a little man with a limp,' and he himself speaks of 'this twist foot God give me'. The anatomy of Satan has often been recorded in the 'pan-ic' terms:

> Often He (Satan) has been described as limping, a symbol of impotence, according to some writers and He is frequently black in colour.[7]

Moustique is Makak's alter ego. It is Makak's compassion for him that makes them live together. Moustique says to Makak:

> ...you find me in the gutter, and you pick me up like a wet fly in the dust, and we establish in this charcoal business. You cut, burn and so on, and I sell, until we make enough to buy the donkey.... (233)

But, this bond of compassion gets undermined when Moustique abandons a fair commercial alliance for commercial exploitation.

Moustique is hurt as he feels he is excluded from Makak's emotional circle. As a result Moustique, whether out of his curious perspective and insight, or, out of hurt, sees the spectral white woman as a 'diablesse.' Therefore, there is a poignant irony in Moustique's short soliloquy:

> The misery black people have to see in this life.... A man not only suppose to catch his arse in the daytime but he have to ride nightmares too.... (238)

The rest of the scene, or, the play itself completely, is a battle for the 'soul' of Makak by both 'devil' and 'diablesse.' Moustique uses forceful practicality, cringing fear (of the spider) and tears and appeals to the old man's compassion, the white woman uses sexuality and an appeal to irrationality. Makak is being tempted into forming a relationship with either the materialistic or the fantastic. The irony is that Moustique wants Makak to compromise belief and truth for greed, whereas the white woman wishes to consolidate the romanticised vision Makak has of himself and Africa. Both invade him on the Monkey Mountain: one resides in the actual landscape and the other in the psychological realm.

In Scene Two of the play we see Makak as a Jesus-like healer and Moustique as a Judas-like exploiter of the former's spiritual strength. The death-figure drawn from the Haitian mythology is presented as Basil in this scene. Speaking about the emergence of the character of Basil, Walcott said:

> .... Now, a strange thing happened: I had a prepared text, but there was one figure at the back of my mind, a death figure from Haitian mythology, that wasn't written in. There was an actor, Albert Le Veau, who had just finished doing THE ZOO STORY and DAUPHIN. We were going on tour, but there was no part in it for him. So I worked in the figure from the center of the play's design, and the part radiated through the whole text—the part of Basil. I think that this figure tightened, webbed its structure. It's one of the beautiful accidents that can happen when you have a good company.[8]

There is a comic element in Moustique joining the prayers of the members of a dying man's procession.

Makak puts a living coal in his palm, 'a soul in my hand,' he invokes his own organic and spiritual beginnings:

> Like the cedars of Lebanon,
> like the plantains of Zion,
> the hand of God plant me
> on Monkey Mountain. (248)

This is the spiritual height. From here Makak sees the rest in their homeless, rootless state, 'like a twisted forest/like trees with no roots,' and encourages them to sing out of the depths of their historical anguish and faith: 'sing as you sing/ in the belly of the boot'.

Moustique proclaims Makak God's messenger as the latter saves the sick Josephus. The argument between Moustique and Makak shows clearly that the white Apparition appeals to the woodcutter's sensuality besides to his psychological obsession with whiteness. To gratify his commercialism Moustique exploits Makak's spiritual power and their friendship also. It is here that Moustique comes into conflict with Basil, the overseeing death-figure. Basil threatens Moustique:

"We go meet again, stranger." (252)

We see, in Scene Two, Lestrade succumbing to the temptation of European postures. His concept of self and home lies in the total and static mimicking of European concepts and in the denial of the Black aspect of his mulatto legacy. Wearing wig and gown he tells Souris and Tigre:

> .... This is our reward, we who have borne the high torch of justice through tortuous thickets of darkness to illuminate with vision the mind of primeval peoples, of backbiting tribes!
> We who have borne with us the texts of the law, the Mosaic tablets, the splendours of marble in moonlight, the affidavit and the water toilet,.... (256)

Here one may see a resemblance to Kurtz's sentiments in Joseph Conrad's *Heart of Darkness*—the colonizer sees himself as the bearer of the torch of civilization and salvation to the 'darkness of Africa.'[9]

Moustique exposes the lie inherent in "the colour of (his) English (which) is 'white.' " In turn the Corporal exposes the fear and insecurity that lie behind Moustique's facade of over-confidence and power. Moustique drops the bowl in fear of a spider. Lestrade asks then: 'A spider? A man who will bring you deliverance is afraid of a spider?' (268). Of course, it is Basil, who finally, exposes Moustique's deception to the people. The crowd beats Moustique. Makak enters to see Moustique dying amidst the spoils of his deceit. Moustique says:

> ...I take what you had, I take the dream you have and I come and try to sell it. I try to fool them, and they fall on me with sticks, everything, and they kill me. (273)

Moustique's confession enables Makak confront the materialist aspect of himself. Makak's vision and so Moustique's advice to 'go back to Monkey Mountain' is unheeded by him. Finally Makak looks into the dead man's eyes and sees there a vision that 'darkens his (own) vision, and he lets out a terrible cry of emptiness' (274).

There is a psychic war between the two worlds of black and white, Africa and Europe, that plays on Makak's consciousness. This is mentioned clearly in the question from Frantz Fanon's *The Wretched of The Earth* that Walcott uses to introduce part two of *Dream on Monkey Mountain*: 'Two worlds; that makes two bewitchings, they dance all night and at dawn they crowd into the churches to hear Mass; each day the split widens...' (277).

Initially, Lestrade mimicks the values and attitudes of white colonizers. Simultaneously the white woman tempts Makak to choose a romanticized, illusory vision of his African heritage. Lestrade believes that his salvation and home lie in the white world. He tells the thieves—'Remind me to ask for a transfer to civilization'—a definite reference to the departure syndrome that plagues the West Indies.

Tigre hears that Makak has money hidden away. He plans to get Makak break them out of jail and have him show where the money is hidden on the Monkey Mountain. Instigated by Tigre, Makak stabs Lestrade and says in horror almost referring to Christian ceremony "O God, O gods: What am I, I who thought I was I will drink blood, you will drink it wit me' (0.286). There is another level of reference for the communion comes into symbolic coincidence with 'jungle law'. It is important to see that the 'killing' of Lestrade springs not from a ritual concept of sacrifice, but from the selfish motivation of revenge and profit. Lestrade is only injured by the stab of Makak. He sees that he must play 'another part'. This implies Lestrade's self-imposed role as descendant of the white slave master who often appears in the history books as hunter of runaway slaves (for instance, the hunting of the Maroons of Jamaica). But, 'another part' also carries an underlying meaning which foreshadows the change in the rest of the play. Lestrade says:

> .... There's nothing quite so exciting as putting down the natives. Especially after reason and law have failed. So I let them escape.... I have good reason for shooting them down...attempting to escape the prison of their lives. That's the most dangerous crime. It brings about revolution. (286-87)

These words echo Kurtz's manifesto in Conrad's *Heart of Darkness*: "Exterminate all the brutes." But Lestrade fails to see that the enslavement and persecution of people engenders in the human race itself a profound self of guilt and torment.

Makak is obsessed with life-denying violence. He talks to his imaginary army. Lestrade's entrance in his role of hunter/explorer/ravager/conquistador disturbs Makak's frenzied speech. He is confronted with Basil who uses the same concepts of law, logic, and reason that Lestrade himself is adept at. Now after seeing Basil, the figure of death, Lestrade quickly becomes cognizant of his other part, his Blackness.

When Makak invites Lestrade into the flock, Tigre and Souris give vent to their hate and revenge on the prodigal. In response to Souris' question "...Tigre, are you sure who you are?," Tigre says 'I am a criminal with a gun in the heart of the forest under Monkey Mountain. And I want his (Makak's) money" (303). This shatters Makak's vision. He is disoriented not only in the realm of dream, but also in the physical/psychical area of Monkey Mountain which he knows so well but which now looms up before him as a strange and frightening place. He, from the depths of tired disillusionment, says: "I was a king among shadows. Either the shadows were real, and I was no king, or it is my own kingliness that created the shadows. Either way, I am lonely, lost and an old man again" (304). Of course, this hopelessness is revocable, for Makak is beginning an unconscious rejection of the static moon image, symbolized by the white woman:

> ...if the moon is earth's friend eh, Tigre, how can we leave the earth. And the earth self...we are wrapped in black air, we are black, ourselves shadows in the firelight of the white man's mind.... (304)

If asked to revolve alone, without sun, moon and other spheres, the earth would be an illusion. The white and the black must coexist, the lunar and the solar alongside the earthly.

In the next scene Makak occupies the position of African Monarch sitting on the golden stool. Lestrade dons African robes, shedding his colonial uniform. The 'enemies of Africa' are called. The list includes both historical and fictional. All those who have committed art or good deeds are condemned to death. "Their crime...," says Basil, "is that they are indubitably white" (312).

After the white are finished, the tribunal turns to black enemies. Moustique is presented (who is already dead) before the court. The charge is Moustique 'betrayed our dream.' Makak yields to popular pressure and condemns Moustique to death. Moustique has already died having been absolved from the burden of guilt. The ineffectuality of the tyrant is mirrored in the death of his victim.

The apparition that has enticed Makak into the present role is now brought before him. Makak does not want to sensationalize the issue. Hence he demands that he be alone with the woman. Now he removes his African robes, pronounces himself free—'Now, O God, now I am free,' and, then, he beheads her. Here, what he kills is the polarised and static romanticised vision of his ancestral past—a vision which has itself arisen out of Makak's obsession with whiteness.

The most central to any interpretation of the play is the Apparition. In the list of characters of the play she is described as 'the moon, the muse, the white Goddess, a dancer.' What matters most is that the Apparition, 'Lady of Heaves,' inspires Makak to a belief in his own dignity. By association with the moon, she appears to be the source of Makak's healing power. Yet, at the end of the play, Makak, enthroned, is enquiring of her: who are you? who are you? and is persuaded to behead the apparition. "That the main persuaders are Basil, the figure of death, and Corporal Lestrade, who has newly discovered blackness, should make us wonder whether the play is inviting us to approve."[10]

There is an ambivalence in the way the Apparition is presented: her song, for example, makes her sound like a siren and, therefore, dangerous though attractive. As described by Robert Graves, the white Goddess may transform herself into something loathsome or dangerous; in the list of characters of the *Dream* play the apparition is called not 'White Goddess' but 'white Goddess' which gives greater emphasis to her colour. Moustique wonders whether what Makak described is really a white woman or a 'diablesse.' At the end when the Apparition is on trial, Corporal Lestrade proclaims her 'the wife of the devil, the white witch.' But, the Corporal can largely be discounted at this point as an anti-white racist. Moustique, by this time, has begun to understand Makak's vision—having died once in betraying it—and, in the trial scene, he is a more trustworthy.

Makak and his vision have been betrayed and corrupted, first by Moustique (for money), then by Tigre (for money and power) and finally by Lestrade (for black power). Makak himself (macaque—monkey, imitator) has been inveigled into complicity in each betrayal. In the trial-scene it is significant that the two victims are Moustique and the Apparition, the two figures closest to the earlier, uncorrupted, Makak. Moustique is very much to the point when he advises Makak: 'Look around you, old man, and see who betray what...who are all these new friends?'

"Getting rid of his overwhelming awe of everything white is the first step every colonial must take," Walcott has said.[11] In so far as she represents whiteness, the vision has to be beheaded if Makak is to be free. He wakes up in prison.

Makak's dream involves the repudiation of the models of racial or cultural superiority. Makak, having rejected them, may voice his real name, Felix Hobain. He may change his 'denomination affiliation' from a stammered singular 'catolique' to 'I believe in my God.' Both Makak and Moustique, having confessed their obsession within the dream, walk towards home (Monkey Mountain)—"this old hermit is going back home, back to the beginning, to the green beginning of this world" (326). The vision is Adamic and hopeful—*Dream* implies that Makak (the Christ figure, the Don Quixote) will descend again. "He has to face reality, too. He has to go down to the market every Saturday to make a living."[12] As Makak and Moustique walk home and the dream fades, we realise that the conflicts wrought from the multiracial, multi-cultural, multi-lingual milieu of the West Indies create a complex heterogeneous socio-cultural body.

Mark A. Mc Watt, in his Essay, observes:

> Unlike *Henry Christophe*, the progatonist in the play (*Dream on Monkey Mountain*) has no royal pretensions, but is a hero in the folk tradition.... Makak, the ugly charcoal burner of *Dream on Monkey Mountain*, using his own resources of imagination and the richness of experience, undertakes the purifying dream of his people, wherein he undergoes suffering but emerges with a clear sense of self and identity, and rid of his fear and hatred of whiteness. It is a revolutionary dream, like Ti-Jean's actions, and these folk heroes (Makak and Ti-Jean) suggest strategies for survival and success in the Caribbean context. The play (*Dream*) also represents Walcott's concern for, and involvement with, the community. Through an involvement with the folk and the community the hero arrives at a true sense of self, whereas in the poems the movement seems to be in the opposite direction—through a contemplation of self towards a vision of community.[13]

The hint that 'Monkey Mountain is home' is given in the

Moustique: Makak, Makak, wake up. Is me,
Moustique. You didn't hear
me calling you from the throat
of the gully? (231)

With the apparition still in his mind, Makak is in a coma. Moustique enters. We have to observe the stage direction here: "We hear a cry far off, echoing." This is the authentic, initial scream that comes from the West Indian, the New World expelled/embraced Adam who is central to the all-embracing and releasing archetype that Walcott is attempting. The 'throat' of the gully amalgamates the images of voice and birth: giving birth to voice and being.

Walcott is clearly capable of superb characterization and in his *Dream on Monkey Mountain* Walcott he offers "an archetype of the white woman which owes something to Jean Genet's *The Blacks*."[14] It is important that this image of white racism is presented as a woman, justified object of hate and violence which lies just under the surface of the adoring lover. Clearly, the white woman was not only the oppressor in the slavery-clolonial period in the Caribbean, but the white man seems less culpable in Walcott's world, for both the Devil in *Ti-Jean* and the grand failure Harry in *Pantomims* are perceived as human despite their evident capacity for tyranny, perhaps, Walcott only makes allowances for male evil, out of the freemasonry of maleness which regardless of race, culture, or history, can unite against woman.

Walcott's protagonists experience the necessary progression through exile and alienation to indifference and to a sense of belonging, so the naming of the 'nothing' of history is a necessary preamble to celebrating what is there: this entails going beyond the fact of history to emotion and writing a comprehensive fiction of his people.

In *Dream* on *Monkey Mountain* Walcott contends that what would deliver the New World Negro from,

> servitude was the forging of a language that went beyond mimicry, a dialect which had the force of revelation as it invented names for things, one which finally settled on its own mode of inflection, and which began to create an oral culture of chants, jokes, folk songs and fables; this not merely the debt of history was his proper claim to the New World.[15]

The recurrent theme of Subaltern writers has been 'establishing both a social and a personal identity.' Most of the writers choose to examine the ways in which oppressive ideologies undermine personal identity and lead to madness. Treating the disintegration of personal identity in the face of oppression, post-colonization literature has tended to focus on women. "Walcott is an anglophone post-colonial writer who has taken up the problem of racism. Identity and madness, developing and extending Frantz Fanon's observations through a literary medium."[16]

Dream on Monkey Mountain is a play that explores the ways in which racism defines an unlivable identity for oppressed people, an identity which pushes towards madness. Walcott draws the epigraph for part one from Sartre's prologue to *The Wreched, of The Earth*: as a result of 'always being insulted,' the self becomes dissociated, and the patient heads for madness (211).

Walcott devotes much of the play to exploring the absolute valorization of whiteness, and the absolute devaluation of blackness, in colonial racist ideology. For instance, Moustique says in the play "when I was a little boy, living in darkness, I was so afraid.... God was like a big whiteman, a big whiteman I was afraid of" (290). Walcott is less concerned with the details of racist ideology than with the effects of this ideology on black people. Blacks seek to repudiate their blackness when all value is associated with whiteness. Corporal Lestrade says in the play: "...is this rage for whiteness that does drive niggers mad" (228). Colonial valorization of whiteness has connections with traditional African beliefs. In the yoruba pantheon the circle of deities surrounding the creators Obatala and Oduduwa are called "Orisa funfun" or white deities. As Hallgren points out, "This connection with the colour white is usually interpreted as symbolic: white = holiness and purity."[17] In cases such as, this colonial racist ideology takes up principles from African culture to create a colonized identity. In this way, colonial ideology is not purely foreign. Part of the colonized, subaltern identity is a perversion of a prior, indigenous identity—here the valorization of whiteness.

The play *Dream* centres round a character who foregoes his legal name for the derogatory and implicity recial epithet 'Makak' or 'Monkey.' This use of 'Makak' operates not only to denigrate people, but to undermine African cultural values as well. The monkey is sacred in parts of Africa—among the yoruba. To use the monkey as a derogatory image is simultaneously to dehumanize the person who is called a monkey and to devalue the culture which considers the monkey sacred. "This sort of inversion of African cultural values is the obverse of the perversion and misuse of indigenous identity."[18]

When arrested for disorderly conduct, Makak forgets his legal name. The delirium from which he suffers is connected with this inability to link himself to family or culture. He is formed by an ideology which strips him of the individual and human identity implicit in the name and which seeks to structure his personal identity around a racial typology according to which black is to white as monkey is to human. Lestrade summarizes Makak's condition:

...this is a being without a mind, a will, a name, a of its own. (222)

Though Lestrade adopts a colonial and racist perspective, he articulates Makak's total alienation from any culture which might provide a positive alternative to colonial, racist ideology.

Patrick Colm Hogan refers to Mimeticism and Reactionary Nativism in the *Dream* play, and, relates them to Makak's madness and Lestrade's pathetic and cruel conformity. Mimeticism is "the formation of one's identity in terms of the concepts and values ascribed to one by one's oppressors." It is what leads to racial despair, to the sense that one has no value, as well as to the imitation of white culture, devotion to white law and rule, white ideas and language. Reactionary Nativism is the obverse of mimeticism. It is "the general inversion of colonial and racist hierarchies such that members of the oppressed group affirm their racial and cultural authority in precisely the manner of the colonizers."[19] It is a reaction to the physical and mental brutality of the oppressors, which it denies, but does it overcome.

The plot of the play *Dream* is organised by reference to mimeticism and reactionary nativism. Walcott divides mimeticism into the figures of 'racial despair' and 'mimetic collaborationism'. Racial despair is the popular tendency for those who suffer racial despair and identify themselves with the people. It is exemplified in Makak. The collaborationist tendency, in contrast, is marked by an insistence of difference. We see this in Lestrade who is proud of being part white and who refers repeatedly to blacks in brutally racist terms as 'animals, beasts, savages, cannibals, niggers' (216).

The most significant image of Makak's mimeticism is probably the mask. Makak carries a white mask at the time of his arrest. This is the mask that imitates white people. Moustique, on finding the mask in Makak's hovel, calls it "cheap stupid black children putting on" (240). Facing a crowd seeking release from oppression Moustique says "All I have is this," and explains pulling out the mask, "black faces, white masks" (271).

Makak's love for the white woman gives him pride in his heritage: "She say that I come from the family of lions and kings" (236). Makak is still linked with nature, not humanity. Later in the play Walcott sets up three parallels: milk and coal, day and night, lion and monkey (283). The primary significance of lion is as a signal of whiteness. Through the imagined love of the white woman Makak has gained access to values which need not constrain his identity to that which is worthless. Etymologically, 'lion' derives from Greek and Hebrew roots making it firmly Jude-European. While the values place on Makak by the white woman give him a sense of worth, it is worth that derives from colonial valorization of whiteness and European culture. The values allowed to Makak to celebrate are thus mimetic.

However, from mimeticism, Makak moves into reactionary nativism. Walcott represents two stages of reactionary nativism. The first is that tends to precede national independence which is called 'Romantic nativism' in its popular form, and 'opportunistic nativism' in its anti-popular or indivisualist form. Romantic nativism is an idealization of the culture and history of subordinated group. Makak's Romantic nativism tends to be a romantic naturalism related to his new self-image as the lion, the king of the jungle. Makak urges Souris to find himself 'at home' as 'one of the forest creatures' and makes himself, as Souris says, 'Half-man, half-forest' (289-90).

Opportunistic nativism, on the contrary, is the cynical manipulation of the people's hopes and desires through an insincere celebration of non-European values and customs—a celebration aimed at one's own advancement. The best example of this is Moustique's fraudulent preaching and impersonation of Makak after the latter's sucess as a political and religious leader. Walcott criticises such demagoguery, but, at the same time, allows Moustique to recognise the close connection between romantic nativism and mimeticism, as already quoted in the passage concerning 'black faces, white masks.'

In the play the characters change role, assume aspects of the protagonist's dominant personality traits, and serve as symbols; one who is killed twice returns alive again in the epilogue. Complying with the subliminal continuity of dream sequence, without defying logic, the plot unfolds as Makak attempts to explain the vision he has seen and the event leads to his arrest on charges of being drunk and disorderly. Makak's assistant Moustique, the mulatto jailer Lestrade, two fellow prisoners, Tigre and Souris, merge with his (Makak's) hallucination and participate in his experiences. All of them constitute a beast fable: mosquito, mouse, tigre and the Caribbean macaque. Makak is identified as mimic monkey, remote mountain gorilla, King Kong. But, these were the racist epithets of the colonial period. Now, in the area of independence and black consciousness Makak is toured as King of Africa, Lion of Judah. Looking at this problem of naming we may wonder as to where the actual man is on that spectrum from ape to lion.

Makak's journey to Africa is presented as a Jordan crossing to the promised Land. Besides the central relationship between Makak and Moustique several details of the play owe something to Cervantes' *Don Quixote* "The overall pattern of the action—descent from the mountain, Saturday delirium, and Sunday ascent—alludes to the passion and resurrection of Christ, while Tigre and Souris stand for good and bad thieves crucified with Christ."[20] The historical connection between Easter and Carnival is also exploited: this dream is a brief mardi gras of role-playing, self-dramatization, wish-fulfilment. The white-faced mask of the apparition that Makak carries with him is surely a Carnival mask (and Lestrade's comment that "everybody round here have one" speaks less to the St. Lucian characters than to the Trinidadian audience).

In the production of the play the end is an apotheosis. Makak becomes a pantheon of one on an unregarded tropical olympus. In the details of Makak's final speech, it is clear that Makak remains ambivalent about who he is in relation to this place and its people. He asks to be "swallowed up in mist again," (326) but at the same time he imagines a future when people will look up to the mountain and say "Makak lives there. Makak lives where he has always lived, in the dream of his people" (326). This is precisely the ambivalence of Walcott's contemporaneous poems. In his '*Hic Jacet*' he writes: "Commoner than water I sank to lose my name."[21]

Dream on Monkey Mountain suggests a nativist moralism in which the rejection of 'Europe' and Eurocentrism is taken to its extreme limit. It can be seen as analogous of certain forms of the 'Black Aesthetic' rubric of sixties and early seventies in the United States. The underlying impulse here is a total change of nomenclature, models, inspiration; the call for an autochthonous, pristine, originally aesthetic is so total that any trace, or, influence of European techniques and forms in literature, and any European critic and school in literary criticism is condemned as infinite. *Dream on Monkey Mountain*, according to Biodun Jeyifo, "effectively dramatizes the falsity and pitfalls of the 'decolonization' claimed by this form of nativism."

To conclude one may tune with Walter J. Meserve and say:

> Themes involving God and justice are most persistent in Walcott's plays as he writes about the condition of the common man. God is always a factor in the lives of his characters and the social conditions with which they must contend is dominant in his plays. Although the hero's 'dream touched everyone' in *Monkey Mountain*, it was only a dream, a bitter irony. Yet Walcott's plays must also 'touch every one' as he makes use of along career in the theatre to provide the innovative dramaturgy which transforms his thoughtful concern for man to the public theatre.[22]

Thus, in *Dream on Monkey Mountain* Walcott introduces Makak who sets up a judgment on the history of racial oppression. Makak's journey to Africa serves as a necessary intermediary towards personal liberty. In his reverie he discovers his essential self. Thus, he is a new man living in the dream of his people. "Other men will come, other prophets will come, and they will be stoned, and mocked, and betrayed, but now this old hermit is going back home, back to the beginning, to the green beginning of this world" (326).

NOTES

1. Robert D. Hamner, *Derek Walcott*, Updated Edition, New York: Twayne Publishers, 1993, 66.
2. Walter J. Meserve, "Walcott, Derek (Alton)," *Contemporary Dramatists*, ed. James Vinson, London: St. James Press Ltd., 1977, 814.
3. Errol Hill, "The Emergence of A National Drama In The West Indies," *Caribbean Quarterly*, 18.4 (Dec. 1972), 33.
4. 'A Note on Production' (Dream on Monkey Mountain), *Dream on Monkey Mountain and Other Plays*, New York: The Noonday Press, Farrar, Status and Giroux, 1970.
5. Daizal R. Samad, "Cultural Imperatives In Derek Walcott's Dream on Monkey Mountain," *Postcolonial Literatures: Achebe, Ngugi, Desai, Walcott*, ed. Michael Parker and Roger Starkey, London: Macmillan Press Ltd., 1995.
6. Derek Walcott, "Meanings (1970)," *Critical Perspectives On Derek Walcott*, ed. Robert D. Hamner, Boulder & London: Lynne Rienner Publishers, 1997, 49.
7. R.E.L. Masters, "The Anatomy of the Devil," *Eros and Evil* (Maryland, 1962), 120.
8. Derek Walcott, *Critical Perspectives On Derek Walcott*, 47.
9. Daizal R. Samad, *Postcolonial Literatures: Achebe, Ngugi, Desai, Walcott*, 236.
10. Mervyn Morris, "Derek Walcott," *West Indian Literature*, ed. Bruce King, London and Basingstoke: Macmillan Education Ltd., 1995, 189.
11. Selden Rodman, "Derek Walcott," *Tongues of Fallen Angels*, New York: New Driections, 1974, 249.
12. Derek Walcott, in 'Man of the Theatre,' report of an interview with Derek Walcott, *The New Yorker*, 26 June, 1971, 30.

13. Mark A. Mc Watt, "Derek Walcott: An Island poet and His Sea" in *Third World Quarterly*, Vol. 10, No. 4, Oct. 1988, 1607-15—Reproduced from *Contemporary Literary Criticism*, ed. James P. Draper, Gale (Detroti), Vol. 76, 1992, 274.
14. Elain Savory (Fido), "Images of Dream: Walcott, Soyinka and Genet," *African Theatre Review*, 1: 1 (May, 1985).
15. *Ibid.*, 17.
16. Patrick Colm Hogan, "Mimeticism, Reactionary Nativism, and the Possibility of Postcolonial Identity in Derek Walcott's Dream on Monkey Mountain," *Research in African Literatures*, Oxford: Hans Zell Publishers, 1994, 104.
17. *Ibid.*, 117.
18. *Ibid.*, 118.
19. *Ibid.*, 109.
20. Laurence A. Breiner, "Walcott's Early Drama," *The Art of Derek Walcott*, ed. Stewart Brown, Dufour: Seren Books, 1991, 78.
21. *Ibid.*, 80.
22. Walter J. Meserve, "Walcott, Derek (Alton)," *Contemporary Dramatists*, ed. Jamse Vinson, London: St. James Press Ltd., 1977, 814.

18

Metaphors of Rain and Fire in Salman Rushdie's Recent Story *The Firebird's Nest*

Prabhat K. Singh

'Myths and cultural past of India' has been a favourite choice of Salman Rushdie partly because he has a tenuous link with this land which gives tremendous leaps to his thoughts and fancy and partly because India as a major literary subject helps him win the favour of his western audience by catering to their devious curiosity about Indian ethos. As a literary strategy he mixes the fiction of his mind with the material picked up from the past for giving such an account of life as may be both relevant and revealing to the contemporary reader. In other words, his linking of the mythical or cultural past with the living present makes his writing a mythocentric historiographic metafiction.

"The Firebird's Nest" is one of Rushdie's recent short stories published in the eighth volume of *New Writings* (1999), an anthology of the best in contemporary literature brought out by Vintage in association with the British Council.[1] Conceived in the mythical image of Phoenix, as the title reflects, and the Ovidian terms of metamorphosis, as the epigraph reads, this story explores the mythical, historical, economic and sociocultural facets of contemporary life through two dominant metaphors—rain and fire. Rushdie has chosen these metaphors for their elemental nature that lends them infinite association with the collective unconscious of human race. This paper intends to look into the multiple applications of these metaphors to the given context and underline their suggestiveness.

The story opens with a description of drought which has engulfed the entire domain of a princely state (rains have successively failed its thick forests and singing birds) and has turned it into a dying place, a wasteland, forcing both man and animal to migrate and seek water, the life giving element. Staggering cattle move to the south and east while the Prince, now only Mr. Maharaj after the abolition of stately privileges, moves to America in search of good fortune. The story progresses with the return of Mr. Maharaj with his American bride (bearing a child in her womb) in a limousine driving to his crumbling palace now six-hundred-year old, a virtual ruin of a gothic novel. She has been described as a "rich" and "fertile land" that will bring both "sons and rain" (234). She is a "rainmaker" capable of combining "capital" with "idea" and conjuring up "monetary nourishment" for any project. She had joined the enterprising Maharaj while he was exploring possibility of economic rainfall. Thus water or rain becomes a metaphor of survival in the story. Rushdie has intensified the irony of life by showing that "cascades of precious water flow ceaselessly" (232) in the palace while the rest of the kingdom is dying for a drop of water. Prince's gluttony is his subjects' famine. People assemble in large number at the palace spring to fill their pitchers. Even though those people who consider the American bride a "barren woman" whose "breasts are dry" for she embodies drought and therefore will bring "despair and gloom" to the region, Rushdie has made the necessity of rain metaphorically more pronounced.

To impress on his American bride the glamour and strength of his princely heritage Mr. Maharaj displays the aura of his highness by inviting dignitaries and nobles to dinner by moonlight and arranging an extravaganza of horse-race, camel-race, dancing, songs, fire-works etc. in her honour. But this effort to recreate the scintillating wonder of his lost "magic kingdom" proves to be his economic misadventure which he admits in his reaction to his bride's teaching—"is this how you relax every night?"

> We impoverish ourselves to make you happy. How can you imagine that we are able to live like this? We protect the last fragments of what we had, and now, to please you, we plunge deeper in debt. We dream only of survival; this Arabian night is an American dream. (239)

This economic aspect is intertwined with the issue of cultural collision in the story. The American bride is faced with the problem of homogeneity, the problem of leading life according to a custom she never anticipated. She has to remake her home in an alien environment where she feels she has lost directions as symbolized by the disappearance of railway tracks in her favourite movie that recurs in her dream. The images of "burning bridges" and "burning boat" in her dream suggest the loss of links with her previous life and also cast apprehensions about her fate for she feels trapped in a world of fantasies where the idea of conjugal bliss is fraught with dangers of bride burning, a social malady that makes the metaphor of fire in the story still more evocative.

The sacrificial immolation of a woman labourer in her red *sari* in "the amphitheatre of the dry water hole" (233) hoping for a good rain i.e. good luck, as reported by the labourers digging a reservoir for rain water, is another facet of this mythical narrative. The metaphor of rain here joins the metaphor of fire. Rushdie describes women in general and the 'demure' ones in particular as creatures of 'fiery heart' and dressed in the colours of fire—not only red and gold but also blue in melancholy, green in envy and white and black in utter rage. Rushdie's penchant for irony converges both on the superstitious beliefs prevalent in the society and the allied inevitability of the fate of woman who, he describes, is most 'combustible' for she 'burns' as easily as a piece of paper and gets lost in the sky as a 'puff of smoke.' His anguish over the dehumanization of society is more than evident. He also directs his satiric anger against gender bias—

> Men are earth, solid, enduring, but the ladies are capricious, unstable,
>
> They are not long for this world.... (233)

Rushdie shows that men may be eaten by their land that opens its jaws, the wide 'cracks,' during drought but women die differently—"they catch fire and die" (231). In the bitterly ironical statement there is a clear inversion of the ancient myth about Sita's survival in fire and her submission to the earth in *The Ramayana*. This inversion has been used to characterize both the fury of nature and the pathetic state of woman in the contemporary society, a tragic transformation.

The rationale of metamorphosis has been further expounded through a story within the story which metaphorically accentuates the social evil of bride burning and mythically demonstrates the emergence of life from death. Miss Maharaj, the sixty-year old fierce looking spinster sister of Mr. Maharaj, narrates to the American bride of her brother the horrible tale of a gigantic mythological prince of that kingdom who had married a dancer of unfading beauty. Old age infirmities gripped the prince but his bride, even at fifty, looked a woman of twenty-one. The prince suspected his bride of taking lovers and subsequently developed sexual jealousy that led him to set his fort on fire in which both of them died. Only their children survived—a daughter who became a dancer and a son who grew into a sportsman. It was said that the old prince himself was metamorphosed into 'a giant bird' composed entirely of flames and had burned his bride. Since then the same firebird has been appearing from time to time to burn other brides at their husband's instance by "brushing their bodies with his malevolent wings"—

> All brides in these parts are brought from far a field. And once the men have spent their dowries, then the firebird comes. (242)

Miss Maharaj tells her that even Mr. Maharaj, though a man of modern outlook, was equally helpless in this regard because all were bout to the metaphor of fire. Her question— "Do you know how many brides he has had?" (242)—terrifies the American bride to her bones. Looking at her body she says, "You have a strong body.... Younger, but in other ways not so unlike mine" (240). When the American bride is sleeping, she sits by her side and murmurs—"Yes, a fine body, it could have been a dancer's. It will burn well" (242). Besides, she also describes how a princess "recently" committed suicide by "drinking fire"—"she crushed her heirloom diamonds in a cup and gulped them down" (241).

Since the gossips about the fable keep burning throughout the yarn the whole atmosphere looks ghostly. The panic and bewilderment of the American bride ends only when the mystery of the fable gets blasted. Miss Maharaj, following her confrontation with her brother (in which she admits that the American bride was only the first bride of Mr. Maharaj) divulges the secret—"I am the firebird's nest" (246)—and then turns into flames like Phoenix, the mythological bird. However she does not rise again. Instead, the bodies of the other dancers who were also spinsters symbolizing infertility or dry earth like Miss Maharaj, burst and water pours out drowning the firebird and its nest. The entire "drought hardened land" gets flooded and the region gets "cleansed of its horror." The fairy looking dancers metamorphose into their normal selves and the rhythm of dance turns into the waves of flowing water which symbolizes the regenerative energy of nature. The story finally closes on a note of synthesis as suggested by the American bride's "caressing of her swelling womb" and thinking that "the new life growing within her will be both rain and fire" (247). The metaphors of rain and dire thus become existential.

"The Firebird's Nest" is, therefore, a fictionalization of the myth of Phoenix. It makes an inquiry into the nuances of Indian life and suggests radical transformation for redemption from its delusions. The American bride's fascination about the grandeurs of princely India has served as a narrative strategy and Rushdie, exercising full freedom of imagination, has skillfully interwoven reality and fantasy, history and gossip in the texture of his story using the mythical mode of apprehending reality, a mode most favourite with James Joyce or T.S. Eliot. He has used the ghost element as a technique of romance to comprehend the mythological past as well as to enact the concept of metamorphosis because the mystery about the firebird's nest is hidden in it. And by contrasting the rich past of a princely state with its present phase of economic depression Rushdie has exploded the myth of royalty. However, the recourses Mr. Maharaj take for revival, like turning his palace into a casino run in partnership and owning a satellite-dish franchise smack of Rushdie's endorsement of the modern commercial and high-tech weapons of American imperialism. His story forms a liaison between the east and the west by negotiating cultural identities through the hyphenated existence of Mr. Maharaj who awaits rain to flood the chamber of his dilapidated palace, dry for ages, and his American bride who nourishes the fire of love for continuing human race. Metamorphosis thus works through the metaphors of rain and fire which contain the emotional complexities of both private and public lives.

REFERENCE

1. Rushdie, Salman: "The Firebird's Nest," *New Writing*, Vol. 8, ed. by Tibor Fischer and Lawrence Norfolk, Vintage in Association with the British Council, London, 1999, 231-47.

PART-D

19

Humanitarianism in Mulk Raj Anand

M.K. Naik

Humanitarianism is under a cloud in the present cage. A world dominated by violence, and the culture of the Kalashnikov rifle can obviously have no use for what it evidently thinks is an outmoded creed. The totally negative view of Humanitarianism is well illustrated in Somerset Maugham's plays, *Sheppey*. Here, a barber wins a big lottery prize, and wants to give it away in charity. His relations naturally think he has gone mad; and even the doctor supports them, "because a sane man is not going to give all his money away to the poor. A sane man takes money from the poor.... Philanthropy in general could always be ascribed no repressed homosexuality" (*Collected Plays*, III, 285). That the term, "Humanitarian" has a whiff of the pejorative associated with it, is clear from the definition of it in *The Oxford English Dictionary:* "One who devotes himself to the welfare of mankind at large—a philanthropist. *Nearly always contemptuous*...connotes one who goes to excess in his humane principles" (Vol. V, 445). (Italics mine)

But Humanitarianism is too well rooted in human consciousness over the ages, to be summarily obliterated by passing popular whims. It is an essential part of human nature, and will continue to survive as long as culture and civilization continue to thrive.

The Humanitarian creed has been succinctly analysed by H.S. Salt (*Encyclopedia of Religion and Ethics*, Vol. VI, 836-49). He points out that the creed is not only a principle, but a faith...the ethical belief of the future—the faith of universal kinship.... "Humaneness is an integral part, if not the actual basis of morals. It includes and comprehends both philanthropy-love of mankind, and zoofily-kindness to animals." Humanitarianism is based upon the acceptance of compassion as a moral force, and upon the conviction, with Schopenhauer, that "compassion is an undeniable fact of human consciousness, residing in human nature itself."

The note of Humanitarianism is strongly struck in the work of several writers belonging to different ages. Cowper was "the friend of every animal that breathed;" Blake believed that "A Robin redbreast in a cage/Puts all Heaven in a rage;" Burns knew his animals as intimately as if they belonged to his circle of friends; Sterne's Uncle Toby would not hurt a fly, for "This world is wide enough to hold both thee and me;" and for Thomas Hardy, the "Blinded, Bird" that sang zestfully forgetting the indignity inflicted upon it by Man, is a symbol of divine charity.

Humanitarian compassion has animated the work of several writers of note. This compassion embraces a wide range of unfortunate human beings whose lot it is to suffer at the hands of forces too powerful for them to negotiate. Among these are victims of an unjust political regime, as in Kafka and Orwell; or of a suppressive social order, as in Dickens and Galsworthy. And the compassion can be wide-ranging enough, to take under its wings the disgraced and the fallen, the mentally warped and diseased, and even criminals and so-called enemies of society, as in Dostoevsky. One also remembers that in Shakespeare, even the wicked Caliban is not a hopelessly lost soul. Finally, as in Hardy, there is compassion for the very human condition itself, in which Man is seen as a helpless victim of Fate and Chance.

What effect do humanitarian tendencies in a writer have or his work? Understanding and compassion, sympathy and fellow-feeling seem to endow such a writer's work with a catholicity or outlook, a deep human warmth, an insight into the human heart, and a nearness to life.

At the same time, there are some pitfalls in the path of the humanitarian writer, the most obvious and dangerous being that of sentimentalism. Perhaps the worst offender in this respect is Dickens. One remembers how he refuses to let Little Nell die, before he has extracted the last tear out of the situation (in his defence it can be said that the needs of serial publication necessitated this). To take another example, do not Dickens's Cheeryble Brothers in *Nicholas Nickleby*, appear to be too good to be true, though he claims that they were "drawn from life"?

Another danger is that compassion may sometimes sweep the writer off his feet, and consequently, his work may suffer on the formal side.

Dickens is again the culprit here, and so is Shakespeare in *The Merchant of Venice*, where his sympathy for the Jew, howsoever powerfully expressed, does not quite harmonize with the total ethos of the play, which is that of romantic comedy.

In spite of these possible pitfalls, however, humanitarianism can endow a writer's work with some great gains, as already suggested.

Though the humanitarian ideal is universal, it is perhaps in Indian culture that it has attained its fullest glory, far surpassing Western culture in this respect. Take the question of compassion. In western culture, this extends theoretically to both Man and the animal kingdom; but it seriously restricted by the Biblical injunction that Man has "dominion over the fish of the sea, and over the fowl of the air, and every living thing that moved upon the earth." In contrast with this, in the Indian tradition, God Himself assumed various animal forms, including Fish, Tortoise and Boar. Furthermore, this tradition also includes the vegetable kingdom, thus embracing the entire gamut of the living world. Hence, in Kalidasa's *Shakuntala*, the deer and the trees and creepers weep, when Shakuntala leaves the hermitage, and in *Raghuvamsha* (XIV, 69), Sita's abandonment in the forest is lamented by peacocks, which abandoned dancing, trees that shed their flowers, and deer that gave up their feed. Therefore, a legend like that of King Shibi could only be the product of Indian culture. When this king tries to save a pigeon from the attack by a falcon, the predator argues that if he wants to save the pigeon, he must give the falcon an equivalent amount of flesh, by way of compensation. Shibi agrees and sets out cutting up his own breast; when God suddenly appears to him, telling him that was just a test of the quality and extent of his sense of compassion.

In fact, compassion is only a *value* in Western culture; it is a *way of life* in Indian thought. Hence the Buddha gave a high place to *Karuna* (compassion) in his teaching, so did Mahavira, and the *Mahabharata* proclaimed, *Ahimsa paramodharmah* (Non-violence is the highest way of life).

Actually, Sanskrit poetry was born in a moment of deep compassion when Valmiki commiserated with the *Krauncha* bird, whose mate was killed by the arrow of a hunter, and the poet burst out spontaneously into song, his *shoka*, (lament) becoming externalized into *Shloka* (stanza).

As a modern Indian writer, Mulk Raj Anand is heir to both the Indian and Western thought. That he is very much conscious of this is clear from his statement that he carries "the double burden on my shoulders, the Alps of the European tradition and the Himalaya of my

Indian past" (*Apology for Heroism*, 67). Since Anand's humanitarianism springs from both these traditions, his fiction is perhaps the most complete presentation of humanitarianism in Indian English literature so far. It follows that we see humanitarianism both at its best and at its worst in Mulk Raj Anand.

It is highly significant that Anand's very first novel, *Untouchable*, is a triumphant assertion of his humanitarianism. To choose an untouchable as hero in the year 1935 was, in a sense, a revolutionary gesture in Indian fiction. It was the privilege of handsome middle class youths to play that pivotal role, in most cases. In fact, with the solitary exception of U. Laxminarayana's *Malapalli* (*Colony of Untouchables*, 1921), the untouchable does not figure at all in fiction in the several Indian languages, until then. Even in Marathi, one of the most progressive of Indian literatures, the untouchable first appears in 1941, with S.M. Mate's evocative short stories about the lives of the untouchables in Maharashtra.

Equally significant is another feature of Anand's choice of his hero. We generally think of (or atleast used to, in the pre-Independence days) all untouchables as a single class occupying the lowest rung of the social ladder; but ironically enough, there was an accepted hierarchy within the class, and the lowest of the low were the sweepers, especially the latrine-cleaners. This was obviously because they were not only ritually impure, like others in the same class, but physically impure, owing to the very nature of their work, during the course of which they came into actual contact with human excreta. To make Bakha, the latrine-cleaner, the hero of his novel was, therefore, a brave gesture on the part of Anand.

In describing one eventful day in the life of Bakha, Anand skillfully avoids the temptation to be swept off his feet by his humanitarian compassion. There is no tear-mongering here over the bottom-dog, no tearing of the hair over the downtrodden, no breast-beating over the lot of the oppressed. The novelist maintains an admirable detachment, and a sense of balance, and with one unfortunate exception, refrains from direct preaching. That one exception is the long harangue on the caste-system by the Poet, in the concluding pages of the novel, where one gets the impression that this particular character (who really has no place in the novel) is only the mouthpiece of the author.

The chief reason why Bakha strikes us as the authentic article, and not a pasteboard, romantic low-class hero, is that Anand as a boy, had actually played with untouchable boys, when his father was working in a regiment, to which a sweeper colony was attached. This was a kind of an experience rarely available to a middle class boy. And since childhood experiences leave an indelible mark on a writer's consciousness (Dickens being perhaps the best example of it) Bakha was probably at the back of Anand's mind over the years awaiting his fictional destiny. E.M. Forster aptly said, "*Untouchable* could only have been written by an Indian, and by an Indian who observed from the outside. No European, however sympathetic, could have created the character, because he would not have known enough about his troubles. And no untouchable could have written the book, because he would have been involved in indignation and self-pity" (Preface to *Untouchable*, vi).

Objectivity is vitally important in a novel of protest, because without it, the work is in danger of becoming more protest than novel. Anand seems to be fully aware of this, and avoids the temptation to make Bakha's entire day a chronicle of misery. Bakha is of course humiliated, cursed and bullied in turn, and above all, has to suffer the mortification of finding his sister being molested by the lascivious temple priest. But the day does provide a few sunny moments also. After a termagant of a woman has scolded and driven him away from the wooden platform outside her house on which he rests for a moment, a kindly woman consoles him by handing over a *chapatti* to him, with the gentle admonition, "My child, you shouldn't sit on people's door-steps like this." Similarly, Havildar Charat Singh, who seems to be above all caste prejudices, actually asks him to go into his kitchen and bring him coal for his hubble-bubble; and later, he even pours out tea from his own tumbler into the pan in Bakha's hand. And the day brings Bakha two great gifts: a brand-new hockey-stick, a present from the generous Havildar Charat Singh, and secondly, a gift far more previous—the gift of hope, that some day he will be set free from his dirty duty of latrine-cleaning imposed on him by the accident of his birth as untouchable.

The same kind of objectivity is discernible in the portrayal of character also. The obvious temptation in a novel of protest is to divide characters neatly into the sheep and the goats. Anand withstands the temptation very well. The untouchables in the novel are not all angels, nor are the caste Hindus all devils. It is made clear that Bakha is not a run of the mill untouchable. He looks intelligent, even sensitive, with a sort of dignity that does not belong to the ordinary scavenger, who is, as a rule, uncouth and unclean. The point is driven home when Bakha's brother Rakha is described: "His tattered flannel shirt, grimy with the blowings of his ever-running nose, obstructed his walk slightly.... Flies congregated in abundance...(on) his dirty face...to taste the sweet delights of the saliva on the corners of his lips."

The neat and compact structure of *Untouchable* provides enough evidence of how Anand has not allowed his humanitarian zeal to stifle the formal values of the narrative, which shows three clear stages of development, all during a single day. Each stage shows pleasant and unpleasant experiences mixed with each other. If Bakha's day begins unpromisingly with a harsh dressing down by his father and the rigours of his morning task, he can still look forward to getting the gift of a hockey stick from Charat Singh later in the day. And the proposed visit to the Market-place is another coming attraction. The climax of his felicity is reached when, with a packet of *jalebis* in his hand, he is moving through the market-place. Suddenly, he collides with a caste Hindu, and both his *jalebis* and his felicity bite the dust. The first stage of the narrative, which ends here, occupies less than one third of the novel.

The second stage is longer, occupying as it does about half the book. There are several meaningful incidents in this phase. There is the shocking episode of the temple priest's molestation of Bakha's sister, Sohini; the hockey match, which begins with the triumph of Bakha's scoring a goal with his new hockey stick and ends with the tragedy of a fiasco; and another encounter with father, which leaves a bad taste in Bakha's mouth. This stage occupies slightly less than half of the book.

In the third and final stage, three possible solutions toy his problem are suggested to Bakha: (i) Conversion to Christianity, (ii) Abolishing of untouchability and (iii) the acceptance of the Flush system. The ending of the novel also shows how the artist in Anand does not allow the social reformer in him to overpower the artist. Bakha is not shown accepting a particular solution. "He was thinking of everything he had heard, though he could not understand it all."

It has perhaps not been widely noticed that *Untouchable* carries a critique of what Anand calls the "white-livered humanitarian" (121). The humanitarian, in question is Colonel Hutchinson, chief of the local Salvation Army. He has "swamped the overbearing strain of the upper middle class Englishman in him by his hackneyed effusions of Christian sentiment" (*Ibid.*). He is sincere and well-meaning, but without imagination and real empathy. He utterly fails to establish a rapport with Bakha. All his talk about "Jesus, the Son of God," and "Sin and forgiveness" is meaningless to the simple Bakha. In spite of all his proselytizing zeal, the worthy Colonel represents humanitarianism at its worst—unthinking, blundering and ineffectual.

Untouchable is structurally the least flawed of Anand's novels, the only blemish in it being the long harangue of the Poet towards the end.

Apart from that, theme and form make a "seamless whose" in the novel. *Untouchable* remains the most triumphant assertion of humanitarianism in Anand's fiction. This becomes clear when one finds Anand returning to the same theme twenty-five years later, in *The Road* (1963). During these years, untouchability had been legally abolished, and caste-distinctions had lost their edge in the cities at least. But, in the villages, things remained almost the same, though reform was definitely in the air. This new situation had raised a different set of problems, and one naturally expected Anand to confront them. He does mention some of these changes, but does not allow his awareness of them to be expressed in terms of character and situation. On the other hand, he drags in the hoary romantic convention of the children of two adversaries duly falling in love with each other. Sequels are dangerous animals; they almost always devour their creators!

The two chronicles of the coolies: *Coolie* (1936) and *Two Leaves and a Bud* (1937) lack the near-perfection of *Untouchable*, but do continue the humanitarian affirmation effectively. *Coolie* is the ignoble odyssey of Munoo, an orphaned village boy from the Kangra hills. His several roles include working as a domestic servant in an urban middle class family, a labourer in a Bombay cotton mill, and rickshaw-puller in an Anglo-Indian family in Simla. The theme of the exploitation of the poor by the rich and powerful is driven home quite effectively. Particular care seems to have been taken to see that the picture does not remain one-sided. Munoo is no doubt ill-treated and underfed most of the time; but once he also comes across an employer who treats him like a son, and his Anglo-Indian employer who treats him like a son, he is seriously ill. So Munoo's odyssey is not all trailing clouds of sorrow. It is this sense of balance that saves the humanitarian motif from the pitfalls of sentimentality and tear-mongering.

In spite of this, *Coolie* remains flawed in one major respect. Throughout the narrative, the protagonist remains passive figure. Things happen to him, but nowhere does the author try to let us have a peep into his mind. Munoo is sensitive and intelligent, and the varied experiences he undergoes during highly impressionable period of adolescence should ordinarily make for an almost total transformation of personality. This would have added a new dimension to the narrative, but for some reason, the author avoids meeting this challenge. An uncomfortable question to ask here would be: did Anand do so, because he was so busy emphasizing the social inequity motif that he was content to leave his protagonist a passive figure? This is probably a classic example of what may be called the "humanitarian overkill," which is quite common in this kind of writing.

The theme of exploitation of the underprivileged is dealt with even more effectively in *Two Leaves and a Bud*, where the entire tragedy is unfolded against the backdrop of a tea plantation, which is a microcosm in itself. It is a world in which British officials and their Indian subordinates on the one hand and the indentured coolies on the other are ranged in two separate camps of the exploiters and the exploited. And the colonialism of the British official adds another dimension to the theme of exploitation.

The exploitation of the protagonist, Gangu begins even before he is aware of it. He is lured to the plantation with false promises but finds himself to be virtually a prisoner in the plantation. He is underfed, has to live in unhygienic conditions, and bullied all the time. His wife dies owing to the harsh living conditions, and on top of all this, an over-sexed British official tries to rape his daughter, and Gangu who tries to save her is shot dead. He had come here to start a new life; he ends by dying.

Here again, Anand refuses to allow himself to be swept off his feet by his compassion for the underdog. The coolies are not all presented as paragons of innocence and virtue. Most of them cheat at work; and even a friendly British official is exasperated at their stupidity, their abject humility and their cowardice. The British officials too are not uniformly wicked. Hence, Reggie Hunt, the *Pukka sahib* is pitted against the liberal minded de la Havre, a sensitive, good-natured Englishman.

Two Leaves and a Bud could have emerged as a flawless work, had not Anand succumbed, as in *Untouchable*, to the temptation of direct statement. Here the author's mouthpiece is de la Havre, who treats us to a long harangue on Indo-British relations (135-40).

The Lal Singh trilogy (*The Village*, 1939, *Across the Black Waters* 1941, and *The Sword and the Sickle*, 1942) does not feature the humanitarian strain prominently, but it returns to dominate two later novels: *The Big Heart* (1945) and *The Old Woman and the Cow or Gauri* (1960). The two novels separated by fifteen years, but they are, in a sense, complimentary to each other. *The Big Heart* shows a low class youth, who boldly champions modernity, being destroyed by tradition; while the second novel represents a mystic girl, docile as a cow being transformed into a veritable tigress, under the impact of modernity.

In *The Big Heart*, the negative forces are the narrowness and obscurantism, the defeatism and fatalism of tradition; and the crusader against them is Ananta, the young coppersmith. The most emancipated member of his community, he is a champion of modernity. He has been to Bombay and Ahmedabad, and is well acquainted with the trade union movement. He even dreams of going to *Vilayat* one day and see with his own eyes the wonderful machines invented by the "Sahibs." A man with a "giant frame," Ananta is noted for his generosity (hence the nickname, "Big Heart"), his zest for life and his high spirits. In spite of these assets he however fails to become a new Messiah for his people. He flaunts his atheism, and his disregard of moral taboos, and lacks the tact and patience to carry people with him. His sudden death at the hands of a friend perhaps comes as a retribution for having wasted his opportunities so wantonly. But his fall is tragic because he had really been betrayed by "something false within."

The Big Heart seems to present another aspect of humanitarianism. When larger forces crush an individual, the victim is not altogether without blame, it cannot put on the mantle of lilywhite innocence. If all tragedy is simply waste, the life and death of Ananta represents such a tragedy.

Anand's weakness for direct statement in place of externalizing his vision in terms of meaningful situation involving characters in action, once again comes to the fore in *The Big Heart*, violating the artistic integrity of the novel. As in *Untouchable*, the Poet holds forth here with greater and more disturbing frequency of Anand's favourite topics such as exploitation, the Humanist faith, and modernity. In fact, the novel could certainly have done without the Poet's long harangue to Janki in the closing pages of the narrative. This is a sad blot on a novel, which has otherwise a well-ordered structure, particularly because the entire action takes place on a singleday, as in *Untouchable.*

In *The Old Woman and the Cow* (or Gauri, 1960), Anand's humanitarianism leads to the creation of one of his finest novel, by endowing him with enough empathy to enter successfully into the mind and the heart of a rustic women, and to show the wonderful transformation in her character, personality and fortunes over the years. When the narrative opens, Gauri is just like any ordinary hill-woman. With the deeply ingrained fatalism of the traditional Indian woman, she knows what to expect after marriage and is resigned to her lot. Persecuted by a shrewish and cruel mother-in-law, and a suspicious and brutal husband, Gauri, driven out of the house, goes back to her mother, who is not exactly well-endowed with love and affection. She actually sells poor Gauri to a rich merchant, explaining her decision with impeccable Utilitarian logic: "it was a choice between my Gauri and my cow," the four-footed variety evidently ranked higher.

Returning to her husband once again, she is driven out of the house for a second time. Her plight reminds her of the great Sita, abandoned by Rama. But this latter day Sita need not pray to the earth to swallow her up, like her legendary counterpart. The anonymous crowds in the city can do the job equally well. Gauri becomes a nurse in a city hospital. The rustic, mute, passive Gauri in the opening of the narrative is now a bold, self-confident and self-reliant woman. In suggesting this parallel, Anand has once again shows how a modern narrative can be made to resonate with a deeper meaning, when the author can successfully run a continuous parallel between contemporaneity and antiquity, as Eliot did in *The Waste Land.*

Unfortunately, *The Old Woman and the Cow*, like Anand's earlier successes, is not entirely without a blemish. Here again, Anand succumbs to the temptation of direct, inartistic preaching, spelling out crudely at length, what he has already shows effectively through meaningful incident, and the recordation of the changing face of the protagonist. The main culprit here is Colonel Mahindra, head of the Hoshiarpur hospital. The worthy Colonel's harangues are not only long and shrill; they also are sometimes so misplaced and mistimed as to sound almost ridiculous, as when he solemnly pontificates on effete traditionalism and post-Independence materialism to two rustics who clearly do not understand a single word.

The Old Woman and the Cow is perhaps the last of Anand's novels in which humanitarianism has successfully activated action and developed character. No later novel rises to the level of Gauri's saga. The failure of *The Road*, that pale sequel to *Untouchable* has already been noted earlier. Tall claims have been made for *The Private Life of an Indian Prince* (1953), particularly on the grounds of the putatively autobiographical element in it. It is argued that since the tragedy of the protagonist is based on that of the author himself, the novel must be a masterpiece. This is a copybook example of the Genetic Fallacy; surely the actual work before us should matter more than its putative genesis. The tragedy of the novel begins with its title itself: *The Private Life of an Indian Prince.* No putatively serious novel perhaps had a more titillating title, particularly because the sexual excesses and outrageous escapades of Indian princes are common knowledge.

Anand, of course, had every right to turn the springs of his humanitarian compassion in the direction of a royal prince. But the question is, how successful in artistic terms is the operation. The answer is an unequivocal "no," mainly because Anand does not know his prince as intimately as he knows his Punjabi peasant, his rustic woman and hill-boy. In the event, the protagonist turns out to be only a pathological case, and little more. The central situation also fails to satisfy the acceptable norms of realistic human conduct. It is hardly plausible that the Prince should have a nervous breakdown, because a prostitute rejects him, for a Prince of Colonial India had almost unlimited power over his subjects and he could with impunity drag as many women into his bed as he liked. In any case, the spectacle of a committed writer, and a champion of the underprivileged trying to lave a royal prince in the waters of his compassion is almost comic!

Anand's swansong as a humanitarian writer is *Death of a Hero: Epitaph for Maqbool Sherwani* (1964). This short novel tells the tragic story of a nationalist Kashmiri muslim, who is captured by Pakistani invaders and put to death. Here again, as in the case of the story of the schizophrenic Prince, there seems to be a failure of the imagination. There is paucity of enough situational detail, and the character seems to lack flesh and blood. Even the protagonist fails to come to life, and the one thing one remembers about him after reading the novel is his loquacity. Anand's humanitarian compassion, which rings so true in his native Punjab, seems to become only a routine gesture outside of it.

Morning Face (1968) marks a definite departure in Anand's fiction. From the world of social realism, he now turns inward, and it is the autobiographical vein which dominates most of his later novels, like *Confession of a Lover* (1976), and *The Bubble* (1984). Numerous other minor works have followed, but should be of interest to the bibliographer alone.

Perhaps the most prolific novelist of his generation, Anand has also half a dozen short story collections to his credit. The theme of humanitarian compassion is at the heart of many of these short narratives, with both positive and negative results, as in the case of novels. In his "Short Fables," Anand shows rare empathy in trying to enter into the little minds of a dove, chicks, and a peacock, which in another story the protagonist is a leaf ("A Leaf in the Storm"). And "The Lost Child," which deftly presents at once child psychology and adult philosophy, is easily one of the finest short stories in Indian literature. To set the record straight, one must also mention "Lament on the Death of a Master of Arts," a long short story, which no one could wish had been longer. Sickeningly sentimental, it only shows the author's humanitarianism overflowing the banks of artistic creation to drown the reader in a deluge of tears. Be that as it may, "Humanitarianism in the Short Stories of Mulk Raj Anand" is certainly a subject that deserves separate treatment; but that task had better be left in younger (and abler) hands.

20

Breaking the Borderline: A Note on Narayan's People

R. Ramachandra

A significant feature of Narayan's world is that it is densely populated by borderline people: sanyasis, sorcerers, recluses, criminals and the like. In fact, Narayan's creativity expresses itself, to a great extent, through a fascination for people who are at the borders of social life. A priest exists well within the Hindu social system, but the priest in *The Financial Expert* who gives Margayya the mantra which will make him rich, calls himself a sanyasi; and a sanyasi, strictly speaking, stands completely outside the social system. Perhaps this fascination for the sanyasi will partly explain the conspicuous absence of cast in R.K. Narayan's works. The concept of sanyasi—because it recognizes the equality of not just all human beings, but all living creatures—disapproves the rigid caste system. The sanyasi in *A Tiger for Malgudi* who calmly walks around with a tiger reassures a frightened crowd:

> you need not fear; he has only the appearance of a tiger ...inside he is no different from you and me.

Chinna Dorai who takes Jagan to a secluded spot outside the town, says this about his master's way of life:

> People were afraid to come here because of snakes, but my master loved them and never approved of clearing the wild growth around. This tree was full of monkeys. 'I'll share the fruits of those trees with them,' he used to say. He enjoyed the company of snakes and monkeys and every thing. Once there was even a cheetah in the undergrowth. 'We must not monopolize this earth...,' he used to say....

In Narayan's world, such people who stand about the peripheries of society are more numerous than one notices at first. This is perhaps because they are introduced rather casually and without the burden of the 'metaphysical.' Consider, for example, an episode from *The Vendor of Sweets*. Young Jagan and his wife are being taken to Santana Krishna—the deity who grants progeny to devotees—on the Badri Hill. The journey is by bus. Jagan sits next to his father and on the other side of Jagan sits a 'threshold' figure:

> On Jagan's other side there was a man from the forest with a string of beads round his neck, bolding on his lap a small wooden cage containing a mottled bird, which occasionally let out a cry, sounding like does moving on ancient, uncoiled hinges.

This figure is a combination of a small-statured sanyasi, a petty circus-performer, a tribal and a sooth-sayer. The vehicle holds fifty passengers, double the number it can 'legally' accommodate. Since one of the passengers is sick, the bus stops every "now and then for him to lean out and relieve himself." It is an impressively slow-progressing society containing representations from almost all its sections. And every time the forest-man's bird gives out a cry, it drowns the conversation of the passengers:

> Remarks, enquiries; advice, announcements, the babble of men's talk, women's shrill voices and children crying or laughing formed a perfect jumble and medley of sounds *constantly overwhelmed by the shriek* let out by the mottled bird. (Italics added)

The expression 'constantly overwhelmed' is to be noted, for there is a need to recognize the ability of the peripheral characters to "overwhelm." One such overwhelming presence is that of the Vagrant in *The Vendor of Sweets*. He goes down the streets late in the night, crying at every door "O good mother, give a handful of rice for this hungry one," and he has a voice that easily reaches the innermost recesses of my house:

> He had a deep voice which penetrated the door and reached the kitchen beyond; his tone also quietened troublesome children as he was described to be a man with three eyes.

Jagan has often asked him: "You are sturdy: why don't you seek work?" the unfailing reply is:

> When have I the time, master? By the time I have gone round begging and returned here, the day is over.

This man who is too busy to do any work, provides the frame, as it were, to Jagan's routine life: Jagan meets him in the morning as he goes out to his shop and again, as he returns home late in the evening after closing his shop. He narrates to this Vagrant pictures of America (the Grand Canyon is one of those pictures) as described in his son's letters and even mentions his son's plans of opening a factory.

Narayan's world—whether its social texture is thin or otherwise—is convincing, compelling, because most of his people are not so much characters as figures, or characters aspiring to become figures. Narayan's preferences for 'figures' is quite in consistence with his reverence for the liminal. This is what he says (something which most Indians would reiterate) in his Introduction to *A Tiger for Malgudi*:

> ...when one becomes a sanyasi, one obliterates one's past. A sanyasi is to be taken as he is *at the moment.* You never ask a sanyasi about his ealier life. He has freed himself from all possessions and human ties. (Italics added)

The sanyasi within the novel (*A Tiger for Malgudi*) attests to this belief:

> My past does not exist for me, not a future. *I live for the moment* and that awareness is enough for me. I have erased from my mind my name and identity and all that it implies. (Italics added)

Narayan's characters aspire to become such liminal figures because of an inner compulsion. Such a passage from a full-fledged social status to a peripheral condition appears to be the inevitable destiny of every person in the fictional world of Narayan. "God knows I need a retreat" tells Jagan to Chinna Dorai in *The Vendor of Sweets*, "...at some stage in one's life one must uproot oneself from the accustomed surroundings and disappear so that others may continue in peace," to which the bearded man approvingly replies:

> It would be the most accredited procedure according to our scriptues—husband and wife must vanish into the forest at some stage in their lives, leaving the affairs of the world to younger people.

Even as a confrontation between him and his disobedient son Mali takes place, Jagan feels that his own identity is undergoing a change and he reminds himself that "one ought not to resist when circumstances pushed one across the threshold of a new personality." Retirement becomes for him a "magic word." "If one had to shake off things, one did it unmistakably, completely, without leaving any loophole or a path back." We do not however, feel that this decision to retreat is escapist or even abrupt, because the play of liminality in Narayan is concerned with creating a world and not erasing one. An episode from *A Vendor of Sweets* should amply illustrate this. Jagan's father is a practical man of the world who knows how to get a good coconut crop. "Show me the man who can grow a coconut tree properly and I will show you one with a practical head on his shoulders," is his constant boastful remark. Yet such a man must make a trip to the liminal environment of Lord Santana Krishna, because his daughter-in-law, coming from a family of one hundred and three members, is childless; and a visit to Santana Krishna temple is "the only known remedy for barrenness in women." The temple itself is located on Badri Hill, the base of which is twenty tedious miles away from Malgudi. "Ten months in the year it is raining up there" and is full of "leeches and such things." The liminal nature of the god who grants progeny is further comically stressed by a rule Jagan's father has to respect: pilgrims are not permitted to take coconuts from their own places to the temple, but must buy them at the temple gate. Hence Jagan's father, an expert in coconut cultivation, pays an exorbitant price for a single coconut at the temple. He must not grudge a little extra expense, says the coconut woman, for he will be rewarded with a grandson, she prophesies. The prophecy is fulfilled, of course, with the birth of Mali who increases the number of family members on his mother's side to a hundred and four. So then, celebration of life within society has been made possible, ironically, by a trip to the fringes of social order.

In Narayan's world people seem to be placed on paths that lead to peripheries of society. Raju (in *The Guide*), Jagan (in *The Vendor of Sweets*), the anonymous Sanyasi (in *A Tiger for Malgudi*) have all, before making a final departure from society, made tentative ventures into the liminal atmosphere of prisons. Paradoxically, such ventures to the borders seem to uphold all that is precious and ineradicably human within society. On learning that his son Mali has laned in prison, Jagan comments:

> A dose of prison life is not a bad thing. It may be just what he needs now.

It is from the liminal position of a dead man that Jagan speaks of the validity of the social world to his distressed cousin:

> Everything can go (on) with or without me. The world doesn't collapse even when a great figure is assassinated or dies of heart failure. Think that my heart has failed, that's all.

It is because Jagan has become a liminal figure at the end that he can speak with conviction of the society he is about to give up and the fate of his unsympathetic, non-cooperative son:

> Open the shop at the usual hour and run it. Mali will take charge of it eventually. Keep Shivaraman and the rest happy, don't throw them out.

The 'liminal' is to a great extent responsible for the juxtaposition of the tragic and the comic in Narayan's works. An episode form *A Tiger for Malgudi* should perhaps bear this out. News has gone round that a sanyasi is living with a tiger. Among the many who go to take his 'darshan' is a woman. She bitterly complains to him about her husband who has deserted her. She had to go through a forest to seek out the sanyasi, and the three men who accosted her in the forest have relieved her of her jewellery. This is mere robberly, less heinous, she tells the sanyasi, than deserting one's family and home. The reader's suspicion that the sanyasi is her husband keeps growing. The man, however is not at all affected by her accusations. But his equanimity is for a moment disturbed when she refers to one of her husband's mannerisms, peculiar only to him: rubbing his finger across the brow. Even when reading a newspaper, he would "hold it in one hand so as to leave the other free to trace his forehead." Before going to office, if she asked for cash,

> ...he would say, "If I should conjure up the money," and while uttering the word conjure, he'd send his fingers dancing across his forehead—whether joking or serious, he always took his fingers to his forehead.

This sanyasi has the same habit. The man's past, then, is not totally eased! "Don't deceive me or cheat me" says the woman becoming bolder:

> Others may take you for a hermit, but I know you intimately. I have borne your vagaries patiently for a lifetime. Your inordinate demand for food and my perpetual anxiety to see you satisfied and my total surrender to you night and day when passion seized you and you displayed the indifference of a save....

The poignancy in her tone as she starts obstinately addressing him as 'husband' is set against his gentle but detached kindness and the firmness with which he refers to himself in the third person: "please know that he left home not out of wrath, there was no cause for it, but out of an inner transformation." He neither denies nor affirms that he is her husband. The comic manner in which she detects the husband is juxtaposed with the tragic failure of the woman to persuade the man to consent to his past. In other words, the episode is comic and tragic at once because the man refuses to become a 'character' (through acquiring a past) and chooses to remain a 'figure' (by granting validity only to the immediate moment).

Liminal figures like these make us aware of a sadness that pervades Narayan's works—sadness that has its roots in separation. The sanyasi philosophizes to the tiger:

> No relationship, human or other, or association of any kind could last forever. Separation is the law of life right from the mother's womb. One has to accept it if one has to live in God's plan.

This law of separation seems to operate consistently throughout Narayan's works. People drift away from one another, and to the fringes of civilized life. There is a desparate need for a counter principle to retain people within the social frame. Money provides such a principle in Narayan's world. It may not be morally and emotionally satisfying but Narayan's characters pursue it as long as they want to stake their identities within the social order. It is important for Chandran (in *The Bachelor of Arts*) to earn money through the agency of 'The Daily Messenger,' and so is it for Margayya, Jagan and Raju and others.

To summarise: Narayan's fictional world is populated by people who exist at the outskirts of society; such threshold characters paradoxically validate life within society and it in turn, appears to cherish borderline values; the tragic coexists with the comic.

The proliferation of 'marginal' people largely explains the absence of any great sense of evil and the lack of scope for strong passions in Narayan's works.

WORKS CITED

Narayan, R.K. *The Financial Expert.*

— *A Tiger for Malgudi.*

— *The Vendor of Sweets.*

— *The Guide.*

— *The Bachelor of Arts.*

21

An Interview with Raja Rao

P. Bayapa Reddy

> "I am a man of silence. And words emerge from that silence with light, of light, and light is sacred."
>
> —Raja Rao

The 'Big Trio'—Mulk Raj Anand, R.K. Narayan, and Raja Rao—made a substantial contribution to the novel in English. In fact, they established 'the suppositions, the manner, the idiom, the concept of character, and the nature of the themes' which were to give the Indian novel its particular distinctiveness. With his genuine concern with the villages, with the ferocious poverty and the cruelties of caste, with orphans, untouchables, and the urban labourers, Mulk Raj Anand may aptly be called a 'leftist high Gospeller.' With his delicate blend of gentle irony and sympathy, quiet realism and fantasy, R.K. Narayan stands out as one whose fiction is imbued with a strong sense of place and a 'genius locus.'

Raja Rao, 'a scholarly Sanskritist' has expanded from a modest mountain spring into the huge and majestic flow of the holy Ganges. In fact, he rose from the archetypal village of Kanthapura to Paris, London, Austin; from village realism to a Joycean polyphony of language, languages, and mythologies. As a senior Fulbright scholar I conducted advanced research in English at the University of Texas, Austin where Raja Rao taught philosophy. Just then, Raja Rao won the most prestigious Neustadt International prize for his seven-hundred page narrative, *The Chessmaster and His Moves*. With his challenging radiance and silence Raja Rao gave me an interview which I furnish below for the lovers of literature. Though he passed away on the morning of July 8, 2006, his work remains everlasting amidst the creative artists' minds.

PBR: Do you feel that your background of the ancient Brahmin descent has had any influence in making you a writer?

RR: I think it did a little.

PBR: You seemed to have learned philosophy in Urdu and some Islamic theology in Salar Jung's Madarasa-e-Aliya in Hyderabad. Do you think this philosophical background has ever shaped you as a creative artist?

RR: I learned Sufism there. This appears in my short stories.

PBR: It was said that you were interested in the river Ganga and that you were busy in writing a book on her. Have you ever published any book dealing with the Ganga?

RR: Just ten days ago, it was published in India. Someone sent me a copy of it. The title is "The Ganges Remembered."

PBR: In an Interview published in *The Illustrated Weekly of India* (January 5, 1964), you came out with your view of literature thus: "Literature as 'Sadhana' is the best life for a writer.... All this may sound terribly Indian, but it is not so really. Valery, Rilke and Kafka, for instance, are as close to this view as Tagore in looking upon literature as Sadhana." Will you please elaborate on the Western writers' dedication to the spiritual discipline?

RR: Kafka deeply felt literary creation as Sadhana. Similarly, Rilke looks upon literature as Sadhana.

PBR: E.M. Forster, like you, aligned himself with the city of Hyderabad. Did you ever meet him there? If so, what impressions have you formed on Forster as a writer?

RR: It was I who was instrumental in asking Natwar Singh to edit a book on E.M. Forster. I even contributed an article to it.

PBR: In your earliest writings in Kannada, you eulogize your motherland thus: "O Mother India, at your feet I have been blessed with a glimpse of the supreme spirit. I may leave you and go to your sisters, but I can never forget you." Having lived in the USA for long, do you still hold the same view of owing your inheritance to India?

RR: Yes I do. I tell my American friends that America has only a four hundred year history, Europe has about a 1500 to 2000 year history, but India has four thousand years of splendid heritage. I also tell them that Greece and Rome are the suburbs of India.

PBR: This pertains to the epigraph to your *The Cow of the Barricades and Other Stories.*

On all the roads I go, they suffer
The hermit and the householder
When I tell them the truth, they are angry
And I cannot lie.

How far is this realized in your first collection of short stories?

RR: They mostly deal with the sufferings of human beings. So the epigraph.

PBR: In the Foreword to your novel *Kanthapura*, you said, "Our method of expression has to be dialect which will someday prove to be as distinctive and colourful as the Irish or the American. Time alone will justify it." Do you feel that Indian English has acquired distinction and colour as American English?

RR: Yes, I certainly feel that Indian English has acquired such distinction. When I read some of the journals from India, I feel that they have overcome their Victorian English. They write very good English.

PBR: The epigraph to *The Serpent and the Rope*—waves are nothing but water. So is the sea—is from the sayings of Atmananda. But I find this to be more parallel to Sankara's Hymn on clouds and water. What is your comment on this?

RR: You are absolutely correct. My guru is an advaita. Naturally, he explains the advaita philosophy of Sankara.

PBR: In *The Serpent and the Rope*, Rama declares, "Bombay is a barbaric city...it had no right to exist." Do you think that Aryan wisdom, symbolizing beauty, wisdom and purity, is not preserved there in the city of Bombay?

RR: It is really dirty. It is more westernized.

PBR: Between Indian philosophical and religious thought and the Western philosophical position—which has influenced you more in the writing of your latest novel, *The Chessmaster*?

RR: I always follow the Indian tradition, but I cannot understand where exactly I have been influenced by the Western philosophical position. *The Chessmaster and His Moves* expounds the cosmic tapestry of India. India contributed "Zero" to the world. I took a cue from Ramanujan's concept of

Mathematics and proceeded. There is no question of western influence on me.

PBR: Have you any particular message to convey in *The Chessmaster and His Moves*?

RR: You read it and react to it.

PBR: Did you suffer from critics' lack of experience of the impersonal and the Absolute? If so, will you please specify?

RR: Many a time, especially, with regard to my *Chessmaster*, critics have not understood the seven or eight levels of meaning of the text. So, most of them have written bad reviews of the book. Similarly, they have searched in my work for the East-West dialogue which is not there at all.

PBR: In your fiction, I find your protagonists are always modelled on you. Do you agree?

RR: No. The imagination of mind found a concrete shape in the protagonists in my work.

PBR: You seemed to have conducted research on the influence of India on Irish literature under the guidance of Prof. Cazamian at the University of Paris. Can you possibly explain the Indian factors that have influenced Irish Literature?

RR: Yes. I find similarities between India and Ireland. Mysticism is one such element. W.B. Yeats translated some Upanishads into English. Tagore had some influence on Ireland.

PBR: What comments can you offer on present Indian writing in English in general and of Indian fiction in particular?

RR: I am not a critic at all.

PBR: What is your answer to the critics who say that your novels sometimes overdo the scenes relating to love and sex?

RR: They are not correct. What is Sivalinga in a temple? It is the Yoni of Parvati and the linga of Siva. In temples, we find a similar picture. Read Kalidasa's *Abhignana Sakuntala*. You find more passages which are highly romantic as they seem to be erotic. Critics are not justified in saying that my works overdo scenes relating to love and sex.

PBR: Will you please comment on your theory of fiction?

RR: I have written puranas but not novels.

PBR: Have you ever taught your own creative writing to your students? If so, how did the students react to your works?

RR: I have taught only Indian philosophy. I never told them about my writing.

PBR: To your knowledge, has any comprehensive bibliography appeared in the recent past? If so, can you give me the details?

RR: *The Journal of Commonwealth Literature, World Literature Today* seemed to have brought about some Bibliographies.

PBR: What advice do you give to young artists and critics from India?

RR: They have to practice writing as Sadhana.

22

Tradition and Change in the Novels of Kamala Markandaya

Shiv K. Kumar

Of all the contemporary Indian novelists writing in English, Kamala Markandaya is the most accomplished, both in respect of her sensitive handling of a foreign medium and her authentic portrayal of the Indian scene. What distinguishes her most incisively from other Indian novelists is her acute awareness of a gradual shift in values that has been taking place in this subcontinent during the past two decades or so. Poised delicately between a nostalgic idealization of traditional values and a new compulsive urge for modernity, India has yet to choose between these two postures. Should she allow herself to be swamped by the rising tide of Western materialism or resuscitate older concepts of spiritual contentment and self-abnegation? But, in an age of jet travel and space exploration, she is finding it increasingly difficult to retain her cultural identity.

Kamala Markandaya's novels attempt to present in symbolical characters and situations this thrust toward modernity, which often assumes in her work the guise of a malignant tumor infecting the vitals of a culture traditionally quietistic. It is this evil force that drives her rustic characters from idyllic tranquillity to the disquieting pressures of city life. The exodus from the villages here symbolizes the disinheritance of the human soul, its recantation of the age-old commitment to faith, peace, compassion, and truth.

Change is, therefore, the focal theme in her novels; it is the pivot round which her fictional world revolves. There is hardly a novel which does not derive its aesthetic validity from the interlocked polarities of religion and science, possession and renunciation, empiricism and transcendentalism.

Nectar in a Sieve (1954), her first novel and her magnum opus, captures this dichotomy of values in a most compelling manner. Rukmani, devoted wife of a tenant farmer, living in the soulful quietude of her little village, suddenly finds within this Garden of Eden a serpent in the form of a tannery that begins to rear its ugly head, devouring green open spaces, polluting the clean, wholesome atmosphere, and tempting simple, gullible peasants into greed, ambition, and immorality. Like marauders, the townspeople come, with carloads of bricks, stones, and cement, to build this hideous superstructure, while their supervisor directs the operations "with loud voice and many gestures but doing not a stroke of work himself."[1] The proprietor, "the red-faced white man," does not live in the village "but came and went...," thus laying the foundations of an industrial society based on the principles of exploitation of labor and absenteeism. Prices now rocket sky-high, inflation grips these helpless villagers, and lust begins to prowl around unashamed and unchecked. Suddenly, Rukmani feels concerned about her beautiful young daughter: "I think the end of my daughter's carefree days began with the tannery. She had been used to come and go with her brothers, and they went whither they wished. Then one day, with many a meaningful wink, Kali told us that it was time we looked to our daughter."[2]

Most of the villagers now bow to the winds of change, heralding the tannery as a great landmark of progress. One of the wenches in the village, Kunthi, asks Rukmani to be jubilant over the new developments. "Are you not glad that our village is no longer a clump of huts but a small town? Soon there will be shops and tea stalls, even a bioscope, such as I have been to before I was married. You will see." And Rukmani's own husband, Nathan, joins this chorus of universal exultation: "It is well to accept these things." But Rukmani's intuitive perceptions warn her against the impending disasters; the tannery, she knows, does not augur well for the village; her spirit revolts against this deflowering of pristine innocence.

"'Never, never,' I cried. 'They may live in our midst but I can never accept them, for they lay their hands upon us and we are turned from tilling to barter, and hoard our silver since we cannot spend it, and see our children go without the food that their children gorge, and it is only in the hope that one day things will be as they were that we have done these things.'"

"'Foolish woman,' Nathan said, 'there is no going back. Bend like the grass, that you do not break.'"

And so bend Nathan's children, and Kunthi's, and others', before the winds of change, until the tannery, like the mythical monster, devours the entire village, turning it into a spiritual wasteland. The little village is now transformed into a small town; Rukmani's own daughter, Irawaddy, is forced into prostitution by the inexorable laws of necessity and destitution. The prelapsarian peace of the village is disturbed beyond all redemption. Rukmani's pain pierces deeper and deeper, till she cries out in utter despair:

> "'...our money buys less and less. And for living in a town—if town this is—why, there is nothing I would fly sooner if I could go back to the sweet quiet of village life. Now it is all noise and crowds everywhere, and rude young hooligans idling in the street and dirty bazaars and uncouth behavior, and no man thinks of another but schemes only for his own money.'"

Urged partly by greed and partly by the soaring prices, the villagers demand higher wages, and when denied and thwarted, they threaten to create trouble for their employers. This builds up menacing tensions all over the village. Rukmani's sons return one day, "long after dusk, with the faces of angered men, though neither is twenty."

"'What has happened?' We ask with trepidation. They are still our sons, but suddenly they have outgrown us.

"'Trouble,' they say. 'We asked for more money and they took from us our eating time.'

"I bring out some dried fish and rice cakes. They are ravenous. 'More money?' I say. 'What for? Do they not pay you well already?' 'What for?' one echoes. 'Why, to eat our fill, and to marry and for the sons we shall beget.' And the other says, 'No, it is not enough.'"

Pollution of the body and mind—this is what the new social revolution brings in its wake. But this spiritual wilderness may be reclaimed, Markandaya seems to suggest, by the resilient humanism of an individual like Rukmani, whose unbounded faith looks defiantly beyond all physical suffering, and partakes of that peace that surpasseth all understanding.

Against the backdrop of the turbulent autumn of 1942, when "Englishmen spoke of joining the army, and Englishwomen of driving the ambulances,"[3] Indians were preoccupied with their own political future. *Some Inner Fury* (1957), Markandaya's next novel, presents an India caught up in the maelstrom of her sanguine struggle against British rule. Provoked by constant humiliations and repressions, the younger generation rises against both foreign domination and parental tutelage. The split between the generations, embodying tradition and change, widens unbridgeably. Revolution, both political and social, electrifies the atmosphere. "Let us not talk of change," says Govind, one of the young firebrands. "That is pastime and preoccupation for the middle-aged, not for us. We are young."[4] Flushed with a new sense of independence, the young protagonist in this novel, Mirabai, of rich and orthodox parents, falls in love with Richard Marlowe, one of the governor's aides. This liaison with an Englishman is a rude assault on the powerful and seemingly impregnable citadel of convention. But Mira rides roughshod over all social taboos and inhibitions, and goes on long honeymoonish expeditions with her lover, in utter disregard of decorum and propriety. They are sundered only when political and national barriers intervene.

Roshan Merchant, another emancipated young lady, Oxford-educated and divorced, feels equally torn between the demands of East and West, orthodoxy and nonconformism. "Born in one world, educated in another, she entered both and moved in both with ease and nonchalance. It was a dual citizenship few people had, which a few may have spurned, but many more envied, and which she herself took for granted." "She went to dances wearing lacquered slippers and saris as bright as butterfly's wings and not only Indians but Englishmen as well were eager to partner her...." Both Mira and Roshan are members of a newly emergent society, labelled ultra-modern—"young men in Western clothes and English accents who flaunted their unorthodoxy, and (rather fewer) self-possessed girls with shingled hair and advanced views which they were not afraid top air."

Entrenched against these angry young people is tradition, which often wields subtler weapons to vanquish and befuddle its opponents. When, for instance, Kitsamy returns from Oxford, still in the hold of Western culture, "its brazen ways, its painted women, its easy morality," his mother ingeniously maneuvers him into a prearranged liaison with a girl of her own choice. Premala is let loose on this unsuspecting man till he capitulates willingly, and the marriage is solemnized with the customary ostentation.

> " 'The girl pleases you?—you think your mother has chosen well?"
>
> " 'You have chosen well,' he said, 'I am very fond of Premala.' "

A Silence of Desire, published three years later (1960), brings into sharp focus another aspect of the conflict between tradition and change. Here, the novelist is essentially concerned with the tension between faith and reason, spiritualism and scientific rationalism. Dandekar, a junior clerk in a government department, is painfully disturbed to learn that his wife, Sarojini, has a growth in her womb. A "second-generation city dweller," his pragmatic and scientific outlook on life, partly influenced by his "contact with Europeans," he is shocked when he discovers that his wife is seeking some kind of faith-cure for her serious ailment. Equally disturbing is her idolatrous worship of the tulasi plant, although deep in his soul he feels the beauty and potency of her uncompromising faith. "He had been at pains to bring up his children, with a correct understanding of these matters, and to educate his wife. Not that she did not understand; her religious tutelage had been rather more earnest than his won, and she often had answers to the conundrums which his less amiable, non-Hindu friends set him—not, of course, that she would supply them, until he had indicated that, perhaps, she might. So it was not that she did not understand; it was just that sometimes she might forget, tending the tulasi with a reverence which it did not merit. And yet he had to concede, it was a fine point, the difference between the reverence due to a symbol, and to its actuality, between the tulasi tree, and its maker. Still sometimes she went too far."[5]

He feels still more upset when, one day, his cousin Rajam also tries to defend Sarojini's visits to the Swamy, the faith-healer:

> "'And what makes you so gullible,' cried Dandekar, 'as to believe these hearsay stories, these cures that have happened always to someone else.'"[6]

Dandekar, of course, would rather have his wife treated by some competent doctor at some ultramodern clinic; he would not brook any nonsense about faith-healing. But Sarojini would not yield either; in fact, one day, she flashes back with an unusual vehemence:

> "'.... You would have reasoned with me until I lost my faith, because faith and reason don't go together, and without faith I shall not be healed.... I do not expect you to understand—you with your Western notions, your superior talk of ignorance and superstition when all it means is that you don't know what lies beyond reason and you prefer not to find out. To you the tulasi is a plant that grows in earth like the rest—an ordinary common plant. And mine is a disease to be cured and so you would have sent me to hospital and I would have died there.'"

For a few moments Dandekar feels nettled; his self-complacent scientific rationalism is somewhat shaken. But he soon lapses into the earlier positivism which he daily shares with most of his colleagues who constantly keep drumming: "'The Times are changing!'" There is, for instance, Joseph who "believed in free love and was even said to practice it;" and there was Ghose, a senior officer, who always derived sinister pleasure from puncturing primitive superstitions. When asked by Chari, the head of the department, to probe the mystery surrounding the Swamy, Ghose produces a report, rationally conceived, mechanistically itemized, and logically concluded. "'Here is a man,' he posits before his boss, 'living in apparent poverty whose storerooms are crammed with food and clothing like an Arabian Night's treasure house.... Whose claims to spiritual healing make women flock to him, paying for his illusory cures in cash and kind...who deals in an atmosphere of drugs, devils, incense—things that healthier countries got rid of centuries ago.'" He suggests that this impostor's circus be dismantled and he drummed out of town forthwith. And yet, behind this façade of rational analysis, circumstantial evidence, and irrefutable deductions, there lurks a deeper truth—a truth that remains intractable to any logical reasoning. This transcendental view of experience dawns upon Dandekar when he himself visits the Swamy. In his presence time comes to a stop, all questionings and misgivings are suspended; all activity is petrified, and all nagging urge to investigate and scrutinize is blunted and overcome. Now he realizes the illusion of all material possessions; he who had come to scoff, remained to pray.

"The Swamy was not looking at him, he did not seem to look at anything, he was simply there. Dandekar sat down, glancing overtly at the thin face, the weatherworn skin, and the calm, deep-set eyes. After a while he forgot even the externals, aware only of a quiet that seeped into him, a stillness in which he seemed to float, detached from every care, warm and serene like a child in the womb." And then the Swamy's prophetic words ring out, with a compelling urgency: "'One is not rich until one has nothing left to give away.'" The ancient scriptural emphasis on self-abnegation is reiterated. But as soon as Dandekar moves away from the holy presence, back into the banalities of his humdrum existence, doubt and negation reassert themselves, and a vacuity grips his soul. He even implores Mr. Chari, his executive head, to have the Swamy turned out of town. But when the faith-healer is gone, he again realizes how his disciples, particularly his wife, have been deprived of their only spiritual anchorage.

Markandaya's next novel *Possession* (1963) attempts yet another variation on the theme of acquisition and egocentrism. Lady Caroline Bell, a divorcee—beautiful, rich and imperiously self-willed—visits India, and is fascinated by the amateurish paintings of Valmiki, a rustic boy, whom she encounters in the course of a bizarre search for Indian country liquor. She at once decides to "acquire" him as her protégé, and, after negotiating with his parents, carries him off as a "possession" to London where, under her patronage, and in a congenial environment, he flowers into a mature artist. Caroline now organizes exhibitions of his paintings, and also grooms him for the urbane sophistication of modern living. As a Londoner, Valmiki strays into emotion liaisons with women, flirt with a Jewish maïdservant, Ellie, then with Annabel, a beautiful eighteen-year-old English girl, and lastly with Caroline Bell herself, who, in spite of being old enough to be his mother, tempts him into this incestuous relationship. But even these ephemeral excitements do not completely dry up the springs of traditional religious convictions so deeply ingrained in his soul. He particularly feels an inalienable attachment for his Indian Swamy, whose blessings he invokes in all moments of crisis. When he realizes that his callous indifference toward Ellie has driven her to suicide during pregnancy, he experiences great anguish:

> "My child, living, fighting to live while her blood ran cold. I let it happen...I cared nothing for the sanctity of life—I, a Hindu, wearing the mantle of a Brahmin, and it was a shame, a hypocritical mockery...."[7]

Pursued by this acute sense of guilt, he returns to India, to his guru. When Caroline follows him there to reclaim him, if possible, she is surprised to discover that none of the checks, her material emissaries ("symbols all of power and influence"), that she has sent him for England have been cashed. Valmiki has now gravitated into a new sphere of influence—his Swamy's, his art is now dedicated to the Divine Spirit, not to the god of modernity. Infuriated and crestfallen, Caroline is forced to receive the bitter truth from the Swamy's lips:

> " 'Not only me, I am the least: there is also a divine spirit,' said the Swamy gently, and the chasm between them widened, carrying them to different continents. 'He works for that, and therein is the glory...it gives men a satisfaction so rich they cannot explain it, and mostly they do not even wish to.' "[8]

Her latest novel, *A Handful of Rice* (1966), portrays the milieu of Indian city life in which Ravi, fresh from a village, feels constrained to choose between conscience and violence, compassion and cruelty, integrity and cunning. Hounded by police from pillar to post, he drifts into a coterie of criminals, whose leader Damodar represents human nature at its lowest. If Ravi wishes to offer his beautiful young wife, Nalini, the basic comforts of life he must, Damodar argues, compromise with his conscience, accept the dictates of a new morality, and subscribe to the ethics of bootleggers and smugglers. But in the midst of an orgy of mob fury, Ravi is caught up in an existential moment of soul-searching. "Ravi took aim, posing the jagged brick level at his shoulder. But suddenly he could not. The strength that had inflamed him, the strength of a suppressed, laminated anger, ebbed as quickly as it had risen. His hand dropped."[9]

If Kamala Markandaya's novels carry a peculiar contemporary relevance, it is because her world is peopled with warm and pulsating individuals, caught existentially between momentous choices and commitments. And in this agony of choosing between spiritualism, sometimes denigrated as "passive withdrawal," and materialism, often glorified as "dynamic progress," the novelist's verdict rings out unequivocally. Beyond the ramifications of reason, the hallmark of modernity, lie those indefinable zones of the spirit where alone abides peace. If technological advancement has ushered in only frustrations and neuroses, faith can cure all human ills. The world is indeed too much with us, and little do we realize that "there is also a divine spirit." Interpreted in terms of tradition and change, therefore, Markandaya's novels acquire a new coherence and meaning.

NOTES

1. Kamala Markandaya, *Nectar in a Sieve* (New York: Signet, 1954), 30.
2. *Ibid.*, 33.
3. Kamala Markandaya, *Some Inner Fury* (Bombay: Jaico, 1957), 92.
4. *Ibid.*, 94.
5. Kamala Markandaya, *A Silence of Desire* (London: Four Square, 1960), 5.
6. *Ibid.*, 114.
7. Kamala Markandaya, Possession (Bombay: Jaico, 1963), 212-13.
8. *Ibid.*, 232.
9. Kamala Markandaya, *A Handful of Rice* (New York: John Day, 1966), 297.

23

Evam Indrajit: Prototype of Modern Human Consciousness

K. Nirupa Rani

The history of the drama shows that it has always been dependent on the stage for its development and really good drama can only be born out of a whole movement and not as the outcome of the individual efforts of one or two dramatists. The most fortunate occasion that could happen in the history of Indian drama is the enthusiasm and initiative of the regional writers to translate their plays into English and by way of doing they have paved way for a phenomenon called 'The National Theatre Movement.' The main exponents of this particular sensation are Bengali, Hindi, Marathi and Kannada writers. These writers have engaged themselves in different kinds of experiments ranging from psychoanalysis to Thesis plays which are latest trends in drama. Around mid-sixties when the world drama is busy dealing with a somewhat parsimonious or eccentric or out of sorts of dramatists scouting non-verbal territories giving greater, more subtle and flexible range of expressions both intellectually and emotionally, Indian writers too competed with them with their innovative techniques. This is the time when Girish Karnad came out with his *Tughlaq* (1965) in Kannada, Badal Sircar with his *Evam Indrajit* (1965) in Bengali and Vijay Tendulkar with his *Silence! The Court is in Session* in Marathi. Karnad's play has explored the psyche of a medieval monarch reflecting the political mood of disillusionment which followed the Nehru era of idealism in the country. With irreducible and puzzling quality, symbolism, theme of disguise and dualism of man, shape shifting and elusive and haunting quality, Karnad could successfully relate historical characters of Tughlaq to philosophical questions on the nature of man and destiny of a kingdom headed by a dreamer. Karnad himself has translated the play into English and this translation was first staged at Bombay in August 1970. The same year witnessed another marvellous play in English at Madras translated and directed by Karnad that is Badal Sircar's *Evam Indrajit* followed by *Silence! The Court is in Session* in March 1971.

Evam Indrajit uses myth to examine some of the dilemmas of the urban middle class minority, their class roots, surroundings and his times basically the monotony of existence, tedious conditioned conventions and the allusive idealistic world elsewhere ruminating the meaninglessness of this existence resulting in metaphysical anguish. With illusion of reality use of 'Middle marchers' and prototypes as commentators on society, shift in scales and opting for a flexible, portable and inexpensive third theatre Sircar could recount the story of mythical rebel Indrajit the name of Meghnad who defeated Indra to the futile ambition of man to prove superior to death-in-life attitude in modern life. Vijay Tendulkar's *Silence! The Court is in Session* deals with the deep seated instincts of violence and sexual compulsions that lie beneath respectable exteriors. Using mock-element, theatrical edge and making the structure revolve round the idea of a game and being tight lipped about legal remedies for social problems and unwholesome comments on human nature Tendulkar commented on the lack of self-knowledge and resources to self-justification which is distinctive trait of the present day society.

Of all the forms of literature, the drama perhaps affords the greatest scope of realism. If the term 'naturalist' is used to indicate a dramatist who dealt with contemporary issues in a prosaic way, realist could be idealistic, poetic, fantastic, impressionistic—almost anything except romantic. To this category belongs Badal Sircar. For Sircar theatre has become a real human event 'a real meeting of human beings, not mask to mask, armour to armour, but man to man'. Knowledge about human existence and feeling for the saga of life are essentials of life. This integration of feeling and knowledge forms the basis for consciousness and this in return induces and guides man resulting in meaningful action which can change the colour of the world for the better. To realize human values on the stage there is no need to have auditorium, costly paraphernalia of non-essentials like sets, props, costumes, etc. just a free theatre and human body would do he proved. These two conditions could propagate progressive ideas and values to sophisticated audience who would like to be mentally stimulated and emotionally entertained. There is a cold fire of intellectual display in his art. *Evam Indrajit* is a fine testament on human condition presented in absurd tradition. He explored both the indigenous and western theatre to cover a very wide social and emotional range. Maybe growth of mass-communications has brought this artist nearer to the frontline, so to speak of his society. The play presents the phenomenon of life, selected but not distorted by the vision of the dramatist and the public is left to draw its own conclusions. He is like the inspector in a public inquiry who does not make the law but tries to be impartial about the relevance of evidence. He is a committed observer.

The Indian mind is always fond of attributing the finer thing of national culture—and even the cruder things to a hoary past, to the days of the Gods. The central character of the play 'Indrajit' has all the qualities that one can easily identify in the mythical Indrajit. The Indrajit here figures as a true representative of the author's own age, an arrogant, adventurous spiteful man, a dangerous combination who realizes at the age of thirty-five that "Age is afraid of joy, of happiness. It only wants comfort and peace. Now Indrajit only wants the comfort of a dark, cloudy sky."[1] He is sure of his credentials but doubtful about his existence in terms of space. At once one realizes that inevitable doom darkness the life of such a character. He is not an exceptional person but he is part and parcel of his society capable of coming out of the story crossing the barriers of illusion and reality, willing to play into the hands of his creator the playwright; if the playwright adept in using characters without definite identities to put forward his treatise on human condition effectively. When characters are limiting in their individuality and the story is too specific a subject like—urban middle class people, an important minority and are intimately known Sircar says prototypes rather than characters would be more suitable to express that the problems are not of one, but of many. He adds saying the writer can:

> ...use four prototypes having rhyming names like Amal, Vimal, Kamal, Nirmal to emphasize the generality. He can give one of them another name—say Indrajit, to show that this person is in some ways different from the other three; but Indrajit is also a prototype, not a character. To express the problems of Indrajit effectively, he may also put somebody as one of the dramatic personae who is neither a character nor a prototype but a kind of alter ego of Indrajit. As a story would be too specific to project the Universal nature of the problems, he uses a cycle of typical events in their life instead— examination, interview, marriage, career.[2]

Against this backdrop the action is set in motion and the strength of the theatre is explored by involving spectators, establishing direct communication with the prototypes from audience making the situation three dimensional reality. At this juncture he made theatre a human event and the structure far from naturalistic. Continuity of time and separation of space are not respected: the action flows from one time to another, one space to another without any break. Events occurring at two or more different places at two or more different times are enacted simultaneously. In the process 'space is expanded, sometimes time is telescoped'. Events are suggested rather than actual actions—like a series of abstract movements and gestures—dependence on the performer's body and the spectator's imagination increases reminding us of Beckett's world. The absurdity of the human existence is made clear with the depiction of the two worlds with equal clarity of vision and fairness of view. Climaxes which occur in the one are reduplicated in the other—human values are questioned! One world has a protagonist, so has the other; they are utterly opposed in class. Yet in belief, principle, motivation and ambition they are curiously interchangeable. If they exchanged positions each would act as the other does. Human values which come up for inspection repeat themselves.

The four prototypes Amal, Vimal, Kamal, and Nirmal along with the alter ego of Indrajit that is the writer rip the society bare mocking and putting the conventional practices to shame using symbols which are more real than reality itself. Time gallops, history repeats but the facts of life remain static for generations. People who were young once grow old, hand over their experience to next generation of Amal, Vimal, Kamal, and Indrajit's but still there is no change in man-made conventions and practices. Generations of students discuss cricket, cinema, physics, politics and literature, try their best to migrate to the world outside geography, make futile attempts to soar high in realms of imagination, nurture romantic thoughts and they graduate from school to college and from college to the world passing examination. Time ticks 'one-two-three!' they go round and round bending 'low to rules'

> Indrajit: One has to study—that's a rule. One has to take exams—that's a rule.
>
> One must take up a job—that's one too.[3]

He tries to fight with the world, the society and the evils of society. Knowing well that the anger is 'pointless anger it's blind. Powerless.' When his female counterpart and first cousin Manasi expresses her incapacity for anger and love for life feeling happy to be conditioned and conventional, preferring to be traditional not encouraging Indrajit to contemplate about marriage. The writer says "one moment, one single moment. Deny that circle. Deny that going round and round. Deny the whole question. One moment, one moment in the present. Life. And let's not add this life to other lives. For that will lead us to the whole problem again—resulting in a zero. Let us save this life. Let us save this one moment in the present—that is life."[4] There is no language that can make authentic statement on this life. 'Language is simile and battered and maimed.' The reality is timelessness of existence:

> The earth is crushed, but it's still alive
>
> The century's old, but it listens still.[5]

The world inhales people and disperses them in search of materialistic pursuits. The spark of life catches the prototypes making them immortals for a brief time. All settle in life except Indrajit. He irreverently cries out against what looks to be the tyranny of convention, tradition and authoritarianism of every conceivable activity of type. Knowledge of life makes man aware of the reality of existence. The new awareness traps life seeking liberty, freedom. Freedom from what? Existence—may not be possible—escape is the answer—escape to unknown land—may be familiar London about which he learnt through history an alternative to this is contemplation and past-time present cannot retrieve the time past in concrete terms making life a burden to carry along. Reasoning and logic loose sense in the last analysis of the world. The writer, the alter ego realizes and suggests to Indrajit:

> Hope, waiting hope, waiting on the banks of death is tired too.
>
> Go, take your questions, arguments with you.
>
> Let me be...
>
> In the dark womb of shadows let me sleep...
>
> I am very tired.[6]

The sleep can only be a short respite from the mechanical turning of the wheel of life. It ends at a particular point but not the hangover of dreams. At every stage of existence something crops up to sustain hopes before one understands the truth about it. Indrajit becomes aware of futility of achievement in this nihilistic world. Life is just a dream in which 'past and present are two ends of a single rope.' In this juncture past instead of waiting for future turns into a well-defined point that is Death! If death is reality in life than what else can be a happy situation? In death future is caught as a mould of past. Time comes to standstill at last Indrajit opts this static stance to overcome his disappointments. In an utterly dejected mood he questions the audience

> One needs faith to live. Faith in
>
> God, faith in fortune, faith in

> man; faith in work, faith in
> revolution, faith in oneself,
> faith in love. Tell me—which
> of them is alive in me today?[7]

Existence has become a lie pervading the consciousness of man. People like Indrajit who can grasp this reality are one among a million. He understands 'The lie in his life is the lie in the lives of millions.' He attains a state where he can stand and watch life passing by. Truth of life dawned on Indrajit but how about the rest? Realization strengthened him and overcoming alienation and death Indrajit settles with life, becomes a clog in a wheel and opts for mundane cycle of life safely tucked in his heart. He says that he walks between the railway line and reality is

> what is behind is ahead. There is no distance between the past and the future. What's there in the past is in the future as well.[8]

He is brought out of the emotional past by the writer and put in a sort of a limbo, a no man's land in unreal time; for a final confrontation with the writer in an unwritten play. A promising subject has fallen prey to his destiny. Life cannot be understood in concrete terms. The journey towards no defined goals on an irrational and futile road is the truth. Indrajit is quick to see the Sisyphus analogy and the play ends with a conclusion that goes beyond our logic and reaches out to us from Indrajit who has experienced inescapable sense of life. He is the eternal question mark. Indrajit realizes this out of personal experience and the audience—you and me still seek an answer. The writer brings back the audience to the present from future and says:

> Walk! on the road! For us there is only the road. We shall walk. I know nothing to write about—Still I shall have to write. You have nothing to say—still you have to talk. Manasi has nothing to live for—she will have to live. For us there is only the road—so walk on. We are the cursed spirits of Sisyphus. We have to push the rock to the top—even if it just rolls down.[9]

For Indrajit to become Nirmal is an easy task, but to accept him as Nirmal is problem for the writer. Indrajit suddenly exits putting the writer back on the road to keep on searching for the subject—life.

> For the questions
> Forget the grief
> And have faith
> In the road—

The endless road
No shrine for us
No God for us
But the road,
The endless road.[10]

In this natural presentation of life, an analysis of the individuals inner difficulties lying at the root of social problems and contempt for superficial idealism are highlighted. The heightened consciousness in the form of 'Manasi' is present throughout the play striking a balance between the dream and reality performing the role of 'anima' in the male psyche. She is an archetype waiting patiently to spring out of the realm of unconscious of the writer to become a part of his consciousness. Probably she is an image performing many roles at various levels constantly keeping us to down-to-earth reality. Many of the conventional resources of poetic communication—rhythm, associative values of words, image-making, tonal effect are exploited. The material was not so much specific in the play but unique symptoms of a restless society such as religion, politics, education, the law, social habits and mores, culture and how all these were beginning to lose what seemed to a young generation to be the 'monolithic unchanging face' of centuries is well analysed. There was no expressly conscious response to outside stimuli at all in the play—the playwright was concerned to write a play as ably as possible. To do this the artist allowed himself to be open, at the very least, to the effect of.

NOTES

1. "Three Modern Indian Plays"—Girish Karnad: Tughlaq; Badal Sircar: *Evam Indrajit;* Vijay Tendulkar: *Silence! The Court is in Session* (Delhi: Oxford University Press), 1994, 5.
2. Badal Sircar, *The Changing Language of Theatre* (New Delhi: Indian Council for Cultural Relations), 1982,19.
3. *Three Modern Indian Plays*, 21.
4. *Op. cit.*, 26.
5. *Ibid.*, 29.
6. *Op. cit.*, 46.
7. *Op. cit.*, 49.
8. *Ibid.*, 55.
9. *Op. cit.*, 59.
10. *Op. cit.*, 60.

24

Music as a Medium in *A Suitable Boy*

I.D. Tiwari

Every art involves some other art to create something else. The exercise results into a creation or a performance. A writer uses his imagination to create a world of characters and happenings while a musician uses his imagination with spontaneity to produce emotive sounds. Thus, every artist celebrates human experience, because art, in general, is the celebration of life in varied contexts.

Music, in a wider perspective, is the essence of all living things in nature. All natural things, most of the time, are rhythmical and regular. Abnormality breaks the rhythm but for a very brief period. Normally there is a period of action followed by a period of rest.

The diversity among various cultures has resulted into vividness of music and dance. All forms of arts deal with human being and his attitude towards an unknown power. Generally complex societies nurture complexity in their arts. Indian society, for example, is one of the most complex societies of the world. It is due to this complexity that our arts are complex. Indian dance, in particular, as an aesthetic experience, is a sensorial phenomenon. It is as old as man's earlier effort to express his most early coordinated sensibility. The forms of arts mirror the contemporary social and political conditions. Artists record history unrecorded by the historians. Novelists make use of art and artists as medium in their writings.

Thus, interdependence of arts provides wider and better scope of creativity to a creative person. It also presages parallel movements in different arts. T.S. Eliot, poet and critic, believed in 'synaesthesia'—a term coined by his teacher Baudelaire. The term denotes that all arts are complementary to each other. He extensively used arts and artists as media in his poetry. In his famous poem, *The Love Song of J. Alfred Prufrock*, renaissance artist Michelangelo's recurring reference brings new meaning to the poem.

Eliot uses Michelangelo's name to highlight the culture hollowness of a class. The line 'In the room the women come and go, Talking of Michelangelo,' is not only an ironical thrust at conversational level. Again, these words are not being used as a mode of fashion. It is a significant and a successful attempt of the poet to juxtapose the contrasting values of past and present of the same culture. He is referred to expose the trivialities of a society represented by Prufrock. Besides Eliot, there have been many other poets and writers who used art as medium to express their point of view. Virginia Woolf visited the Post Impressionists Exhibition in London (organised by Roger Try in 1910) and after that characters in her novels changed. Art movements always influence literary movements of the time. Twentieth century Indian English literature exhibits obvious influences of art movements on it. The name that catches our attention first is of Rabindranath Tagore. He was as great in music as in poetry.

One of the many tasks of the artists is to nurture their culture. Here the term 'culture' has been used in the sense of growth of an individual, a class and a society. It involves areas like music, fine arts and literature etc. The culture of an individual as a writer or as a musician cannot be isolated from that of his community or society.

The growth in culture at regional or local level contributes towards the growth of national culture. Indian music and art at local and national level present India's unity in diversity. This is one of the reasons why Indian writers so often use Indian musicians and music as medium to express their viewpoint. R.K. Narayan made a serious effort to depict social realism through music and musician at regional level in his much acclaimed novel *The Guide*. The story of the novel moves round a female dancer and her friend. On the surface level *Guide* is a simple love story with different shades of relationships ending in death of the protagonist. The undercurrents of the narrative reveal socio-economic fabric of Indian society. R.K. Narayan has successfully used art and artist as medium and revealed the cultural constraints of a period.

A Suitable Boy[1] by Vikram Seth is written in the background of social, economical, political and cultural upheaval of newly independent India. It would be interesting to investigate how a novelist chooses a particular set of characters to depict his point of view. Any novel owes its existence to the interest 'which men and women everywhere and at all times have taken in men and women in the great panorama of human passion and action.'[2] Every piece of fiction, whether it is a novel, a drama or a short story, presents a view of life. In fact, time and place of action embrace entire milieu of any society, including political and economic life. Very often reputation of the novel rests on skillful portrayal of life and manners of a particular class, social group or place. *A Suitable Boy* deals with glorious and most eventful period of Indian history.

There are four prominent groups of characters in the novel. They are: Meharas, Kapoors, Khans and Chatterjees. Another important group of characters is the one of musicians that consists of Saida Begam, Ustad Majid Khan, both vocalists of considerable fame, and two accompanists, Ishaq Khan and Motu Chand.

Khans represent a collapsing feudal system. They are proud of their past and apprehensive about their future. Chatterjees represent values of new India. They are forward-looking, innovative, well-educated family. Vikram has used musicians and music as medium to explain and comment upon the social and cultural conditions of early sixties i.e., 1950 to 1955. The novel opens in the early winter of 1950, in a period when India had been free for over three years.

Mahesh Kapoor, a freedom fighter, is a Minister of Revenue of Congress Government in Purva Pradesh. He lives in Prem Niwas—a C shaped, cream coloured, two story family house at Brahampur, an overpopulated city. His son, Maan, is an amateur poet and a lover of classical music. Mr. Chatterjee, head of Chatterjee family, is the Judge at Calcutta High Court. He has five children and all are music lovers. Mahesh Kapoor, as the Minister of Revenue, is the prime mover of a bill that will abolish large and unproductive land holdings in the state. Nawab of Baitar, who owns a large landed estate, is his close friend. Nawab's father, the later Nawab, was an active and dedicated worker of Muslim League. The birth of Pakistan was his life's mission. Unfortunately he died before Pakistan's birth. The present Nawab has two sons—Firoz and Imtiaz. Firoz is a lawyer while Imtiaz is a medical practitioner. Nawab himself is a person of refined taste and loves books. The reader, for the first time meets him in his library expecting his two grand children. He says to a fellow guest in a party, 'I need help in cataloguing. It is a gigantic task and in some way not very heartening. Some of the early editions of Ghalib can't be traced now and some valuable manuscripts by our own poet Mast. My brother never made a list of what he took with him to Pakistan.'[3]

Like many, late Nawab had golden dreams of a new nation. The new nation symbolized cultural identity and material affluence. The cultural ethos of feudal system of the time is dealt with in detail through Nawab's family and their relationship with Saida Bai and his clan and dependent. Mahesh Kapoor invites Saida Bai to sing Ghajals at his residence on the eve of Holi. He is worried about her mood. She is known for making commitments and then not fulfilling them. She is guided by her inclination rather than by her commitments. This tendency could have done a great harm to her professionally if her voice and manners had not been as captivating as they were. At last Saida Bai Firozabadi (although she never lived at Firozabad) arrives at Prem Niwas with her three accompanists. She looks stunningly beautiful. Every action and movement of her body is musical. She goes to Pandal and sits with her harmonium that a servant of the house has carried from the car she came in. It is a known fact that in forties and sixties there were specific dresses for male and female artists. Female singers wore Saris and male singers put on Achakan. Saida Bai wears Sari. Before she begins her song, she moves her silk pallu further forward over her head. Every time it tends to slip down, she moves it further forward. This she does to insure that her head is not left uncovered. The musicians—a Tabla player, a Sarangi player and a Tanpura player sit down and start tuning their instruments. The audience adjusts itself and gives way to newcomers. Men—young and old—sit with eagerness to listen to Saida Bai Firozabadi. Shallow bowls filled with rose and Jasmine petals are passed around. The less modern women sit up stair on the balcony and look through thin drape.

Their discussion about Saida Bai's dress, ornament, face, manner and voice exposes the feudal social structure of the time. The conversation is among the women of two respected families about a high profile artist of the time:

> "'Nice sari, but nothing special. She always wears
> Banarasi Silk.
> Red to night. Last year it was green. Stop and go.'
> '[Hoon] look at that zari work in the sari,'
> 'Very flashy, very flashy'—but I suppose all that is
> necessary in her profession, poor thing.
> 'I would not say 'poor thing.' Look at her jewels. That
> heavy gold necklace with the enamel work—'
> 'It comes down a bit too low for my taste.'

'—Well any way, they say it was given to her by the Sitagarh people!'

'And many of those rings too, I think she is quite a favourite of the Nawab of Sitapur. They say he is quite lover of music'...

'She is exchanging greetings with the Governor now. Look at him grinning. What a fat little man—but they say he is very capable.'

'Are, what does a Governor have to do except snip a few ribbons here and there and enjoy the luxuries of Governor House? Can you hear what she is saying.' "[4]

Both women are from high class families but are not allowed to sit in open with common audience. Although in veil, they are well aware of the decorative authority of the Governor.

Artists of the time depended on their patrons but this did not deter them from breaking their commitments. Saida Bai, aged thirty-five, is a Thumari Singer. In the words of the novelist she has "natural talents, musical training and a touch of heart ache." Saida Bai symbolizes composite culture and interwoven relationship among different social groups. She has mastered her art so well that no one can guess about her religion while she performs her art. She sings so artistically and convincingly that one thinks as if she might have seen the whole thing with her own eyes. After singing some Holi songs she begins to sing the Ghajals of Ghalib and Mast. She asks Mahesh Kapoor, "What will you listen to next Mahesh ji? What a good audience you always provide in your house and so knowledge that I some time feel redundant. I need only two words and your gentlemen complete the rest of the Ghazals. 'The audience responds back with 'no, no,' what are you saying.... We are your mere shadows Saida Begam.' Saida Bai replies very patiently, 'I know it is not because of my voice but through your grace—and that of the one above.' "[5] She continues singing till late in the night. After dismissing her Tabla Player and Sarangi Player she sings with Harmonium.

Saida Bai symbolizes indivisible cultural bond among different religious groups in free India. She entertains Hindus and Muslims alike without giving any consideration to their faith or political belief. Arts stem out of culture. It can be said, specially in Indian context, that cohesiveness or variance of any culture percolates to the bottom line of the society through its arts. Music or art can be used to control divisive forces and at the same time they provide ample changes to study the different components of culture. Music traditions in India were enriched by all sections of the society. Their differences shrink to lowest level at least in this sphere. Vikram's deep interest in anthropology helped him a lot in shaping such characters as Motu Chand and Ishaq Khan with their plausible backgrounds. Motu Chand, the Table Accompanist is a Hindu by faith but this does not impede him in defining sarangi in its real perspective. He says to Ishaq Khan, "Now for me sarangi is not what is made of but what makes-these divine sounds. In the hands of artist even this gut and skin can be made to sing."[6] Ishaq augments Motu Chand's view, "When we pray to such lofty art, we are praying to God himself."[7] Thus music unites, elevates and finally leads to salvation. It is due to their commitment to music that Saida Bai, Motu Chand and Ishaq Khan work as a team. Islam does not consider music as a medium to attain spirituality but for Ishaq 'playing music and praying to God are the same. His statement is in tradition with Indian belief in theory of Naad Brahama,'[8] a belief that God expresses himself through his eternal music and can be realized through earnest music efforts.

Peter Sellars, a theatre producer, writes in *A World of Ideas*, "Vocal music is an attempt to take the whole human being and project it into space. It is the ultimate gesture of getting out of yourself. You take a part of you that is most private, most personal, most inward, and you hurl it out into space—you project it as for as you can. That gesture of opening this whole region of the body results in an enormous spiritual release, and is felt by other people with tremendous impact" (Quoted from *Readers Digest*, 101, Feb. 2000).

The feudal approach to music and culture of that period has been vividly described through the portrayal of feudal character like Raja of March and Nawab Sahib. Raja of March, a fanatic Hindu and staunch enemy of Muslim community once was blinded by Saida Bai's bewildering beauty and had proposed her for marriage. Saida, who hated him but entertained under professional compulsions could turn down his proposal and save her life due to the stringent laws of British India. Even after the independence things have not changed for her. She is as helpless as she was ever. The helplessness of her class and uncouthness of the feudal lords are well portrayed through the following conversation that goes on between Saida Bai and her pet parrot, "Now look at me," said Saida Bai. "I still fell young, though I admit I am naturally not as young as you. I am waiting to spend the evening with its disgustingly ugly man who is fifty-five years old, who picks his nose and belches, and who is going to be drunk even before he gets here. Every one thinks that I am epitome of romance, Miya Mitthu, but what about my feelings? How can I feel anything for these ancient animals, whose skin hangs from their jaws like that of the old cattle straying around Chowk?"[9]

Begam Abida Khan who preferred to stay back in India against the wishes of her husband, expresses concern about art and music in the Assembly of Purva Pradesh when she speaks against Zamindari Bill, "The class of people who preserved the culture, the music, the etiquette of the province is to be dispossessed, is to be driven through the lanes to beg its bread."[10] Saida Bai too is anxious about the preservation and patronage of music and musicians who have been orphaned due to the collapse of a system. Almost same views are expressed by Saida Bai when she asks her parrot what the fate of the birds living in the trees would be after the tress are uprooted. The only ray of hope is A.I.R. controlled by bureaucrats. Ustad Majid Khan, who is an All India Radio graded top class artist passes comment on the then bureaucracy as to how they made or mar career of the artist during the early years of A.I.R. His abrupt comment during the conversation of junior artists exposes the corruption and mismanagement of the system.

> "It is a silly system to grade someone in Delhi on the basis of a single tape of a performance but that is the system we have." Ishaq does not agree with him and says, "It is impartial and insures some degree of competence."
>
> 'Competence!' It was Ustad Majid Khan speaking. The word was spoken with a contempt that seemed to come from the deepest level of his being. 'Mere pleasing competence is not worth having.'

Thus, the novelist has used musicians and their predicament to give tongue to his viewpoint because they represent a living tradition and provide a kaleidoscopic view of the social and cultural life of the particular period under study.

REFERENCES

1. Seth, Vikram, *A Suitable Boy*, New Delhi: Penguin Books India (P) Ltd., 1993.
2. Hudson, William Henry, *An Introduction to the Study of Literature*, London: George G. Harrap and Co., Ltd., 1963, 129.
3. *A Suitable Boy*, 22.
4. *Ibid.*, 80.
5. *Ibid.*, 83-84.
6. *Ibid.*, 107.

7. *Ibid.*
8. "Sound to the Hindus is a form of God referred to in the Shastras as the Naad Brahman and music a part of the whole cosmology. The history of Indian Music is the history of Hinduism beginning with the Vedas. Indian Music in its highest form means the sound of Krishna's flute and god Shiva's dancing to the beat of his Damru." Edit., P.C. Mehta, *On Music, A Collection of Essays*, Bombay: Indian Music Society, 1989; 62.
9. *A Suitable Boy*, 119.
10. *Ibid.*, 281.

25

India and the U.S.A. in Kiran Desai's *The Inheritance of Loss*

Shyamala A. Narayan

Kiran Desai's second novel, *The Inheritance of Loss* skilfully intertwines two strands of narrative, two stories of voluntary exile. The judge (we are told his name only in the sixth chapter) lives in retirement in a decrepit old house in Kalimpong, with his old cook, and his orphaned granddaughter Sai. The only object of his affection is his aging dog, Mutt. The other story is of the cook's son Biju, who is an illegal immigrant in New York. *The Inheritance of Loss* begins with a violent incident in February 1986. "Sai was seventeen, and her romance with Gyan the mathematics tutor was not even a year old" (8). Young boys from the Gorkha National Liberation Front are looking for weapons; they take away the judge's rusted guns "which date from his days in the Indian Civil Service. A BSA five-shot barrel pump gun, a .30 Springfield rifle, and a double-barreled rifle, Holland & Holland. They weren't even locked away: they were mounted at the end of the hall above a dusty row of painted green and brown duck decoys" (5). The two stories come together at the end; Biju is reunited with his father in Kalimpong, though he has been robbed (by the G.N.L.F. boys) of all the money he painfully earned in America. They take away all the things he has lovingly bought to take home, even the clothes he is wearing. But the ending is redeemed from bitterness if we recollect the thought provoking lines which occur earlier in the novel:

> Anyway, he said to himself, money wasn't everything. There was that simple happiness of looking after someone and having someone look after you.

Kiran Desai handles the shifts in time with great expertise. Events of the past, such as the judge's early life and marriage, or details of Sai's parents and her childhood, occur as flashbacks. The atmosphere of Kalimpong, and of Biju's life in New York, is built up through minor characters. Both strands of narrative have a compelling psychological realism; however, some of the scenes set in India lack the sureness of touch that characterizes the social realism of the American scenes.

Since her grandfather has totally retreated from all human relationships, Sai's only emotional ties are with the cook. But they can never be close, because of the class barrier:

> She was rarely in the cook's hut, and when she did come searching for him and enter, he was ill at ease and so was she, something about their closeness being exposed in the end as fake, their friendship composed of shallow things conducted in a broken language, for she was an English speaker and he was a Hindi-speaker. The brokenness made it easier never to go deep, never to enter into anything that required an intricate vocabulary, yet she always felt tender on seeing this crotchety face, on hearing him haggle in the market, felt pride that she lived with such a difficult man who nonetheless spoke to her with affection, calling her Babyji or Saibaby. (19)

There are certain discrepancies in Kiran Desai's depiction of the relationship between Sai and the cook. When she returns late from her meeting with Gyan, the cook reprimands her:

> "Why don't you leave me alone?" she said....
>
> The cook felt hurt to his chutney core. "I'll give you one smack," he shouted. (143-44)

This is inconceivable, considering the class hierarchy. One feels that Kiran Desai has not conceptualised the characters clearly, she seems to be echoing a similar situation in Anita Desai's novel *Fire on the Mountain* (1977), where Nanda Kaul's lonely life is disturbed by the arrival of her great granddaughter, Raka, who turns out to be more of a loner than herself:

> Like an insect burrowing through the sandy loam and pine-needles of the hillsides, like her own great-grandmother, Raka wanted only one thing—to be left alone.... If Nanda Kaul was a recluse out of vengeance for a long life of duty and obligation, her great-granddaughter was a recluse by nature, by instinct. (*Fire on the Mountain* 47-48)

If Raka is "like an insect," eight-year-old Sai is a "little stick figure":

> She had first met the cook when she had been delivered from St Augustine's in Dehra Dun. Nine years ago now. The taxi had dropped her off and the moon had shone fluorescently enough to read the name of the house— Cho Oyu—as she had waited, a little stick figure at the gate, her smallness emphasizing the vastness of the landscape.
>
> ....
>
> There was age in his temperament, his kettle, his clothes, his kitchen, his voice, his face, in the undisturbed dirt, the undisturbed settled smell of a lifetime of cooking, smoke and kerosene. (*Inheritance* 19)

Nanda Kaul realises that Raka "was the finished, perfected model of what Nanda Kaul herself was merely a brave, flawed experiment" (*Fire on the Mountain* 47). In *The Inheritance of Loss*, the judge realises that

> Sai...was more his kin than he had thought imaginable. There was something familiar about her; she had the same accent and manners. She was a westernized Indian brought up by English nuns, an estranged Indian living in India (210).

Nanda Kaul lives all alone in an isolated house, Carignano, in the Himalayan hill station of Kasauli. "It had been built in 1843, by a Colonel Macdougall..." (6). Anita Desai tells us about the history of this cottage, as the postman recollects the various people who lived there:

> "She was the first in a long line of maiden ladies who inhabited Carignano—all English of course.... There was a Miss Lawrence who had ridden across the Thar desert wearing a linen hat and veil.... The two misses Hughes.... Suddenly it was all over. It was 1947. Maiden ladies were not thought to be safe here any more.... Carignano was up for sale and Nanda Kaul bought it". (10)

Like the judge in Kiran Desai's novel, she lives alone with a cook, and avoids all company. Anita Desai does not just state this, she shows it through dialogue:

> "No visitors yet?"
>
> Ram Lal merely shook his head.
>
> The postman gave a snorting laugh. Ram Lal turned to stare at him with his small, red-streaked eyes. The postman immediately looked apologetic. "Every house in Kasauli is bursting now," he explained. "It is the season."

"We have none," said Ram Lal, firmly. (*Fire on the Mountain* 12)

Nanda Kaul "did not want him [the postman] to stop at Carignano, had no wish for letters" (3). Her body language when she receives the letter shows this:

> In the meantime, the postman had detached one letter from the rest and silently handed it over to Nanda Kaul who said clearly but in a voice of suffering, "thank you." Holding it with her fingers, at a little distance from her side, she walked slowly up the flagstone path....
>
> Here was a letter and she would have to open it. She resolved to say "No" to whatever demand or request it contained. No, no, no. (12-13)

The letter is from "the least loved or, at any rate, the most exasperating of her daughters. Asha, the beauty, had dedicated her life to the cultivation of long glossy hair and unwrinkled skin and had little time left over for her unfortunate daughter, the one who married a diplomat" (*Fire on the Mountain* 14). Tara's husband ill-treats her, but her mother callously insists on her going with him to his new posting at Geneva, on her making "another try at being a successful diplomat's wife." Their child Raka has just recovered from typhoid, and so Asha decides to send her to Kasauli; her brother-in-law is going to Shimla with his family, so he will take Raka with them till Kalka, and "put her in a taxi and send her up to Kasauli" (16). Anita Desai carefully prepares the ground for the child to disturb Nanda Kaul's isolation at Kasauli.

Kiran Desai does not take the same interest in the psychological working of her characters. Anita Desai individualises the minor characters, like the cook or Nanda Kaul's daughter by giving them names: Kiran Desai does not give names to Sai's parents, or even the cook, who is a very important character. Her representation of the nuns at the convent school is not quite credible. We can believe that they are avaricious, and so want to get rid of the child from their boarding school because "This month there would be no Mistry bank draft in the convent coffers, no mandatory donations to the toilet renovation fund and bus fund, to fete days and feast days" (*Inheritance* 28). So why don't they simply ask the judge for money? "The older nuns remembered her mother and the fact that the judge paid for her keep but never visited" (28). Sai is despatched to Kalimpong with "a visiting nun who was studying convent finance systems, on her way now to Darjeeling" (30). They travel together by train to Siliguri, and take a taxi; later, the nun goes off to Darjeeling by jeep, while the taxi goes on to Kalimpong. It is difficult to believe that nuns would send an eight-year-old girl all alone in a taxi on a dark evening. Kiran Desai is either mindlessly echoing Raka's arrival in Carignano (which involved the child travelling alone in a taxi for a few kilometres from Kalka to Kasauli, in broad daylight), or she seems to be interested in a purely negative portrayal.

Girls' schools run by nuns were the first to ban corporal punishment, so six-year-old Sai's experiences at school ring false:

> "Good-bye," said Sai, to the perversities of the convent, the sweet sweety pastel angels and the bloodied Christ, presented together in disturbing contrast.... Good-bye to four years of learning the weight of humiliation and fear,.... Good-bye to:
>
> (a) standing in the rubbish bin with dunce cap on.
>
> (b) getting heatstroke in the sun while on one leg and with hands up in the air.
>
> (c) announcing your sins at the morning assembly.
>
> (d) getting paddled red black blue and turmeric.
>
> "Shameless girl," Sister Caroline had told Sai, homeworkless, one day, and delivered her bottom bright as a baboon's, so that she without shame quickly acquired some.
>
> The system might be obsessed with purity, but it excelled in defining the flavour of sin. There was a titillation to unearthing the forces of guilt and desire, needling and prodding the results. This Sai had learnt. This underneath, and on top a flat creed: cake was better than *laddoos*, fork spoon knife better than hands, sipping the blood of Christ and consuming a wafer of his body was more civilized than garlanding a phallic symbol with marigolds. English was better than Hindi (29-30).

As Sai is in boarding, there is little chances of her being "homeworkless," it is day scholars who attract punishment. There is a discrepancy in the time she has spent in the school: on page 27, we learn that "six-year-old Sai had been hastily entrusted to the same convent her mother had attended", but on page 29 (quoted above), the eight-year-old Sai has spent four years in the school. The system's obsession with purity and sin would be apparent to an older child. A child of six or seven would not be so aware of the titillation in "unearthing the forces of guilt and desire." Such a comment would be more relevant to the experience of Rahel in *The God of Small Things*, who is expelled from school when she is eleven and a half years old, for "hiding behind doors and deliberately colliding with her seniors...she had done it to find out whether breasts hurt. In that Christian institution, breasts were not acknowledged" (Roy 16); the experiences of her aunt Baby Kochamma, also reveal the convent's unhealthy attitude. However, the convent's looking down on everything Indian is probably true, and provides a link with the judge's psyche.

Kiran Desai's description of the train journey from Dehra Dun to Siliguri could come straight from Naipaul's *An Area of Darkness:*

> Out of the window, from Dehra Dun to Delhi, Delhi to Siliguri, they viewed a panorama of village life and India looked as old as ever. Women walked by with firewood on their heads, too poor for blouses under their saris.... It was early in the morning and the railway tracks were lined with rows of bare bottoms. Close up, they could see dozens of people defecating onto the tracks, rinsing their bottoms with water from a can. (30)

Later on in the narrative, there is an account of the police checkpoint. The tone of the description, the casual way in which the waiting bus passengers are de-humanized, is reminiscent of V.S. Naipaul:

> At the other end of the bridge the checkpoint guards were inspecting some vehicles going through. Careful in this time of trouble, they had opened the bundles and cases of everyone in a bus and turned their belongings inside out. The passengers waited impassively inside; poor people, their faces squashed against the windows, hundreds of pairs of eyes half dead, like animals on their way to death; as if the journey had been so exhausting, their spirits had already been extinguished. The bus had vomit-strewn sides, great banners of brown flared back by the wind. Several other vehicles waited in line.... (215-16)

One wonders why all the passengers have "eyes half dead." This probably comes of treating the mass of Indians as the Other. If we look at a recent novel centred on a bus journey, Tabish Khair's *The Bus Stopped* (2004), we find that the passengers are generally a feisty lot; of course there is poverty, deprivation and hopelessness, but all the passengers are not "like animals on their way to death" (*Inheritance* 216).

That Kiran Desai can present an authentic picture of India when she concentrates on particular persons and incidents is shown in the continuation of this passage. Sai is just recovering from a bout of retching; she is on her way back from Darjeeling, with Father Booty, Uncle Potty, Noni and Lola, and they are waiting on the bank of "the beautiful transparent Teesta" (215). It is not so much the food as the rejection by Gyan, who is marching in a G.N.L.F. rally, that has made her sick. The Teesta valley is famous for its butterflies; Father Booty sees an unusual butterfly and takes a photograph of it. Unfortunately, it sits on a cable of the bridge, and everyone in the jeep gets into trouble:

> He was about to try again when the guards began to shout and one of them came racing up. "Photography strictly prohibited on the bridge." Didn't he know?
>
> Oh, dear, he did, he did, a mistake, he had forgotten in his excitement. He knew, he knew....
>
> It didn't help that he was a foreigner.
>
> They took his camera and began to search the jeep. (216-17)

What follows is Kiran Desai at her comic best; when they search the jeep, they find Father Booty's cheese: "It smelled far too suspicious and one of them reported that he thought it smelled of bomb-making materials" (217). The anglicized people in the jeep are quite out of touch with local reality. When the guards start examining the books borrowed from the Gymkhana Library, Lola makes matters worse by her supercilious behaviour:

> "Why are you reading it?"
>
> "To take my mind off all of this." She gestured vaguely and rudely at the scene in general and the guard himself. Who had his pride. Knew he was something. Knew his mother knew he was something. Not even an hour ago she had fed her belief and her son with *puri aloo* accompanied by a lemony-limy-luscious Limca, the fizz from which had made a mini excitement about his nose. (217-18)

The guards confiscate Father Booty's camera, and "the red-hot library books were taken carefully away" (219).

Kiran Desai beautifully sums up the attitude of the anglicized class of Indian society, educated in schools which believe that "cake was better than *laddoos*,.... English was better than Hindi." This is what Sai has in common with her neighbours, the two Bengali sisters to whom she goes for tuition and their friend, "Uncle" Potty. The judge has deliberately cut himself off from society, but people like Lola and Noni have just drifted into this alienation, "it was natural they would incite envy, they supposed" (241). It is only when poor people take over the Mon Ami vegetable patch and put up huts there that they realise that "The wealth that seemed to protect them like a blanket was the very thing that left them exposed":

> Just when Lola had thought it would continue, a hundred years like the one past—Trollope, BBC, a burst of hilarity at Christmas—all of a sudden, all that they had claimed innocent, fun, funny, not really to matter, was proven wrong.
>
> It *did* matter, buying tinned ham roll in a rice and dal country; it *did* matter to live in a big house and sit beside a heater in the evening, even one that sparked and shocked; it *did* matter to fly to London and return with chocolates filled with kirsch; it did matter that others could not. They had pretended it didn't, or had nothing to do with them, and suddenly it had everything to do with them. (242)

The portions of the novel that deal with the life of Lola and Noni reveal Kiran Desai at her best. The beauty and power of the style (as in the passage quoted above) is impressive. She goes into the minute particularities of their life, and gets all the details just right, including the names:

> And finally there was Noni (Nonita), who lived with her sister Lola (Lalita) in a rose-covered cottage named Mon Ami. When Lola's husband had died of a heart attack, Noni, the spinster, had moved in with her sister, the widow. They lived on his pension, but still they needed more money, what with endless repairs being done to the house, the price of everything rising in the bazaar, and the wages of their maid, sweeper, watchman and gardener. (41-42)

The main characters, Sai and the judge, are not equally convincing. The names are not very satisfactory. "Sai" does not ring true as a name chosen by a Parsi father and Gujarati mother for their child. The judge's father-in-law is called Bomanbhai Patel, a typical Parsi name—I have never come across a Hindu (Patidar) Patel calling himself "Boman." Kiran Desai situates the judge precisely—he is born in 1919, in a low caste family[1] in Gujarat.

> Jemubhai Popatlal Patel had, in fact, been born to a family of the peasant caste, in a tentative structure under a palm roof scuffling with rats, at the outskirts of Piphit where the town took on the aspect of a village again. The year was 1919. (56-57)

The Patidar Patels in general are not such an impoverished community. They are landed peasantry, with a flair for business (half the motels in the U.S.A. are owned by Patels). When the rulers of Gujarat allotted land, "To maintain a record of the annual crops on each Pat (a parcel of land) the ruler appointed a record keeper known as the Patlik. This name was later shortened to Patel."[2] The Patels are classified as "Other Backward Caste" in some states of India, but they occupy a high place in the caste hierarchy, coming just below the twice-borns. Kiran Desai tells us that Jemubhai was the first member of their community to go to study at Cambridge, "The year was 1939" (35). But this is unlikely; as early as 1910, Vallabhbhai Patel (the "Iron Man" of India)[3] went to London to qualify as a barrister, and joined the Middle Temple.

It is the socio-economic details of life in India that often strike a false note; the judge's daughter meets Mr. Mistry in a public park in Delhi:

> They became acquainted in this grassy acre, cows tethered to enormous rusty lawn mowers slowly grinding back and forth before a crumbling Mughal tomb. (26)

Cows may be ill-treated in India, and left to roam the roads, but they are never "tethered" to lawn mowers, Kiran Desai must be thinking of oxen yoked to lawn mowers.

In the description of Jemubhai's school days, Kiran Desai presents an authentic picture of the care lavished on the only son. His mother "shook him awake in darkness so he might review his lessons" (58). The child pleads to be allowed to sleep longer, but to no avail:

> There was nothing but black against his eyes, though he knew it was really a cluttered scene, rows of opinionated relatives asleep outside, *kakas-kakis-masas-masis-phois-phuas*, bundles in various colours dangling from the thatched roof of the veranda, buffaloes tethered to the trees by rings in their noses. (58)

This passage works better if the reader does not understand the italicised Indian words, and read it as a representation of innumerable relatives in exotic India. If you understand the relationships, you start asking questions: *kakas-kakis* are the paternal uncle and his wife, who would be a natural part of Jemubhai's father's household. But *masas-masis* (a masi is a maternal aunt, and a mausa is her husband) and *phois-phuas* (paternal aunt and her husband) would not normally be in Jemubhai's house. It was considered improper for a married woman to stay in her maternal home; especially in the nineteen-twenties and 'thirties, she would visit only during special occasions like a marriage.

When the taxi driver reaches Cho Oyu with the eight-year-old Sai, "a little stick figure at the gate," he rattles the gate and shouts, *Oi, koi hai? Khansama? Uth, Koi hai? Uth. Khansama?* (19). "Koi hai" ("is anyone there?") makes sense, but what does one make of "Uth, Khansama" (O Chef, Get up)? Why would a taxi driver from Siliguri call for a chef/cook? There is no problem if the reader does not know Hindi.

Kiran Desai gives no explanation for the judge's poverty during his retired life in Cho Oyu—this is another example of her poor grasp of the socio-economic scene. The Indian Civil Service was very well paid—the novelist herself mentions that "Jemubhai, who had lived on ten pounds a month, could now expect to be paid three hundred pounds a year by the secretary of state for India for the two years of probation" (*Inheritance* 118). "In 1947, a mid-level District Collector would have been paid Rs. 2,000 a month while his Commissioner would draw Rs. 3,500.... For 1947, these were large sums" (Majumdar). The judiciary were equally well paid. Jemubhai cuts off all contact with his parents and wife, and refuses to return the Rs. 10,000 they had borrowed to send him to England. Describing his life in the I.C.S., we are told:

> he rode into the fields with the local officials.... Farms were growing less than ten maunds an acre of rice or wheat, and at two rupees a maund, every single man in a village, sometimes, was in debt to the *bania*. (Nobody knew that Jemubhai himself was noosed, of course, that long ago in the little town of Piphit in Gujarat, moneylenders had sniffed out in him a winning combination of ambition and poverty... [*sic*] that they still sat waiting cross-legged on a soiled mat in the market, snapping their toes, cracking their knuckles in anticipation of repayment...[*sic*]. (61)

One wonders why the moneylenders took no action against Jemubhai: they would certainly not write off a loan given to a person who is now earning more than a thousand rupees a month. This is another example of Kiran Desai using a Hindi word, *bania*; it is not only unnecessary, it is not the most appropriate term, *sahukar* would be better.

With independence, Indians in the Indian Civil Service rose rapidly, so the judge's salary also would have gone up. Moreover, he would earn a handsome pension. We are told that he retired in 1957—after seeing Cho Oyu, "He never went back to court" (29). In 1986, he realizes that he has no influence:

> He remembered all of a sudden why he had gone to England and joined the ICS; it was clearer than ever why—but now that position of power was gone, frittered away in years of misanthropy and cynicism. (292)

One can understand that the judge has lost his clout, through years of misanthropy, but how did he lose his money? In Sai's school records (*Inheritance* 28), his position is mentioned as "Chief Justice (Retd.)" So one wonders what he did with his salary, and what he does with his pension. All descriptions of his home in Kalimpong focus on poverty, deprivation and decay:

> ...the judge seemed not to have noticed Sai's arrival. He was a shriveled figure in a white shirt and black trousers with a buckle to the side. The clothes were frayed but clean, ironed by the cook, who still ironed everything. (33)
>
> In her bed later that evening, Sai lay under a tablecloth, for the last sheets had long worn out. She could sense the swollen presence of the forest.... The structure of the house seemed fragile in the balance of this night—just a husk. The tin roof rattled in the wind. When Sai moved her foot, her toes went silently through the rotted fabric.... Suddenly, as if a secret door had opened in her hearing, she became aware of the sound of microscopic jaws slow-milling the house to sawdust. In this climate, she would learn, untreated wood could be chewed up in a season. (34)

Seven or eight years later, the situation has only worsened.

> Through cracks and holes in Cho Oyu, came a sterile smell of winter. The bathroom taps and switches threw off shocks. Sweaters and shawls bristled with aroused fibres, shedding lightning. "Ow ow," said Sai. Her skin was a squamous pattern of drought. When she took off her clothes, dry skin fell like salt from a salt cellar. (151)

Gyan spends a night in Cho Oyu, because the heavy rain makes it impossible for him to walk home; the cook "made up the bed in an extra room, which was actually filled with rubbish but contained a bed placed in the very centre" (113-14). All four inmates are unable to sleep:

> Rainy season beetles flew by in many colours. From each hole in the floor came a mouse as if tailored for size, tiny mice from the tiny holes, big mice from big holes, and the termites came teeming forth from the furniture, so many of them that when you looked, the furniture, the floor, the ceiling, all seemed to be wobbling. (114)
>
> In his bed slung like a hammock on broken springs, leaks all around, the judge lay pinned by layers of fusty blankets. His underwear lay on top of the lamp to dry and his watch sat below

> so the mist under the dial might lift—a sad state for the civilized man. (116)

The cook is described as very poor

> It pained Sai's heart to see how little he had: a few cheap clothes.... (13)

> A poverty-stricken man growing into an ancient at fast-forward. Compressed childhood, lingering old age. A generation between him and the judge, but you wouldn't know it to look at them. (19)

He was hired late in the nineteen-forties or early 'fifties, "'We were always on tour', said the cook" (60). But the Indian reader is surprised at his utter poverty; surely his wages would have gone up, just as the judge's pension would have been periodically revised. No explanation is given for why the cook stays on, in such miserable circumstances. His misery is not the consequence of the Gorkha agitation, the cook is described as old and poor even in 1977, when Sai first comes to Cho Oyu.

A similar lack of credibility pertains to Sai's economic condition. The judge has no money to send her to a convent school; he has accepted the child because "Sai could look after Mutt, he reasoned. The cook was growing decrepit. It would be good to have an unpaid somebody in the house to help with things as the years went by" (210). We are told that her father Mr. Mistry died in Moscow, where he had gone for training. As an officer of the Indian Air Force, he would have been given a family pension; surely that would have been enough to pay for her education in St Augustine's Convent in Dehra Dun.

In the other strand of the story, the socio-economic circumstances are portrayed much more graphically. Biju's various employers and coworkers are mentioned by name. We get a dramatic (at places, melodramatic) account of Biju's struggles as an illegal immigrant, the squalid circumstances in which he is forced to live, exploited by his employers. When he starts working in a restaurant which "served only one menu: steak, salad, fries. It assumed a certain pride in simplicity among the wealthy classes" (135), he tries to rationalise his abhorrence of serving beef,

> Holy cow. Unholy cow. Biju knew the reasoning he should keep by his side. At lunch and dinner the space filled with young unformed businesspeople in their twenties and thirties. (135)

It is not Biju alone who comes under Kiran Desai's delightfully satirical gaze, she talks about other Indian immigrants too.

> But here were Indians eating beef....

> "I'll have the steak," they said with practised nonchalance, with an ease like a signature that's a thoughtless scribble that you *know* [sic] has been practised page after page. (135)

The young students face the same cultural confusion:

> Confusion was rampant among the *haalf 'n' haf* crowd, the Indian students coming in with American friends, one accent one side of the mouth, another the other side; muddling it up, wobbling then, downgrading sometimes all the way to Hindi to show one another: Who? No, no, it was not they pretending to be other than who and what they were. They weren't the ones turning their back on the greatest culture the world has ever seen...[sic]. (148)

Biju starts looking for work in a place where he would not have to cook beef, and ends up at the Gandhi Café, run by Harish (Harry to Americans), who offers "free housing," which means sleeping in the kitchen below the restaurant, amidst the pots and pans and sacks of masala, plagued by rats "exulting in the garbage, clawing through wood, making holes that Harry-Harish stuffed with steel wool and covered with bricks" (147). Here Biju is exploited even more than before:

> By offering a reprieve from NYC rents, they could cut the pay to a quarter of the minimum wage, reclaim the tips for the establishment, keep an eye on the workers, and drive them to work fifteen-, sixteen-, seventeen-hour donkey days. Saran, Jeev, Rishi, Mr. Lalkaka and now Biju. All illegal. (146)

Harish has earned a lot of money, but he is unhappy with his daughter, who is getting Americanised.

Biju has a variety of "fellow dishwashers," the most memorable being Saeed Saeed from Zanzibar, who is always one jump ahead of the immigration authorities, and helps his colleagues outwit them. He legalises his stay by marrying an American woman, but for the rest, the green card remains the unattainable El Dorado:

> The green card the green card. The...[*sic*].
>
> Without it he couldn't leave. To leave he wanted a green card. This was the absurdity. How he desired the triumphant After The Green Card Return Home, thirsted for it—to be able to buy a ticket with the air of someone who could return if he wished, or not, if he didn't wish...[*sic*]. He watched the legalized foreigners with envy as they shopped at discount baggage stores for the

> miraculous, expandable third-world suitcase, accordion-pleated, filled with pockets and zippers to unhook further crannies, the whole structure unfolding into a giant space that could fit in enough to set up an entire life in another country.
>
> Then, of course, there were those who lived and died illegal in America and never saw their families, not for ten years, twenty, thirty, never again. (99)

Kiran Desai presents the miserable life of illegal immigrants so vividly, that one is tempted to quote more passages. Her poetic descriptions have both wit and compassion. There are no inconsistencies in the American background (or none apparent to an Indian reader like me). But there are big gaps in the Indian side of the story: there is no explanation for the judge's poverty; there is a singular dearth of names, even the cook is nameless (and the choice of names leaves something to be desired); we are told very little about the eight years of Sai's life from the age of eight (when she comes to Cho Oyu) to the age of sixteen, when Gyan is appointed as her tutor. In an interview with Mukund Padmanabhan, Kiran Desai says that this novel was subjected to a lot of editing:

> I think the structure is very different from the first one, which had a very simple structure.... In this regard, I am not entirely sure it [*The Inheritance...*] has worked. In terms of the momentum of the work, sometimes I wonder whether it is soggy in the middle. That struggle still exists for me. I still think there are little dead bits in the book. But I cut 1500 pages down to about 300... [*sic*].

Maybe the connecting links in Sai's story and the judge's were lost in editing. In the published version of the novel, the American social background is better depicted than the Indian one.

NOTES AND REFERENCES

1. "Caste: Patidar" (*Inheritance* 28).
2. http://www.patidarsamaj.org/culture-traditions.htm.
3. http://pib.nic.in/feature/feyr98/fe1098/f1510981.html.

WORKS CITED

Desai, Anita. 1977. *Fire on the Mountain*. Harmondsworth, Middlesex: Penguin, 1982.

Desai, Kiran. *The Inheritance of Loss*. New Delhi: Penguin Books India, 2006.

Khair, Tabish. *The Bus Stopped*. London: Picador, 2004.

Majumdar, Sumit K. "India Must Pay for Good Governance." *Business Line*. Jun 23, 2006.

Padmanabhan, Mukund. "Writing can be a dangerous activity." *The Hindu* October 12, 2006. URL: http://www.thehindu.com/2006/10/12/stories/2006101202791100.htm

Roy, Arundhati. *The God of Small Things*. New Delhi: IndiaInk, 1997.

PART-E

26

The Role of Mass Media in the New Century

Prema Nandakumar

India has posited a tremendous achievement in accumulating, sustaining and guarding a vast amount of knowledge and has raised an unparalleled culture without the help of Mass Media. The Vedas have been transmitted down millennia without the loss of even inflexions. This has been possible because of a person contact view of knowledge; that knowledge is best gained by learning from a teacher in person. Hence the high position given to the Guru in Indian tradition. Even today this clinging to the fellow human being either as a teacher or as a student continues and we speak proudly of our generational (transmission method).

The setting up of printing presses in India was our first introduction to the mass media. The eminent scholar, B.S. Kesavan, sees the history of printing and publishing in India as "a story of cultural re-awakening, consequent on the introduction to India of the art and technique of printing." The newssheet followed not long after and India had entered the age of the mass media. The first Hindi weekly paper was *Oodunt Mortund* that was begun in 1826 with a panegyric on the Governor General, Lord Amherst as "Sriman Governor General Bahadur ka Subha Varnan." However, within a year it had to close down due to lack of government patronage, but a little less than two centuries later, the Hindi newspaper industry commands a top slot in India's socio-political scenario.

The success has come after long years of struggle, of course. For, a newspaper is for mass consumption and this leads to mass reactions as well. It could be for the good of the society or for its detriment, but the spread of news is fast. The rise of the newspaper industry in India in the first half of the 20th century was almost entirely due to the independence struggle. Later it became a formidable instrument of disseminate political news. In its golden moments it has been exposing corruptions in our society but in its worst moments, it has been a weapon of political and social black mail as well. News found in the papers can raise passions with great intensities, as was discovered during the Partition horror.

The Radio, films and the Television joined the mass media in a big way after the coming of independence in 1947. The achievements of the radio are many, and happily, the track-record of India's broadcasting history is very, very satisfying. Because of the inevitable control from the government, its political wings may remain clipped but thanks to its ability to reach out the remotest village, it has spread the best of Indian culture and received knowledge (in agriculture, for instance) to the countryside as well. Governmental control is stressed for films and the television too but, these visual media have been a deep disappointment in many ways for the watcher of the society. I have myself had the Internet at home for more than a year and I am terrified by its capacity to disseminate significant information, as also misinformation and unwholesome information.

But, of course, increasingly "information is necessary at every step and access to information critical" (AIRC Newsletter, Chennai, January-March 2000) in the twenty-first century. Political, scientific and technological developments cry out for such immediate conveyance of information to intercept tragedies and educate the masses. And the challenges posed by the twenty-first century for man are many. As Duane Elgin says:

> Never before has the human family been on the verge of devastating the Earth's biosphere and crippling the ecological foundations for countless generations to come. Never before has the entire human family been required to work together to imagine and consciously build a sustainable future. This is not a concern for the remote future. Current trends in population growth, resources depletion and pollution suggest we will reach a critical turning point or 'evolutionary inflection' within twenty or thirty years—roughly the decade of the 2020s. If this is a valid assessment, then never before in human history will so many people be called upon to make such sweeping changes in so short a time.

One of the major triumphs of the mass media in the twentieth century was in the sphere of atomic war and atomic tests. It is true that Sri Aurobindo perceived the future course man might take if he used the splitting of the atom as a means to wage wars. If man preferred the course of war, mankind was doomed. He wrote a sonnet on 25th September 1939, the year when it was found that by bombarding an atom of Uranium (the heaviest element), with a neutron, the latter could be split to release two or three neutrons which would split further, setting up a seemingly endless chain-reaction:

"One dreamed and saw a gland write Hamlet, drink
    At the Mermaid, capture immortality;
A committee of harmones on the Aegean's brink
    Composed the Iliad and the Odyssey.
A thyroid, meditating almost nude
    Under the Bo-tree, saw the eternal Light
And, rising from its might solitude,
    Spoke of the Wheel and eightfold Path all right.
A brain by a disordered stomach driven
    Thundered through Europe, conquered, ruled and fell,
From St. Helena went, perhaps, to Heaven.
    Thus wagged on the surreal world, until
A scientist played with atoms and blew out
    The universe before God had time to shout."

Man almost did it when the atom bomb was developed by the United States under the direction of Dr. J. Robert Oppenheimer. The first test explosion was at Alamogordo on July 16, 1945. What Sri Aurobindo had hinted at six years earlier now found a curtain-raiser in Hiroshima and Nagasaki in 1945. After this, the Satanic World War Two was over. But the Cold War had begun. The U.S.-U.S.S.R. race for making nuclear tests and stockpiling atomic weaponry could not go unnoticed thanks to the mass media: the newspapers and the radio. There was Frankling C. Stark, National Vice-Chairman of the Campaign for United Nations Reform speaking in 1982:

> The two superpowers have warheads which equate with nearly 4 tons of TNT (Trinitrotolune) for ever man, woman and child now living on this planet. Between these two nations there is the present capacity to destroy the entire globe twenty-seven times over.

This was not poetry but hard facts and figures. The nuclear doomsday clock has been perilously close to the midnight hour and yet, if we have survived and seen the dawn of the twenty-first century, one can say that much of the credit goes to the mass media. The printed word and the broadcasting voice helped in mobilizing people's opinion by leaders like Bertrand Russell and C. Rajagopalachariar. In India, a relentless pressure was set up through the press by eminent scientists, professors, philosophers and journalists (Dhirendra Sharma, K.R. Srinivasa Iyengar, Shivaji Rao and Subba Rao among them) that the world has worked together and has been able to roll back the onward ticking of the doomsday clock. Truly this has been a victory without swords or blood, as Namakkal Ramalingam Pillai happened to describe the Gandhian movement. There is a great deal yet to be done to make the world safe from the assaults of nuclear power. But with sanity prevailing and with the help of the mass media, success can be achieved.

While the nuclear danger promises a total annihilation, there are other dangers of slow poisoning that also threaten the globe. Here too the mass media has been of immense help to the common man. The Narmada Andolan has had a healthy discourse because of the mass media taking the message all over India, helping people to think about the pros and cons of building dams. The role of the mass media in the twenty-first century would have to be purposeful in this regard. Already, it was mass media that made the Chipko movement catch on and made everyone realize the dangers of deforestation. But for the mass media's exposure of the heinous killing of a protect species of deer by a film personality, we would not have become alert of such goings-on elsewhere. The present century would have to turn the focus on environmental degradation in a big way. Else, our earth would become warmer gradually and cease to be productive leading to a state of constant famine and riots. As researchers and activities pile up the statistics, the mass media brings it all to a wide spectrum of readership that helps the planning of campaigns to clean the environment and keep the discourse online.

This is how we learn that the ozone layer is weakening at an alarming rate and might play havoc with the food chain in the oceans as well as on land; that toxic pollution is leaping like a tiger on land, water and air and is spreading over them like an incubus; that man is squandering away his precious resources gifted by Nature without giving room for its replenishment by the same Nature. This asuric consumerism which is denying the future generations a decent life on this planet can be highlighted best by the mass media to knock some sense down on the minds of the common people and the people in power.

But, how far has the mass media helped us in this regard? Percentage-wise, not much: this is the sad tale. In fact, I find myself often weighing the plus and minus of the mass media. There is a lot of good it is able to do but then it is also capable of immense harm. When the good of the community is brushed aside to favour the commercial success of a programme, how can one stop the slide down? Consumerism has caught on so fast that it is holding the middle and poorer classes in a vice-like grip, for they wish to imitate the richer people in the community who are engaged in conspicuous consumption. It is not only asking someone to buy or eat something; the way the advertisements are projected, woman gets a raw deal. She is seen always as the drudge doing nothing but cleaning the floors, washing dirty clothes and cooking with this or that oil; or she is the molly doll of sexist dream-fantasies. The aim of all these advertisements is selling. What does the seller care if the moral fibre of the society gets destroyed completely? I am told the average person sees at least 25,000 commercials a year on the television. It may be remembered that these commercials do not merely sell the particular soap or eatable or bed or biscuit. They also sell certain behavioural patterns that do not help civilized ways of living and certainly inspire violence in thought and deed by attacking the growing minds without seeming to do so. Also, these commercials which posit a uniform richness—plush cars that zoom through ever so smoothly, soft drinks that fizz over while the girls and boys are sailing in a boat or riding a bike, milk and cream and sugar dance together in vast pans to be gobbled as desirable chocolates by well-fed children—affect the psyche of the poor with a terrible despair leading to an increase in juvenile crime and teenage murders. Somehow, one cannot refrain from using strong words and say that the history of the television in India has also been the history of a definite cultural and moral degradation in the society.

It is not the commercials alone that are being inimical to the society's health. Even in the manner of presentation of news, the visual media are playing havoc on the psyche of people. Watching an actual destruction being done—the destruction of a temple or a mosque or a church—could lead to communal flare-ups. Even more reporting can assault one's sensitivities. Last week, this was brought to me in its acute form when conversing on the subject of a gruesome tragedy with some neighbours. We were giving voice to our outrage and sorrow that three promising lives had been snuffed out by an arsonist in Dharmapuri. One of my neighbours assured me that since I did not have a television, I did not see the actual bus in flames. They had all seen it, and how the bus was burning, and the students were screaming, and the people were rushing, how the police came.... But the manner of dramatic description that accompanied the retelling to me made me feel that watching the episode on the screen had de-sensitized the ladies. For, another launched upon the parallel tragedy of how a person was cudgeled and drowned in a Tiruvananthapuram tank in the full view of so many bystanders.... Such daily dose of violent tragedy cannot keep the emotions of a person sensitive. Mechanical reactions, the ayyayyos and appappas and turn immediately to the noodles being served on a plate in a perfect dining room, the newly weds being seen off in the latest luxury car. Ah, the television is at work and all is right with the world!

Mercifully, of all the mass media, including the printed newspapers and books, the broadcasting voice has been able to do the least harm, thanks to its limited range and lack of visual power.

But, because the mass media is thus going off the track, we cannot deny its existence. After all, never before was its help needed so much. The way things are going, the egoistic power-pressures make the governments a non-functioning toy and what is the point in crying hoarse that the government offices, the police, and the judiciary do not work? Especially with regard to a vast sub-continent like India, we cannot depend upon the Sircar to do everything for us. Already we see that people are slowly turning to voluntary agencies for redressal of their problems, and are themselves coming forward to be part of such voluntary agencies. The Mass Media is the answer to band together these non-governmental organisations, and one hopes that the 21st century's mass media would also follow what was best in its actions in the earlier century. Newspapers, broadcasting and television could help us communicate with one another effectively.

As I meditate upon what the communication revolution is going to offer in this century, I contend with available information that says that very soon we would be seeing an integration of television, computers, satellites, fibre optics and such information technology appurtenances. That might lead to a spread of information which would be faster than light, perhaps! As it is, here is Duane Elgin's assessment of the television-oriented present and the immense good in can do to awaken man's conscience:

> Roughly 60% of the world now has access to television and this percentage is growing rapidly. With the speed of light, television extends our involvement to the entire planet. Because we are a visually-oriented species—'one picture is worth a thousand words,' 'seeing is believing'—television embodies a common,

> visual language that makes it the primary source of information and understanding for the human family. Through the eyes of television, we can touch the reality of a starving villager in Africa, we can see the effects of acid rain in Germany, we can feel the despair of ghetto residents in New York City, and we can touch the reality of fighting in the streets of Northern Ireland. Television makes every viewer an active witness—a knowing and feeling participant in what is being shown. By any measure, television has become the 'social brain' or 'central nervous system' for the human family.

But, none of our socially relevant projections can make a mark on the viewer's psyche if it is immediately countered by advertisement glitz. The present century has to come up with its own answers for the mass media in becoming a socially responsible instrument. The criticism has to come from within, and the immense power in its hands must needs be handled with responsibility. In this mass media must act together with the aim of global good in its agenda, instead of racing against one another. Rachel Carson's one single book, *The Silent Spring*, started the entire movement for environmental protection at a global level. It was a demonstration of the power of the published word. Hence we should hope for such purposeful wielding of the powerful instruments in our hands. It can be done, provided we, the public are alert, and the representatives of mass media are prepared to respond. Let us remember how the 1028 Sukthas spread over the ten Mandalas of the Rig Veda conclude with the stirring call of Samvanana Angiras to humanity:

> "Meet together, speak together,
> let your minds be of one accord,
> as the Devas of old, being of one mind,
> accepted their share of sacrifice.
>
> May your counsel be common, your assembly common,
> common the mind, and the thoughts of these united.
> A common purpose do I lay before you,
> and worship with your common oblation.
>
> Let your aims be common,
> and your hearts of one accord,
> and all of you be of one mind,
> so you may live well together."[1]

NOTE

1. Translated by A.C. Bose, *Hymns from the Vedas* (1966), 203.

27

Problems of Translating Literary Work

Jibesh Bhattacharya

Translation is a powerful instrument for dissemination of knowledge. In this world people speaking different language live. But all of them are endowed with the power of thinking and many of them are gifted with individual talents. And development of knowledge is facilitated when there is an exchange of ideas among men. When such men speak the same language the difficulty does not arise. For, they can exchange their views and ideas effortlessly through the medium of their own mother tongue. But they will be totally ignorant of the views and ideas of other men equally talented or more, if those men speak a language different from theirs. Had they known how those men were thinking about a subject, they could have improved upon their own concept and notion about it. Here comes the need for translation.

In the modern days of quick transport from one place to another, thanks to the bewildering scientific and technological achievements of today, the world has shrunk to a very small place. We are coming into contact with people having a rich heritage of knowledge in its different branches. But it is not possible for everybody to be thoroughly acquainted with a large variety of languages so as to have an easy access to the rich store of knowledge couched in them. As the British had expanded their empire almost all over the globe, most of the nations came to learn their language. Hence, English has become the internationally comprehensible language. That is why most of the books written in other different languages of the world are translated into English for the purpose of a larger communication. Such translations are made either by the native speakers of English or by people of different nations, who have learned English.

Now, it is a known fact that the thoughts and ideas expressed in one language cannot be perfectly rendered in another. And this rendering becomes more difficult when the subject is a literary one. For, the task of the translator, and in particular, the literary translator, is not merely to render the surface meaning of the text, but also to interpret the words. He must be sensitive not only to the face value of the words but also to their hidden meaning and significance. He must also pay his attention to sound, rhythm, cadence, imagery and association. Thus, he is, in a sense, an interpreter just like an actor or a musician. A bad actor and a good actor may both understand the meaning of the famous soliloquy of Macbeth, "Tomorrow and tomorrow and tomorrow;" but their interpretations will be very different according to their levels of understanding. A piano-tuner may play the first five notes of a piano concerto of either Beethoven or Bach merely to test the sound of the piano. He might be playing the right notes, no doubt, but not in the right way. Similarly, a translator also may play the right notes, that is, render the words literally, but may not bring out exactly what the original writer wanted to express.

The express and appreciation of a work of translation will be proportionate to the degree of perfection the translator has attained in his work. The difficulty in reproducing the exact mood and concept of a work becomes apparent when the translator faces the task of translating a poem. Words have their associations. The sound, the rhythm, and the associations of words in a line cannot be perfectly reproduced by those in another language. The literal meaning of the words in the original text may be given in a translation, but the sense, the nuance, the rhythm are liable to be absent. It is rather difficult to reproduce them exactly in a different language. For example, the opening lines of Dante's *Inferno* read as under:

> NEL mezzo del cammin di nostra vita
> Mi ritrovai per una selva oscura,
> Che la diritta via era smarita.[1]

They are translated into English by Henry Carey as

> In the midway of this our mortal life,
> I found me in a gloomy wood, astray
> Gone from the path direct.[2]

The translation gives us only an idea of the situation described by the lines, but it does not seem to convey the exact sense of the passage intended by Dante. Thus, for example, the word 'selva' is translated as 'wood,' whereas the actual sense of the word is 'wild.' 'I found myself in an obscure wilderness' would be nearer the sense than the one given in the translation. 'Wood' in Italian is 'legno'. Dorothy L. Sayers' translation of this passage in the Penguin Classics is far from satisfactory. She has included in her rendering words which the original passage does not have. She translates the passage as:

> Midway this way of life we're bound upon
> I woke to find myself in a dark wood,
> Where the right road was wholly lost and gone.[3]

Again, the following lines of Goethe's *Faust* are:

> Es war ein Konig in Thule,
> Gar treu bis an das Grab,
> Dem sterbend seine Buhle
> Einer goldnen Becher gab.[4]

They have been translated by Bayard Taylor as

> There was a King in Thule,
> Was faithful till the grave,—
> To whom his mistress, dying,
> A golden goblet gave.[5]

In this translation 'gar treu' was translated as 'was faithful,' but the sense of 'gar' (very) has been omitted. Again, 'bis an' should be rendered as 'to' or 'unto,' and not 'till' which refers to time, whereas 'bis an' refers to 'grab' or 'grave,' a place. Randall Jarrell rendered the above passage thus:

> There was once a king in Thule
> Faithful unto the grave to whom his dying mistress
> A golden goblet gave.[6]

Jarrell unnecessarily added the word 'once' although he used the adjective 'sterbend' (dying) properly before 'mistress'. C.F. Macintyre in the New American Version of Goethe's *Faust* translated 'Buhle' as 'sweetheart.' He translated the third line as: 'to whom his dying sweetheart'.[7] This change of 'mistress' to 'sweetheart' strikes a discordant note as it does not conform to the solemnity of the first two lines.

Or, take for example, W.M. Thackeray's translation of the following lines from Pierre Jean de Beranger's *Le Roi d'Yvetot*:

> Il etait un roi d'Yvetot,
> Feu connu dans I'histoire;
> Se levant tard, se couchant tot,
> Dormant for bien sans gloire,[8]

Thackeray's translation is as follows:

> There was a king of Yvetot,
> Of whom renown hath little said,
> Who let all thoughts of glory go,
> And dawdled half his days a-bed;[9]

This is a very free translation except for the first line. The second line actually means 'who was little known in the history.' The third line is not translated at all. 'Se levant tard, se couchant tot' should be rendered as, 'got up late, went to bed early,' and 'Dormant fort bien sans gloire' as 'slept very well without glory.' Thackeray's translation may have the over-all sense of the passage, but it misses the humour contained in it.

The three passages selected at random from Italian, German and French show that it is hardly possible to get the taste of the original in translation. Yet we will have to depend on it. For, how many of us can afford to devote our time and energy to learn a foreign language first, in order to enjoy the literature of that language? We accept any translation so that we may peep into the world of literature of a particular nation. We have heard of the novels of Fyodor Dostoevsky, Count Leo Tolstoy and Emile Zola; the fame of Miliere, Luigi Pirandello, and Albert Camus must have reached our ears; we would certainly like to be acquainted with the great works of Homer, Dante and Goethe. But unless we know the respective language in which each has composed his immortal works, our desire will remain unfulfilled. Only a man of genius can learn so many language in his lifetime and enjoy the works of these authors at first hand.

A knowledge of literary works composed in languages other than one's own is also necessary for a proper comprehension and appreciation of the literature composed in one's own native language. For, a comparative study of literature is a useful aid for evaluating and appreciating works of literary art. Matthew Arnold also held a similar opinion. He said:

> And everywhere there is connexion, everywhere there is illustration: no single event, no single literature, is adequately comprehended except in its relation to other events, to other literatures. The literature of ancient Greece, the literature of the Christian Middle Age. So long as they are regarded as two isolated literatures, two isolated growths of the human spirit, are not adequately comprehended.[10]

Besides a comparative study of the literary works in different languages of the world, a knowledge of the literary theories and principles formulated by established scholars and critics will surely help our understanding and appreciation of literature. Particularly, when we are studying the literature of the West, we cannot do without Aristotle's *Poetics* or Plato's *The Republic* or Horace's *Ars Poetics* or Boileau's *L'Art Poetique*. For these critical works guide us to evaluate a literary work properly. These learned critics, after a careful study of the imaginative works of the well-known literary artists of the day, have formulated certain principles which, if followed, would lend to the creation of good literature. Opinions, however, may vary as to the standard of 'goodness.' But, in order to arrive at any such standard, one must be acquainted with the standard of excellence agreed upon by the renowned scholars and critics. And those scholars and critics belong to different nations of the world writing in languages different from one another. So, in order to have an idea of what they have said regarding literary excellence we will have to depend on translations of their works as it is not practicable for everybody to learn Greek, Latin, Italian and French in order to be able to read the original critical texts composed in those languages and have a knowledge of what those critics have written.

Confusions, however, are created when we come across translations of the same text by different translators and editors, not exactly tallying in respect of certain expressions or passages. Such confusions become all the more acute when the translators are eminent in their field of studies. Common readers, not learned in the language in which the original text is composed, do not know which rendering they would accept as perfect.

Here I venture to collect a few sentences from Aristotle's *Poetics* and their English renderings as given by Ingram Bywater and S.H. Butcher. They will illustrate, I think, the confusion a common reader will feel when he will look at both the translations. Thus:

> Ouden gar an echoimen onomasai koinon tous Sophronos kai Xenarchou mimous kai tous Sokratikous logous, oude ei tis dis trimetron e elegeion e ton allon tinon ton toiouton poioito ten mimesin.[11]

has been translated by Butcher as:

> For there is no common term we could apply to the mimes of Sophron and Xenarchus and the Socratic dialogues on the one hand; and, on the other, to poetic imitations in iambic, elegiac, or any similar metre.[12]

Bywater, on the other hand, renders the sentence as follows:

> We have no common name for a mime of Sophron and Xenarchus and a Socratic conversation; and we should still be without one

> even if the imitation in the two instances were in trimesters or elegiacs or some other kind of verse.[13]

Now, both the translations are more or less free translations. And for this the translators are not to be blamed. For, their main purpose was to make the Greek text comprehensible to an English reader. And it is almost impossible to find an exact equivalent for all the Greek words used in the Aristotelian text. In the preface to Bywater's translation of *Poetics*, Gilbert Murray has explicitly spoken of this difficulty. He writes:

> In an average page of French or German philosophy nearly all the nouns can be translated directly into exact equivalents in English; but in Greek that is not so. Scarcely one in ten of the nouns on the first few pages of the *Poetics* has an exact English equivalent.[14]

Even though accepting the difficulty Gilbert Murray speaks of, we feel puzzled when the term 'trimetron' is translated by Butcher as 'iambic,' whereas Bywater renders it as 'trimeters.' Now 'iambic' is the name of a measure whereas 'trimeters' refers to the number of such measure in a verse. Hence a reader without any knowledge of Greek will wonder as to which term to accept. Although in ancient Greek 'trimeter' was a verse form consisting of three 'dipodies' as in classical iambic, it will be rather pedantic to render the term as mere 'iambic.'

> Again, the line, Kal egenonte ton palaion oi men eroikon of de iamban poietai[15]

has been translated by Butchers as:

> Thus, the older poets were distinguished as writers of heroic or of lampooning verse.[16]

But, Bywater's translation of the above line is as follows:

> The result was the old poets became some of them writers of heroic and others of iambic verse.[17]

Here also a reader will have to stumble as he finds in one translation 'lampooning verse' and in another 'iambic verse.' It is possible that lampoons or satires were composed originally in iambic verse. But for that reason to translate 'iambon poietai' as 'lampooning verse' is to take too much liberty in translation.

> Further, there is also a difference in the rendering of the following lines, between Bywater and Butcher: Epei de prattontes poiountai ten mimesin, proton men ex anagkes an eie ti morion tragodias o tes opseos kosmos,[18]

Butcher's translation of the lines is:

> Now as tragic imitation implies persons acting, it necessarily follows, in the first place, that Spectacular equipment will be a part of Tragedy.[19]

Bywater makes a translation somewhat different from this. He translates the lines as follows:

> As they act the stories, it follows that in the first place the Spectacle (or stage-appearance of the actors) must be some part of the whole;[20]

The renderings of both the scholars seem to have some shortcomings. Butcher translates 'opseos kosmos' as 'Spectacular equipment.' But this probably is not the actual sense of the phrase. The proper sense conveyed by the phrase is 'arrangement of the sight,' 'opseos' is the genitive case of 'opsis' which means 'sight' or 'view' and 'kosmos' means 'orderly arangement,' 'decoration' etc. Thus Aristotle probably wanted to mean that the arrangement of the sight or spectacle of tragic action should be a part of tragedy. That is, he wanted to emphasize the importance of plot in a tragedy. Bywater's translation seems to be most free and defective. For, the first part of the sentence, 'epei de prattontes poiountai ten mimesin' does not exactly mean, 'As they act the stories,' rather the rendering of Butcher is more acceptable. Then the second part of the sentence is not correctly rendered. For, it is not the 'spectacle,' but the 'proper arrangement of it' that must be a part of tragedy. Besides, 'part of the whole' is a vague expression, whereas in the text 'ti morion tragodias' means clearly 'a part of tragedy.'

Thus, we find that although we need translations of books written in different languages of the world, the translations available may create some misconception about a text and its author. Hence, the task of a translator is highly exacting. A translator is going to open the gates of an unexplored building, but if he opens the wrong gate, he may lead the curious ones into a stuffy dark chamber and make them have a wrong idea of the house.

A translation of a passage does not mean the rendering of each word in it exactly into another language. Besides, it is not possible to find the exact equivalent of each word in the language into which the passage is being translated. So, the duty of a translator should be to attempt to convey the sense of the word or the sentence as accurately as possible. Therefore, in order to translate from one language into another, a translator ought to have deep and not superficial knowledge of both the languages. He must be acquainted with the subtle nuances of words and expressions in the two languages. A translation is not an explanation. Hence, in translating a passage one must restrain oneself from the temptation of attempting to explain things by introducing extraneous matters in the body of the translation. Anything distracting in the word-order, or in the paragraphing or in punctuation, should be meticulously avoided. A translator should be careful not to misplace stress or emphasis in translating a sentence or a passage. Particularly, in translating an imaginative work of literature, one must pay one's attention to the shape and balance of individual sentences, the visual images of the words created by alliteration, assonance, rhythm, onomatopoeia etc.

There is need today for translations and more translations. Hence the responsibility of a translator has increased enormously. The problems faced by a translator are many. A translator cannot translate a piece of writing from the source language to the target language with a hundred per cent accuracy. But, he must try to reproduce as exactly as possible the main idea conveyed by the source language. Therefore, it is not metaphors used in the source language may not have an exact equivalent in the target language. In that case the translator must be careful enough to choose the right phrase or idiom in the target language to express the idea conveyed by the corresponding phrase or idiom in the source language. But this should be done only as an unavoidable measure when literary work has given birth to translators who may be otherwise creative writers but failures as translators. This reminds us of what Bentley said when asked by Alexander Pope if he had received 'his Homer,' that is his English translation of the Homeric epics. Bentley replied: 'It is a pretty poem, Mr. Pope, but you must not call it Homer: Pope's translations were a commercial success. And in the present century and afterwards the demand for the translations of literary works will go on increasing, requiring more and more translation works to be produced alongside the valuable gems of creative writings in different languages of the world.

NOTES

1. Alighieri Dante, *Divine Comedy: The Inferno* (London: Champman and Hall, 1849), 2.
2. Dante, *The Divine Comedy* edited by Edmund Gardner (1908; rpt. London: J.M. Dent and Sons Ltd., 1961), 3.
3. Dante, *The Divine Comedy* translated by Dorothy L. Sayers (1949; rpt. Penguin Classics, Harmondsworth, Middlesex, 1953), 71.

4. Johann Wolfgang von Goethe, *Goethes Samtliche Werke*, Sechster Band (George Muiller Berlag Munchen), Vol. 6,185.
5. Goethe, *Faust* translated by Bayard Taylore (New York: Modern Library, 1930), 103.
6. Goethe, *Faust*, Part I (New York: Farrar, Straus and Giroux, 1976), 149.
7. Goethe, *Faust*, Part I (New York: New Directions, 1957), 98.
8. Pierre Jean de Beranger, *Chansons de P-J de Beranger* (Paris: Garnier Freres Libraries, 1833), 129.
9. W.M. Thackeray, *Ballads and Verses and Miscellaneous Contributions to PUNCH* (London: Macmillan and Company Limited, 1912), 132.
10. Matthew Arnold, 'On the Modern Element in Literature' in *Several Essays* edited by G.F. Cumberlege, second edition (OUP, 1927; Indian reprint, 1963), 91.
11. *Aristotle's Theory of Poetry and Fine Art*, translated by S.H. Butcher (Indian edition: Ludhiana: Lyall Book Depot, 1967), 8.
12. *Ibid.*, 9.
13. *Aristotle on the Art of Poetry*, translated by Ingram Bywater (1920; rpt. London: Oxford at the Clarendon Press, 1959), 24.
14. *Ibid.*, 5-6.
15. S.H. Butcher, *op. cit.*, 16.
16. *Ibid.*, 17.
17. Ingram Bywater, *op. cit.*, 30.
18. S.H. Butcher, *op. cit.*, 22.
19. *Ibid.*, 23.
20. Ingram Bywater, *op. cit.*, 35.

28

A Case for a Good Dictionary

P. Bayapa Reddy

In learning a language, dictionaries play an important role. A learner of English language doesn't usually know which is the best dictionary and how to consult a dictionary. There are many dictionaries in the market just as there are many courses in English language and literature. It is pertinent to know something about the history of compilation of a dictionary. Robert Cawdrey, a school master in Coventry in England published the first dictionary in English, *A Table Alphabeticall...of Hard Usuall English Wordes* in 1604. It contained 2560 headwords, with very basic definitions and no etymology. In 1702, John Kersey published his dictionary, *A New English Dictionary*. This dictionary had about 28,000 entries. Nathaniel Bailey, a school teacher brought out in 1721 his dictionary, *An Universal Etymological English Dictionary*. His dictionary included about 40,000 headwords and, naturally it became very popular in those days.

It is Dr. Samuel Johnson who, assisted by his 'small staff and copyists and helpers', brought out in 1755, his *Dictionary of the English Language* in which 'the words are deduced from their originals, and illustrated in their different significations by examples from the best writers. With its 1,14,000 quotations and illustrations, it is easily one of the landmarks in the history of English dictionaries. It is interesting to note that Dr. Johnson gave odd meanings of a few words. For example, "Oats: (noun) = A grain, which in England is generally given to horses, but in Scotland supports the people; School (noun) = 1. A house of discipline and instruction, 2. A place of literary education; a university." These meanings are rather idiosyncratic and prejudicial. Thus, he makes a sincere attempt to illustrate his words in practice and he also tries to indicate the connotations of words, as well as offering their exact meaning.

Noah Webster compiled his compendious dictionary, *American Dictionary of the English Language* in 1828. This dictionary contains 70,000 entries and 12,000 new definitions. The landmark in the making of English dictionary is the great dictionary called *The Oxford English Dictionary* under the active guidance of Sir James A.H. Murrary. This dictionary attempts to give a full history of the development of all English words since the 12th century. It also covers full illustrative quotations ordered according to the principal distinct sense of the word. It contains a record of 4,14,825 words. The original title of this work was *A New English Dictionary of Historical Principles* (Abbreviated as NED). The title *The Oxford English Dictionary* first appeared with a section published in 1895. So far, dictionary making has almost remained a dictionary. Robert W. Burchfield undertook his job of the four-column 'Supplement to the Oxford English Dictionary' and completed it in 1957. Even this Supplement needed further revision because of the enormous growth in the publishing of new books and journals in the last five decades.

As English increasingly gained importance in other parts of the globe, there appeared English dictionaries with their regional and typological variability of the language. Frederick G. Cassidy published his dictionary, *The Dictionary of Jamaican English*, which drew much upon the English of the people of Jamaica. Later appeared a similar type of dictionary called *Dictionary of American Regional English* which depended on the Spoken English of the Americans on a massive scale. With the advent of new technology, the Oxford University Press with the help of a reliable team under the guidance of E.S.C. Weiner, compiled *New Oxford English Dictionary*. Though dictionaries with regional varieties like Jamaican English, Bahamian English appeared, it was only the Concise Oxford English Dictionary that served for quite a few years, as a dependable guide to most of the learners of English.

Nowadays, there are many types of dictionaries available in the market. For example, there are Standard and Encyclopaedic Dictionaries with a comprehensive coverage of established and current English. They give extensive biographical, geographical, and other encyclopaedic entries and illustrations. Forever long companions, there are Concise or abridged dictionaries with good coverage of established and current English. In the market one comes across pocket, paperback and compact dictionaries with restricted coverage of established English or emphasis on current English. There are Learners' dictionaries for school children and overseas learners of English. In fact, these dictionaries offer extensive guidance on current English language usage and practice. For general reference, there are Thesauri and synonym dictionaries which classify and alphabetically arrange lists of related words.

There are also Language guides throwing light on modern English usage, grammar, pronunciation, spelling, and vocabulary and 'good' written and spoken English. To other category belong Selected dictionaries and wordlists of: American English; anagrams; antonyms; Australian English; Canadian English; catchphrases; Citizen's Band; clichés; collective nouns; colloquialisms; confusable words; crosswords and other word-games; dialect and regional words; eponyms; etymology and word origins; euphemisms; foreign words and phrases; homographs and homophones; idioms; Indian English; -isms; Jamaican English; jargon; mottoes; names; new words; New Zealand English; nicknames, -ologies; -phobias; phrasal verbs; place names; pronunciation; puns; rhyming; Scots; Scrabble; South African English; Yiddish.

Of the innumerable dictionaries available, one finds it very difficult to evaluate the usefulness of a dictionary and select the right one. We have to remember the following points in selecting and evaluating a dictionary. The editors' intentions and choice must be taken into consideration while choosing a dictionary. Dictionaries reward proper use based on an understanding of their editors' intentions. For example, a dictionary designed for children cannot easily cater to the needs of a journalist. It is advisable to take into consideration the editors' intentions that appear in the introductory material by the compilers or editors.

The user must see whether a dictionary is compiled by a competent team of lexicographers assisted by numerous knowledgeable advisers. If there isn't any reference to this in the prefatory material, the reader must move cautiously while purchasing it. The coverage of words plays a very important role. Here the user must see in the prefatory material, distinct reference to a number of headwords etc. If a dictionary has extensive collections of quotations and citations from contemporary publications and recordings one may not hesitate to buy it. Sometimes the organisation of words and phrases related to the main entries also gains some importance in the value of a dictionary. It is advisable to note whether a dictionary provides accurate definitions and appropriate explanations. The readability of definitions must also be taken into consideration. Also, the appropriateness, number and variety of examples cannot be ignored.

The linguistic conformity/viability is another factor that propels the user to buy a dictionary. For example, if the phonetic script is in conformity with the International Phonetic Alphabet, one may not hesitate to buy a dictionary. It is also important to examine the use of abbreviations and symbols and their readability and comprehensibility as well as their locations either within an entry or elsewhere on the page. Another salient feature is the up-to-dateness of a dictionary. Since language changes constantly a good dictionary must contain the recently coined terms or meanings and thus stand the test of currency also. The date of first publication, subsequent revised editions also play an important role here. Many good dictionaries contain supplementary material like illustrations, tables, charts, maps, and lists of various kinds. If the user feels that the supplementary material would enhance his day-to-day understanding of the language, he may buy it with utmost certainty. Sometimes, the size, binding, typefaces, and the paper used, the legibility, comprehensibility of special symbols used, the general layout of a page would also attract the user towards it. Keeping the aforesaid in mind, one may feel excited as the Seventh edition of *Oxford Advanced Learner's Dictionary*, 2005 that would convincingly offer a big leap forward to the learners of English.

Oxford Advanced Learner's Dictionary, 2005 is one of the best selling English learner's dictionaries in the world. A.S. Hornby who was originally an English teacher ran his own institute of English in Japan and brought out an English dictionary keeping in mind the specific needs of the advanced learners of the language. Since 1948, many editions of Hornby's *Advanced Learner's Dictionary of Current English* appeared. Hornby's great contribution to lexicography was to apply his experience as a teacher of English to producing a dictionary that met the needs of the learners. His success can be measured by the fact that his dictionary has become one of the best selling books of all times. The Seventh Edition of *Oxford Advanced Learner's Dictionary* under the guidance of Prof. Sally Wehmeier appeared in 2005, and easily broke new ground, sharpening further, the learner-centred focus of the original by Hornby. Prof. Henry Widdowson's 'Foreword' gives us the overt intention of the compilers of this latest dictionary. Prof. Widdowson like Dr. Johnson, earnestly feels:

> The value of a work must be estimated by its use; It is not enough that a dictionary delights the critic, unless at the same time, it instruct the learners.

So this dictionary instructs the learners markedly in learning English and thus exhibits its usefulness for learning.

In this unique dictionary, unlike its early editions, a learner can reasonably find some of the words of literary or outdated usage also. It also includes the most high-frequency words called the Oxford 3000 that occur across a wide range of usage. It has also covered words which fall outside such a list, but which are useful for learning as well as relevant for defining purposes. It gains a boundless authenticity with authentic examples from a vast range of attested contemporary usage. In a nutshell, *Oxford Advanced Learner's Dictionary* (*OALD*) is not just another dictionary of current English but essentially a learner's dictionary that takes into consideration (a) how much of the English now current in the world is to be included and (b) how it is to be presented.

Oxford Advanced Learner's Dictionary has been compiled by competent team of editors, consultants, and advisers. For example, Sally Wehmeier, Chief Editor of this dictionary, has gained rich experience as an Editor and publishing manager of ELT dictionaries, Oxford. For her, making sense out of English words is more of a passion than profession. Even other editors and advisers like Michael Ashby, Keith Brown who align themselves with the dictionary, have won international acclaim with their knowledge of English language and literature and also of lexicography. The organisation of words and phrases can easily tempt any learner of English to buy this dictionary. The Oxford 3000 words are used in common day writing and conversations and none can do well without their knowledge.

Another unique feature of *Oxford Advanced Learner's Dictionary* is the different pronunciations given at each headword. For the convenience of the learners of English at global level, Received Pronunciation is effectively used. The current words pertaining to Internet and science and technology are also included in this dictionary. For example, words like Webmaster, broadband, hotlink, click stream, blog, surfer, etc., are the words which have entered the corpus. The regional variations of the spoken and written form also find a place in this dictionary. For instance, the words that are used in Australia, New Zealand, India have their place in this dictionary. A few samples: 'ghat,' 'bandobast,' etc. are the words that belong to Indian learners of English. Naturally this can easily stand the test of readability and usefulness at the hands of Indian learners of English. There are certain words that become a part of a country's spoken English. Those words also have been selected and included in this dictionary. 2600 cultural words incorporated by Walter Mitty would certainly enhance one's own appreciation of any literary text.

The Reference section that contains most knowledgeable items like Grammar, Study pages, Other reference. The Oxford 3000, Pronunciation and phonetic symbols can easily give what a learner wants. Another added advantage of *Oxford Advanced Learner's Dictionary* is that there is a CD-ROM that can offer much more to a learner. You can just use it to check the meaning or the spelling of a word as you do with a print dictionary. You type the word and the entry for it is immediately there on your screen in conveniently large print with all examples and usage information that is advisable in the printed version. However, you can also listen to how the word is pronounced and this surely has to be preferable to reading a phonetic transcription for all. This is surely a much more profitable way of browsing the dictionary than reading from A to Z or just opening it at random.

The Chief Editor has given the right way of consulting the *Oxford Advanced Learner's Dictionary* and also learning new words. According to her, the best way to learn a word is by seeing it and its meaning again and again. Writing it somewhere and consulting it time and again is a good opinion. Generally people refer to a dictionary only when they need to know the meaning of any word. That is also one way of going about the task. So this dictionary readily ensures that the less experienced learners receive all the support they need, while the most advanced will always find something new and interesting to challenge them.

29

The Literary Text—A Threatened Species?

Krishna Rayan

The centrality, by definition, of the text to the literary process—the process from the author to the text to the reader—is obvious and has been widely acknowledged as such down the centuries, and so has the dichotomy between literary and nonliterary writing. In the first half of the 20th century both assumptions were authoritatively reaffirmed, the first by the New Criticism and the second by Russian Formalism. The New Criticism described the text as a solid entity, a container for intended determinate meaning which could be accessed by close reading. Earlier on, Russian Formalism had asserted the difference between poetic and prose language (or literary and standard language) in terms of the devices of foregrounding and defamiliarization.

Both the assumptions have since been interrogated. Postmodernism has sought to erase the opposition between literature and paraliterature on the same grounds as the opposition between "high" and "mass" or "commercial" in cinema, music, painting and the other arts and media. This breaking down of barriers is distinct from the other new position in contemporary thinking, which is that the category "literature" has no ontological standing and that all is writing which can be read in any preferred way. In this essay, however, "without prejudice," as lawyers say, we will continue to use the term "literary" if only for the severely practical purpose of keeping apart, say, Jorg Luis Borges's *Collected Fictions* and Daniel Goleman's *Emotional Intelligence*.

The other major change in recent thinking has been the reaction against Derrida's concept of deferral and undecidability and his scepticism about meaning having a context. Contesting this, Foucault emphasizes the need to attend to the conditions of origin of texts and to the forces that control the meanings which they have produced. This has led to the development of what may be called political poststructuralism.

The New Historicism, which was heralded by the publication of Stephen Greenblatt's *Renaissance Self-Fashioning* in 1980, is based on the assumption that the text is grounded in the historical context of its production. It reproduces or contests the relations of power specific to its time. The new Historicists have tested the assumption on several Renaissance texts, analyzing them with reference to the ruling power structures of the period. Jonathan Dollimore's interpretation of *King Lear*, for instance, is that the play's main concern is not with the human condition, but with power and property. Similarly, in *The Politics of Tragicomedy: Shakespeare and After*, edited by G. McMullan and J. Hope, which is a collection of essays showing how several plays of the time are concerned to present alternatives to the prevailing power systems, David Norbrook demonstrates how *The Tempest* has hints of an ideal society which challenge the power structures of the time. The play is thus read not as a work of literature but as a dramatized political treatise on contemporary power relations. If figurality is regarded as the defining characteristic of literature, then the New Historicist approach to the two plays declines to treat them as figurative presentations of the human predicament and classes them not as *literary* texts but as *literal* texts presenting ideological issues factually.

There have been other attempts in the 1980s to interrogate, roughly from the same premises, the liberal humanist definition of the text as a literary work offering aesthetic (Croce) or moral (Leavis) fulfillment; and more recently, to reject Derrida's concept of the infinite play of plural meaning. Catherine Belsey, for instance, in her 1983 essay, "Literature, History, Politics," describes the text as "raw material for the production of meanings" which "produce practices and generate behaviour" and to her discourse-as-knowledge being identical with power, the history of meanings is a political history, a history of the contest for power, a contest for "meaning in its materiality"—a history, in short, of the struggle for power and of the resistance to power. The texts should be read not for their literary value but as criticism's raw material for constructing a political history of the present. In Belsey's leftist view, the history of the present is a history of the struggle for power, which legitimates radical political action now in the cause of race, class or gender. Catherine Belsey, whose ideas and phrases I have borrowed above sums up her thesis thus: "The text is no longer the center of a self-contained exercise called literary criticism. It is one of the places to begin to assemble the political history of the present."

Catherine Belsey emphasizes the "substantial political ends which replace the mysterious objectives of aesthetic satisfaction and moral enrichment." Ethical value is now *passé*, but aesthetic pleasure, I think, continues to be the drive which takes readers to literary texts as it has done in all cultures and all ages. In India, *rasa* (the reader's aesthetic response) continues to be dominant across the board in the arts. However, there may be circumstances such as failure to obtain enrolment for a more worthwhile subject, or faith in an English major as a passport to employment in an advertising agency. But what is important is that despite these motivations, a student's continued intense exposure to literary texts can breed taste (to use an old-fashioned word) where none existed before, as it indeed does in the other arts. Therefore, there should ever be "a text in this class," generating pleasure and understanding while it is being read and fostering interest in independent reading. But this has always remained a utopian scenario. Devices like continuous or internal assessment have failed to make a dent on the hegemony of the examination system. As Sudhakar Marathe has shown in his *Read First, Criticize Afterwards*, examination questions which are stereotyped, predictable and put a premium on the use of undigested material recycled from critical works make the text itself redundant and irrelevant. As Marathe says, '...students and also many teachers read cribs or "guide-books" (often in language which is simultaneously outdated Victorian and non-standard enough to call Pidgin) *instead* of prescribed texts.' The poison is fed back into the system and regularly replenished, as most of the graduates in English, having missed more attractive careers, become teachers of English. The practice of marginalizing or wholly ignoring the literary text is thus perpetuated.

Jonathan Keates, writing in *The Spectator* recently, refers to the belief among some in "the impending death of books as we know them" and in "a future of screens and scrolling, of laptops and CD-ROMs purchased from stores set out along the lines of present-day record shops with their browser troughs and user-friendly labelling." But Keates is certain that the book is not on its way out: 'Only deliberate pig-headedness rejects the various blessings of information technology, but the demise of the book is surely not among these.' Keates specifies two properties of the book which he is convinced will ensure its survival. The first is its nature 'as an object, a physical construct of paper, cardboard, cloth, ink and glue...as something sensually understood, in the texture of its pages and their noise and above all their smell, indefinable save perhaps to an analytical chemist, but equally unforgettable in its potency of association.' The second property of books is that they 'are the only artefact whose diversity of aspect and anatomy comes near to replicating the enormous range of difference among the species which creates them. They are also, more significantly, the things we make to satisfy our sense that such difference still matters.' Whether the book can be said to be threatened with extinction or not, the literary text is a different case. It originated as oral tradition and then was in the form of manuscript on leaf and later on paper. It is only since the invention of printing that it has existed as book, but it can be trusted to function just as happily on the monitor.

If the literary text today can be said to be endangered, it is not so much by the ground realities of the education system or of information technology as by the currency of certain reading strategies, inspired by theory, which treat the text not as a piece of literature but as a product of ideology, as a document of contemporary power relations and even as an instrument of political action. Whether there will be more changes in the theory of the text and the practice of reading and whether these will be such as to arrest the decline of the literary text or accelerate it is more than one can say, chiefly because the rate of obsolescence and turn-over among contemporary theories is almost as great as the pace of reproduction and mutation among the simpler organisms.

Profile

K. Venkata Reddy (1939) was born in a village in Chittoor district in Andhra Pradesh where he received his early education. He later went to Tirupati to pursue higher studies, and did Ph.D. on Ben Jonson's plays at Sri Venkateswara University. He took up teaching and research and served as a Senior Professor of English, and later as Principal at Sri Krishnadevaraya University, Anantpur.

Apart from remaining actively engaged in teaching for about four decades, he guided research and has to his credit 12 Ph.Ds and 16 M.Phils in English language and literature. He also completed two UGC Research Projects.

Dr. Reddy is an erudite scholar and a prolific writer. He has written and edited several critical studies on English literature. Many of his research papers have been published in reputed literary journals in India and abroad. He has also dramatized Mulk Raj Anand's *Untouchable* into a three-act play, and translated Chalam's Telugu short story 'Jealousy' into English.

Dr. Reddy has received many awards for his contribution to teaching and writing. He was given the Best Teacher Award by the Government of Andhra Pradesh in 1980. He was awarded the 1st Prize for Janma Bhoomi Publications, by the President of India, on the occasion of the Golden Jubilee Celebrations of Independence and Andhra Pradesh Formation Day on 1st November, 1997. He was unanimously elected Chairman of the Indian Association for English Studies at the 42nd All India English Teachers' Conference held at North Gujarat University, Patan, in December 1996, as well as at the 44th All India English Teachers' Conference held at Banaras Hindu University, Varanasi, in December 1999.

He has been a member of several national and international organisations. He served as a Member of Board of Studies in English in various universities like Annamalai University (1989-92); Gulbarga University (1988-91); Kakatiya University (1991-93); Nagarjuna University (1991-94); and Karnataka University (1994-97).

He conducted many national and international seminars, conferences and refresher courses on different aspects of English literature, at Sri Krishnadevaraya University, Anantpur. He also presented papers, chaired sessions at several conferences, seminars and symposia at national and international levels.

Dr. Reddy also served as a Resource Person for the Academic Staff Colleges at the Orientation and Refresher Courses under the UGC Scheme under different universities. He was the UGC Visiting Fellow in six universities. Despite being regularly engaged in various academic and literary activities, he spared time to visit many foreign universities like those in Singapore, Malaysia, America and Australia. He went to Japan to attend the 5th World Shakespeare Congress held in Tokyo in 1991.

Dr. Reddy is a multi-faced personality. Besides erudite scholarship and administrative experience—having served as Principal, S.K. University College; President, Indian Association for English Studies; and University Coordinator for Academic Affairs—he has taken active part in many nationbuilding activities like rural reconstruction; disaster relief and rehabilitation; national integration; anti-dowry and anti-liquor campaigns; eradication of casteism; and fostering of secularism.

His contribution to society at large can hardly be matched.

Contributors

Wail S. Hassan, Illinois State University, USA.

Howard R. Wolf, The State University of New York at Buffalo, Buffalo, New York.

Ramesh Chandra Tungaria, MLV Government College, Bilwara.

V.R. Badiger, Gulbarga University, Gulbarga.

Ronald Knowles, Reading University, UK.

O.P. Bhatnagar, Eminent poet and critic, New Delhi.

R. Saraswathi, Acharya Nagarjuna University, Guntur.

Shikha Misra, CSJM University, Kanpur.

Satnam Kour Raina, University of Jammu, Jammu.

Ms. Nila Das, University of Kalyani, Kalyani.

Deepsheekha Kotwal, University of Jammu, Jammu.

Parmanand Jha, C.M. College, Dharbhanga.

Basavaraj Naikar, Karnataka University, Dharwad.

Neil ten Kortenaar, University of Toronto, Toronto.

P. Suneetha, Karnataka Educational Service, Bangalore.

Gunjan Chaturvedi, B.D.K. College, Agra.

G. Seetha Ramaiah, Government College, Penugonda.

Prabhat K. Singh, Magadh University, Gaya.

M.K. Naik, Eminent critic, poet, Former Professor and Chairman of the Department of English, Karnataka University, Dharwad.

R. Ramachandra, University of Mysore, Mysore.

P. Bayapa Reddy, Sri Krishnadevaraya University, Anantapur.

Shiv K. Kumar, Poet, novelist, short story writer, playwright, translator and critic, Formerly at the University of Hyderabad, Hyderabad.

K. Nirupa Rani, Adikavi Nannaya University, Rajahmundry.

I.D. Tiwari, Indira Kala Sangeet University, Khairagarh, Chhattisgarh.

Shyamala A. Narayan, Jamia Millia Islamia University, New Delhi.

Prema Nandakumar, Eminent critic and creative writer, Trichy.

Jibesh Bhattacharya, Scholar of Comparative Literature, Kolkata.

Krishna Rayan, Eminent critic, Mumbai.